CROCKETT'S TOOL SHED

LITTLE, BROWN AND COMPANY   BOSTON/TORONTO

CROCKETT'S TOOL SHED

JAMES UNDERWOOD CROCKETT

WITH PHOTOGRAPHS BY LOU JONES

Please Note

Price ranges in this book are accurate as of June 1979. They are subject to change and should be regarded as approximations only.

Library of Congress Cataloging in Publication Data

Crockett, James Underwood.
    Crockett's Tool shed.

    Includes index.
    1. Garden tools.   I. Title.   II. Title: Tool shed.
SB454.8.C76   681′.7631   79-18080
ISBN 0-316-16129-2
ISBN 0-316-16130-6 pbk.

First Edition

Designed by
Dianne Smith Schaefer/ Designworks

RM
*Published simultaneously in Canada
by Little, Brown & Company (Canada) Limited*

Printed in the United States of America

PREFACE

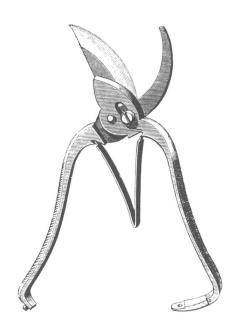

No book is the product of one person's efforts. There are always unseen hands at work, especially with a project as large and complicated as this one. I have been fortunate to have had the help of a gifted and dedicated group of men and women who have worked tirelessly to see this book into print. They deserve to be recognized here for their efforts.

Jane Doerfer was the project editor/coordinator. She did enormous amounts of research on tools, assembled the items to be tested for inclusion in the book, wrote drafts of some product tests, and supervised the assembling of the final manuscript and artwork.

Gregory Stone tested items for inclusion in the book, wrote drafts of product descriptions, and worked on the first draft of the entire manuscript.

Russell Morash, my television producer, tested items, and generously agreed to turn his garage into a photographic studio. He also took the photographs of me you see in this book.

Charles McColough handled many of the mind-boggling business arrangements for this project, organized the photographic sessions, and tested items. He was assisted by Edwin Denty.

Dianne Smith Schaefer of Designworks supervised art direction and designed the book. She was assisted by Mary Reilly and Carol Keller.

Lou Jones was the principal photographer. His assistant was Darcy Hosmer.

Dexter Davis tested hundreds of items and wrote drafts of product descriptions.

Judith Watkins tested items.

Harriet Keaney typed the entire manuscript and Joan Sullivan and Paula Crandell typed many of the product descriptions. Sarah Ellis checked product information.

William Phillips, my editor at Little, Brown, and Laura Fillmore, his editorial assistant, cracked the whip over us all, and guided us through the complexities of getting this book to the printer.

Michael Mattil copyedited the manuscript.

Peter Carr, General Manager of Manufacturing at Little, Brown, supervised the production of the book. He was assisted by Rachel Bunker.

Each of these individuals made vital contributions to this book. Without their sustained effort it could never have been completed. I owe them all a profound debt of gratitude.

I would also like to thank the manufacturers of the many products you will find in these pages. They were generous with assistance without attempting to influence our judgments.

To the Memory of my grand-
father, John Howard Crockett,
my father, Earle Royce Crockett,
and my uncle, Frank Honor,
whose gardening tools I
use and cherish.

CONTENTS

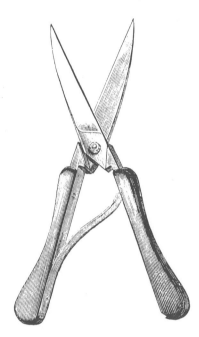

THE WELL-EQUIPPED GARDENER

I grew up at a time when knowledge of gardening and farm tools was basic. If I had a question, I'd quiz a neighbor or the local hardware store owner, who knew just about everything concerning tools. What I learned then has stayed with me all my life and formed part of my love of gardening.

Today this word-of-mouth knowledge is hard to come by. The hardware store owner who tried every tool in stock before recommending one has more often than not been replaced by a clerk at the checkout counter who may never have cultivated with a hoe in his life. I found when I started the *Crockett's Victory Garden* show that people frequently wrote in to ask where they could buy the tools I used on the program or if I could suggest any other useful ones. I decided to write this book to answer their questions. In these pages you will find detailed descriptions, including photographs, of what I consider the best and most useful gardening tools and equipment — over 420 items in all. In addition, I have tried to share my experience of what makes a tool good, which ones are really necessary to do the job well, and how to select the tool you need from the bewildering display at the garden center.

When I'm asked how I choose tools, I tell people I buy the very best quality I can afford. I am a New England Yankee, and as a group we have a reputation for being frugal. A Yankee is not apt to spend any money unless he can see he's investing in something of real value. So I buy the best quality equipment I can find, because I know that's by far the cheapest way in the long run. I want tools I can depend on.

Thus, I always advise that before you buy any tool, pick it up and examine it carefully. Does the workmanship look sloppy? If so, pass it by immediately. If not, see how the tool is constructed: Are stress points reinforced? What kind of metal is used? Is the tool finished carefully? Burrs on a metal blade or rough spots on an axe handle can easily cut your hands. A hoe should be made of a strong though lightweight wood, such as ash or hickory, that won't break when you lean on it. Get the heft of the tool while you're still in the store. A spade, for example, should be easy to lift and not feel awkward. A tool that feels clumsy in your hand when it's idle is going to feel very clumsy indeed when you're using it in the garden. Select a tool that suits your height, weight, and strength; if it's too heavy, you'll never want to pick it up and it will languish on your shelf forever. You know you've made the right choice when suddenly you just can't wait to get out in the garden and start working. Any tool that stimulates such feelings will soon become indispensable.

It's easy to get carried away buying power equipment you don't really need or that you would be better off renting. Recently I read of a person with a 20 × 30–foot plot of land who wanted to raise vegetables and save himself some money. The very first thing he did was go out and spend thousands of dollars for a tractor while his wife invested a bundle in a canning outfit. They are going to have to live a long, long time before their initial investment pays off. That size garden only calls for hand tools. This man obviously overbought for his plot size and didn't gear his purchases to the type of gardening he was likely to do.

Before you go to the checkout counter with your new tool, think seriously about your purchase. Do you really need it? Do you have a place to store the tool where it will be out of your way? (There's little point owning a garden tractor, for instance, if the only place you can keep it is in your cellar.) If you don't have storage space you'll have to build it, which will add to the cost of the tool.

Plan ahead. Do your shopping off season or early in the year when selection is greatest. Shop around. It's a rare merchant who will stock more than two lines of tools. He might have Ames and True Temper top-of-the-line shovels, but it's very unlikely that he will carry merchandise from a third manufacturer. It costs money to keep variety on the shelves. The larger the merchant's inventory, the more manufacturers he has to deal with and the more paperwork he will end up doing. So don't purchase the first spade you see, even if it's the best or only one in the store, until you've examined a number of others from several manufacturers.

If you're buying large equipment, select machines that are easy to service. Check the service reputation of the dealers in your area with your fellow gardeners. There's no point spending $350 on a lawn mower only to discover the first time it breaks down that the local repairman has only a so-so reputation, or that parts are next to impossible to get in your area. Large equipment, like cars, always costs more than the initial investment, and you should keep that in mind when shopping.

A few words about the tools and equipment you will find in these pages and how they were selected. Many readers may be beginning gardeners who want to learn the basics about everyday tools. Others may be eager to discover more about professional tools for specialized gardening activities. This book should prove useful for both types of gardener.

You'll find I've included here a mixture of my all-time favorites, along with some new discoveries. As a professional horticulturist, I'm sent many new tool models each year. Some I consider real improvements upon tools I've always used, and I enjoy adding them to my collection. For you see, I'm a lazy gardener. I welcome anything that makes my job easier and gives me more time to enjoy my peonies or to watch birds flock around my backyard pond.

The bulk of my collection, however, is not new. It's based upon tools handed down to me by my father and grandfather. Some have been in use 75 years — maybe even more than that. These hand tools have passed the test of time — my shovel, spade, hoe, and even a 50-year-old high-wheeled cultivator that I used as a child. I remember when I was a little kid, saving up for the heart-shaped "Warren" hoe that I'm still using today. It's always been my favorite hoe because it's so versatile.

You will notice that I have made no attempt to rate a group of identical items, the way some consumer product-testing magazines do. I have chosen instead the one tool in a category that I think does the job best, or that has features I particularly like. Obviously, this is a personal selection, and there are many fine tools similar to the ones included here that didn't make it into the book. You should also know that these products were not subjected to the scrutiny of engineers with testing machines. However, I can guarantee that every tool in this book was tested by experienced gardeners who used it the way you would at home. Before making any choices, we looked carefully at more than a thousand tools, comparing price and performance.

Although we examined products in all price ranges, you'll notice most tools in the book come from manufacturers' mid- to top-of-the-line ranges. I can't emphasize too strongly that when you buy garden tools you get what you pay for. Cheap tools just aren't worth the money. A cultivator that bends out of shape after three months of use, or a hoe handle that breaks after two afternoons in the garden is no bargain.

Manufacturers make tools differently than they used to. I remember when a manufacturer would not print his name on a tool unless it was a top-of-the-line item. This is no longer true. You'll see tools that look very much the same, but vary significantly in quality. Most manufacturers make at least three lines of tools — top quality, medium quality, and low end. Top- and medium-quality tools look alike; their price will indicate which is which. Low-end tools are usually fairly easy to pick out. You might see a name-brand garden shovel in the $6.00 range and be tempted to buy it. It will never last year in and year out as would a high quality shovel. Manufacturers continue to place tools on the market which they know will not stand up to heavy use in order to be competitive. But no wise buyer will select these tools.

This book will give you a reasonable indication of what a fair price should be for certain items. The prices listed are accurate as of June, 1979; however, the cost of raw materials and foreign imports changes rapidly, so you should consider the price ranges here as merely a general guide.

Should you wish to buy one of the tools listed in this book, write down the model number. Just remembering the brand name and what the tool looked like is no assurance you'll find the same item in the store. If you can't find a tool mentioned in this book, ask your garden center or hardware dealer to special order it for you. Don't write to the manufacturer except as a last resort to get the name of a local distributor. Addresses of manufacturers are included in the Appendix, but remember that very few sell retail.

You'll notice that I've organized this book around gardening activities rather than types of tools, for the wise gardener thinks about the specific chores he's undertaking before rushing off to the store to buy one of this and one of that. Of course, you'll use some tools over and over again throughout the season. A spade comes in handy when clearing the land, planting a tree, or inserting a piece of edging strip — and each of these chores is covered in a separate chapter. In such cases, I listed the tool under the activity in which I believe it is used the most. If you are in a hurry to check on a tool and aren't sure where to find it, turn to the index.

The photographs accompanying most of the items (which are keyed to the entries by number), along with the product descriptions, should give you a good idea of the attractive features of each item. It's important that you learn to judge for yourself what makes a quality tool in case you can't find the one listed here at your local store. You will then be able to choose an alternative wisely.

I've included several professional specialty tools that you may never need but should know about because they're hard to find. For some gardening aids, such as compost bins or cold frames, it's often easier and cheaper to build them yourself. As you design your own version, take a look at the commercial choices and use them as a starting point for your own ideas.

You can't talk about tools without talking about safety. It's extremely important to appreciate the possible hazards of using some of these tools. In a farming community nothing would label a person a city slicker faster than the way he puts down a potentially dangerous tool. Nothing will break a pair of glasses any quicker or is more damaging to a child's bare foot than to step on a rake abandoned tines up. The same goes for a hoe. No matter whether it's dull or sharp, it's still a blade. Most people are careful around power equipment such as chain saws because their dangers are obvious, but don't forget that even little tools can present a hazard if they are not handled and stored properly.

The title of this book is no accident. I want to put special emphasis on the words "tool shed." It's senseless to own good tools and not spend the extra few moments needed to care for and store them properly. It isn't necessary to have a separate shed, although one is always convenient, but you should have a place where you regularly store tools. In your storage area, you should also keep a few rags, some oil, a sharpening stone, and a file. Any tool will benefit from a quick cleaning and drying before it's put away. Metal parts last longer if they get an occasional swipe from an oily rag. And having a file handy will encourage you to sharpen your hoe or shovel before going out in the garden.

If you care for your gardening tools, they can last at least three generations, as some of mine have. Most of the tools in my shed have seen many a gardening year go by, and they are still as serviceable as when they were new. They are old friends now, and each has a special memory. When I pick one up I think of the pleasure I have had using it to help plants grow, and of my family and friends who have shared that pleasure with me. I can only wish as much joy for you.

CLEARING THE LAND
AND HARVESTING WOOD

Whether clearing a patch for a vegetable garden or harvesting a winter supply of firewood, we're going to need special tools that call for a mix of force, skill, and care. With some of the tools in this section, it can be downright dangerous to use them for chores for which they were never intended. If you use your axe head as a sledgehammer, you can damage the connection between head and handle. At some later date, the head could fly off, seriously injuring you or someone nearby.

Many of these tools are expensive. Before you decide to buy a chain saw or some other costly item, look into the rental situation. Many gardeners, for example, will find that for 364 days a year, the only woodcutting tool they want is a single, high-quality pruning saw. On that day when a chain saw is a must, they rent one, saving themselves a large initial investment, as well as the bother of upkeep. But whether you buy or rent, a knowledge of what's available, what it will do, and how to use it safely will be helpful.

Safety deserves special emphasis. The whole question of safety, so critical with any tool, is doubly important with the tools used for clearing the land. After all, they are designed to cut, split, smash, or break anything from a 100-foot pine to a boulder; just picture what they can do to a fragile human limb. Some also pose a threat to eyes and ears, so you'll want to know about special safety equipment and clothing. This doesn't mean you should approach these tools with fear — but rather, with respect.

Keep all your tools oiled, clean, and sharp. At the end of each season, make a careful check of handles to be sure they are still firm and show no signs of looseness or rot. If in doubt, you should replace the handle. Most manufacturers of long-handled tools have detailed information in their catalogs on how to do this. Replacing a handle is a relatively easy job, and is certainly less expensive and less wasteful than buying a new axe or pick, or a trip to the hospital.

SAFETY PRODUCTS

While it's possible to be knocked senseless by a rotten branch shaken loose while cutting down a tree, my first thought is for my eyes.

It is very easy for a wood or rock chip from saw or sledgehammer to find its way into your eye. That's why the first items in this section are protective goggles. (You'll find these are useful as well when you're working with many tools in the home workshop.) Obviously, you want goggles that will take an impact without breaking. You also have to be concerned about perspiration fogging the goggles and impairing your vision. Most goggles handle the moisture buildup with vents, but there are also types that have the lenses treated with an antifogging substance. When you see a pair you want, try them on and walk around for a few minutes. If fogging is going to be a problem, it should show up pretty quickly. Finally, you'll find two basic types of safety goggles. One is designed to protect against impact, which is our main concern when using the tools in this chapter; the other type also protects against splash and dust.

Many of the same activities that send fragments toward your eyes also are a threat to your head. There's always the chance that you'll miscalculate the fall of a tree and be in the wrong place at the wrong time, or get a gash from a split piece of rock. When these things are considered, the money invested in a good safety helmet is well spent.

Such helmets are usually made of high-impact plastic, and the suspension system inside the helmet that keeps it well above your head absorbs thumps from heavy objects. If you're not sure of the quality of a helmet, look for evidence that it has met accepted standards for safety helmets. There usually will be a stamp, or something in the product literature, that will say whether the helmet has been approved by the American National Standards Institute (ANSI) and has met government standards for protective headwear.

It's primarily the gasoline-powered chain saws, brush cutters, and the like that pose a problem for your ears. If you ever had a Sunday afternoon nap interrupted by a chain saw a half-mile away, think of what that noise level is doing to the saw user.

There are two remedies for this. One is safety earmuffs, resembling stereo headphones, which can effectively keep the sound level down to where it is both comfortable and safe. The other solution is soft earplugs. I find the muffs more comfortable and easier to keep in place.

Of course, you can put all this protection together in a single package by purchasing one of the helmets that includes earmuffs and a face mask of clear plastic or wire mesh. With such helmets, the earmuffs and face mask should be attached so that they can be easily slipped out of the way and stay put when not needed. In warmer climates, I suggest a wire mesh, which avoids a fogging problem. When considering a helmet with a transparent plastic shield, give it the safety goggle test: Try it on, put the shield down, and move about for a few minutes. You'll discover soon enough if fogging is going to be a problem.

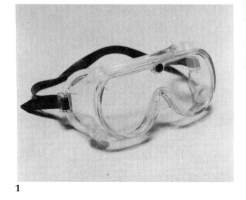

1

Safety Goggles, MODEL 1-484BAF, AMERICAN OPTICAL, $5.00–5.50 **(1)**

Clear plastic goggles with 4 small vents and antifog lenses with "Durafon" coating; adjustable rubber headband.

The main feature of these goggles is the antifog lenses, good for wearing in summer as well as winter. You'll find they won't fog up with perspiration even while chipping stone or chopping down thickets on a humid day. The soft plastic rim makes for a snug, comfortable fit.

2

Safety Goggles, MODEL D66C, WILLSON PRODUCTS, $2.80–3.30 **(2)**

Clear plastic lenses and side pieces; molded construction; hinged over the nose piece with plastic-foam face lining; 2 small direct ventilation screens about ¾ inch in diameter, 1 on each side of the frame; adjustable black elastic band.

These goggles, designed to be particularly lightweight and inexpensive, meet OSHA (Occupational Safety and

Health Administration) standards and ANSI specifications for eye protection. Although the lenses are not coated with an antifogging shield, as are other Willson models, the screens reduce any serious build-up of steam on the inside of the goggles, effectively serving as antifog devices.

Earmuffs, MODEL CP-330, WILLSON PRODUCTS, $11.00–12.00 **(3)**

Constructed of thermoplastic; three wearing positions; fully adjustable ear cups and sponge-filled ear cushions.

These shooters' earmuffs, designed as protection against harmful noise levels, meet OSHA and ANSI safety standards. The sponge inserts in the ear cups help absorb sound, while the three wearing positions — over or behind the head or under the chin — make them convenient to wear. It's still possible, while wearing these muffs, to hear low-level sounds such as warning signals or loud speaking voices. The unit can be disassembled for cleaning with warm soapy water.

3

4

Safety Hard Cap, MODEL BX21, AMERICAN OPTICAL, $5.75–6.25 **(4)**

Red plastic hard cap with adjustable gray plastic suspension and replaceable plastic sweatband; provisions are made for attaching either earmuffs or face visor.

Where it is not necessary that the operator's ears and face be protected, this cap is lighter and easier to wear than more elaborate helmets. It meets ANSI standards for hard caps.

Safety Helmet, MODEL 21710, SANDVIK, $28.00–30.00 **(5)**

Orange plastic helmet with earmuffs and 1/16-inch-wire-mesh face shield; adjustable headband for hat sizes 6 to 8½; suspension snaps into helmet; can be purchased separately without shield or muffs.

This is a comfortable helmet that has been approved by a Canadian testing agency for use in that country and was undergoing tests by U.S. laboratories at the time I looked at it. The helmet sits above your head, offering good air circulation — and of course, with the wire-mesh shield, there's no fogging problem. This shield protects your entire face, extending to chin level. It was a little distracting if kept down while walking, interfering slightly with vision toward the ground. The earmuffs are faced with a soft plastic foam, and both the muffs

5

and the face shield can easily be slipped out of the way when not in use.

Safety Helmet, MODEL 99510, AMERICAN OPTICAL, $35.00–38.00 **(6)**

1-piece white plastic helmet with flexible earmuffs; adjustable for hat sizes 6⅜ to 8; clear plastic visor protects entire face.

This helmet is both versatile and comfortable, and has the standard government and ANSI approval for safety helmets. The face shield slips back over your head when not in use. It is versatile because you can buy a wire-mesh face shield for the same helmet, as well as a special welder's shield. Or you can buy the helmet without any attachments, if you wish.

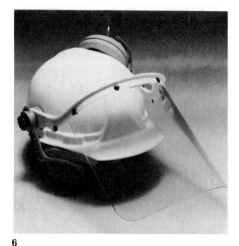
6

GLOVES

It's far easier to lose your grip on an axe or chain saw if your hands happen to be cold, wet, or both. So when you consider buying gloves, think not only of protecting your hands from briars, splinters, oil, and dirt — but also remember that they're an essential part of your safety equipment.

For heavy work in the woods, I prefer leather gloves. The heavy cloth ones I've tried haven't been as comfortable, nor have they given me the sensitive control needed when using the tools in this chapter.

Some leather gloves can be washed with mild soap, but the manufacturer may suggest that other types simply be wiped or brushed free of dirt after every use. If you wash leather gloves, or if they become wet in use, dry them in warm air, but never over strong heat, which can weaken or ruin them.

If your hands are more adapted to the keys of a typewriter or a calculator, wear gloves at the start of your outdoor work. Don't wait until blisters begin to bulge the skin in tender places.

9

Woodcutters' Gloves, MODEL PN25958, OMARK INDUSTRIES, $10.00–12.00 **(7)**

Leather gloves with many yellow plastic dots on the gripping surfaces on palms and fingers; available in sizes Medium (Model PN25958) and Large (Model PN25878).

The special surface of these gloves provides a nonslip grip. They are sensitive enough for normal outdoor tool handling, are water and soil resistant, and may be washed in mild soap and water.

Leather Mittens, MODEL J-980401, IMPORTED FROM SCANDINAVIA AND DISTRIBUTED BY TILTON EQUIPMENT, $15.50–17.00 **(8)**

Soft, brown leather mittens; 3-inch gauntlets; adjustable Velcro tabs; right hand has 3 sections: for the thumb, the trigger finger, and other fingers.

These mittens are flexible, washable, and durable. They're designed with the winter chain saw operator in mind and can be used with an insert pair of gloves, or glove liners, during extremely cold weather.

Glove Liners, MODEL 264, DAMART, $9.25–10.00 **(9)**

Dark blue Thermolactyl knit gloves with wristlets of Vinyon and acrylic; available in Small, Medium and Large.

Developed for Mount Everest climbers, the Thermolactyl fiber in these gloves is meant to let perspiration evaporate while retaining body heat. These are useful, warm liners for leather gloves or mittens.

7

8

BOOTS

Be sure when you get ready to harvest wood or cut brush that you have adequate protection for your feet. There are few moments as miserable as standing on soggy ground or in the snow with cold seeping up through the soles of your boots. But boots for this kind of work should do more than protect against the cold and wet. They should be sturdy enough to resist the tug and tear of undergrowth, ward off flying wood and rock chips, and cushion the impact from a slipping log or rock. Well-insulated boots are not inexpensive, but, carefully cared for, they should last for years.

Heavy-Duty Boot, MODEL 16-21-1137, B. F. GOODRICH, $40.00–50.00 **(10)**

Black rubber boot with distinct heel and deep nonskid design on both heel and sole, curving up each side; top about 12 inches high with 8 pairs of eyelets for lacing; dead-air space surrounding the rear and sides of the foot; steel shank and toe; available in men's sizes only.

Were a limb to crash down on your foot, you would be grateful for the extra protection the steel shank of this boot offers. The sealed-in dead-air space surrounding the rear and sides of the foot gives extra protection against freezing weather. Although the boot is very strong, it feels lightweight and comfortable to wear.

11

Outdoor Boots, "MAINE HUNTING SHOE," L. L. BEAN, $36.00–39.00 **(11)**

Brown or tan 10-inch-high cowhide uppers with rubber bottoms; cushioned crepe innersole with chain-style tread.

Back in 1912, after Leon Leonwood Bean got tired of coming home with cold, wet feet from hunting expeditions, he invented this boot — the concept of which has barely changed in intervening years. Rubber bottoms keep the foot dry, while cowhide tops, treated to resist water, allow the foot to perspire, give arch support, and prevent stiffening while drying. The boots are available in both men's and women's sizes in heights from 6 to 16 inches, and are best worn with an innersole and heavy socks. For a fee, when the boots become worn out, Bean's will rebuild them, attaching new bottoms, reconditioning tops, and replacing eyelets.

10

PROTECTIVE CLOTHING

Forestry Clothing, TUNIC, MODEL 21723, TROUSERS, MODEL 21728, IMPORTED BY SANDVIK, $50.00–55.00 each **(12)**

100 percent nylon; available in European sizes 48–56 (trousers correspond to American sizing as follows: European size 48 equals American 32, European size 50 equals American 34 and so on).

These lightweight, comfortable tunic and trousers come from Finland where they are worn by professional loggers. The partially zippered tunic is bright orange for clear visibility in the forest. Its textured finish resists brambles, snags, and water penetration, while underarm vents allow perspiration to evaporate. Although it is wind resistant, the tunic is meant to be worn over a sweater or warm woolen shirt. The green trousers have an elasticized waistband and feature interior leg pockets for protective padding, which helps prevent chain saw vibrations from irritating the leg.

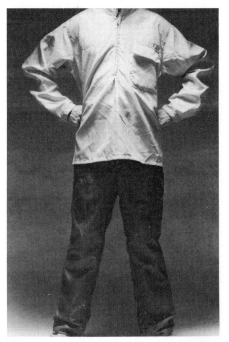

12

HATCHETS, AXES, AND SHARPENING DEVICES

Axes are one of those fundamental tools that have been serving us ever since some Stone Age forebears chipped a cutting edge on a heavy, fist-sized piece of quartz. Today, hard, tempered steel has replaced the quartz, and there are a wealth of regional axe designs that have been popular for more than a century. Blacksmiths traveling with westward settlers often would design patterns to fit individual preferences; a trend that axe manufacturers capitalized upon in the later nineteenth century, when hundreds of axe types were sold. Today you can still buy some of the old favorite patterns such as Michigan, Dayton, or Jersey, and I've included an example of each for you to see. Axe style is a matter of personal preference, but there are some basic points common to all axes and hatchets that you should consider before making a choice. (The one design I'd caution you to stay away from is the double-headed axe. This is the tool of the professional woodsman, requiring plenty of swinging room and an extra measure of skill to use well. It's not really meant for the inexperienced, occasional user.)

In choosing your axe, first think of control. You might be tempted to choose an axe that is outsize, thinking it will give you extra power. When you shop for an axe, heft it, then remember you may be swinging it for an hour or more. Test its balance and feel in your hands. Now look at the head. If it's entirely painted or enameled, examine it carefully — paint can cover up a multitude of sins in metalwork. You want an axe that has been properly tempered so it will hold an edge longer and won't break under normal use. Unfortunately, temper is difficult to judge, so your best guide is to stick with a manufacturer and retailer you trust.

Now look closely at the handle — again, paint can hide defects. First, make sure it is smooth: the axe should slide in your hands. One rough spot or nick can lead to a nasty scratch or splinter. Look at the grain. Is it uniform? Grain indicates the annual growth of the tree. If there were years when the tree grew much faster than others, then the growth pattern would be irregular, leading to weaker wood. Also look for small twists and whirls, which would indicate knots, another sign of weakness.

The same basic rules apply to hatchets, but remember, you'll be using these one-handed to chop off small branches or to split or point stakes for marking a row of carrots or providing support for beans, peas, tomatoes, and the like.

After you've selected an axe or hatchet, treat it with care. When it has been stored for a time, check the handle at the point that it enters the socket (eye) in the head of the axe. If the handle has dried out, this connection may be loose. A quick remedy is to soak it in water, while a more long-range treatment is an application of linseed oil. The last thing you want is the head flying loose as you're chopping down a tree.

Keep your axe sharp. A dull axe is far more dangerous than a sharp one, for it is more likely to glance off the wood and end up in your leg or foot. Sharpening an axe, however, is not a casual skill. It can be done carefully with a file, followed by use of a whetstone or hone to remove all scratches. A file scratch left on tempered steel can cause the axe to break at that point. Never try to sharpen your axe on a high-speed, dry grinding wheel. This will heat the steel, drawing the temper. Grind slowly on a wet wheel, or use a file. Your goal is to create a sharp edge that will stand up under the heavy blows it will be subject to. This means a sharp edge with a rounded, convex bevel just above it. Such a bevel leaves support for the edge. An axe that's been ground to a consistent, straight taper will probably break.

Axes also can break when used in very cold weather, since frost crystallizes tempered steel. Before using an axe under such conditions, warm it slightly over a stove or fire.

Usually, an axe breaks from poor sharpening or other mistreatment. This type of break will be crescent-shaped and the exposed edge will have the color of frosted silver. Breaks caused by a defect in manufacturing will be straight or irregular, and the color of the steel will be dark, or the grain coarse. Such an axe should be returned to the dealer for credit.

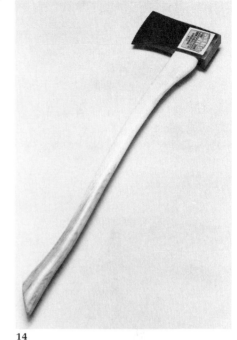

14

still widely used in the northeast and central states. Each side of the head is hollow-ground about 1 inch from the cutting face. (A hollow-ground head does not bind as easily, allowing for a deeper cut and quicker release.) Blades are specially hardened and tempered to stay sharp longer.

Axe, "OUR BEST,"
SNOW & NEALLEY, $19.00–21.00 **(14)**

3½-pound, 7½-inch-high head; 4-inch cutting edge; 32-inch-long handle.

Bangor, historically headquarters of the Maine lumbering industry, is home to the 115-year-old firm of Snow & Nealley, manufacturers of axes and other tools for professional loggers. This axe of their own design is a modified Dayton — a style which remains popular in the mid-South and West. Its balance is good and the head is made of heat-treated high-grade steel. The style is available with 2¼- to 3½-pound heads.

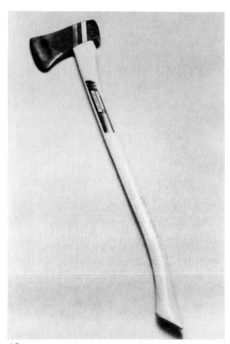

13

Axe, MODEL 301-01,
VAUGHAN & BUSHNELL, $20.00–21.75
(13)

Michigan-style, single-bit axe with 3½-pound, 8-inch-high head; 4½-inch cutting face; pure white hickory handle 36 inches long.

Vaughan's most popular style is the Michigan single bit, a regional style

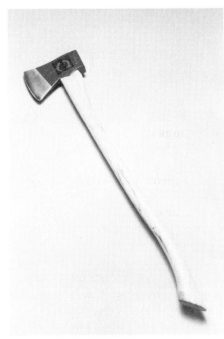

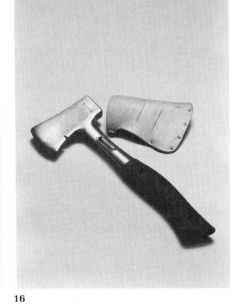

15

16

17

Axe, MODEL H3½JE,
COLLINS AXE, $17.00–18.00   **(15)**

3½-pound, 7-inch-high head; 5-inch cutting face; 36-inch-long handle.

Collins has been known in the axe industry for 150 years; in fact, the town of Collinsville, Connecticut, is named after the founder, Sam Collins. This Collins axe has a head that is slightly hollow ground about 1 inch from the cutting edge. Notice it's the Jersey pattern, a style still very popular in the South, from Washington, D.C., to Florida. The triangular-shaped "ears" on the lower part of the axe help prevent loose handles.

Camp Axe, MODEL AS1¼,
VAUGHAN & BUSHNELL, $16.00–17.25
(16)

1-piece steel hatchet, 13 inches long; cutting head about 5 inches long and 3 inches deep; nail-pulling slot on lower edge of head; 6-inch grip of perforated black rubber; natural color leather case with slots for carrying on a belt.

This small, modified Dayton-style tool is very strong and will hold an edge for a long time when it is used prop-

erly on wood. The back of the head can be used for driving stakes. (It must not be used for driving wedges or striking other metal objects.) The slightly curved handle makes it comfortable to use, the wrist held rigidly so the hatchet becomes an extension of the forearm. The camp axe is good for cutting sticks for bean poles or stakes for tents.

Hatchet, "HUDSON BAY KINDLING AXE," SNOW & NEALLEY, $14.00–15.50   **(17)**

3½-inch cutting face; 6-inch-high head; 16-inch-long hickory handle.

The wide cutting blade style makes it easy to split kindling or make stakes, while the enlarged base of the short handle reduces the chance of its slipping from your hands. This hatchet comes in 1- to 3½-pound sizes.

Sharpening File, ÖBERG MODEL 153,
DISTRIBUTED BY SANDVIK, $3.30–3.60
(18)

8-inch file, 1-inch wide; One side single cut, the other side a double cut; 4-inch yellow plastic handle with hang-up hole.

This file, from the largest file manufacturer in Europe, can sharpen most of the heavy cutting tools used to clear and prepare the land for planting. The single-cutting side of the file can be used for fine work on axes, pruning shears, and mower blades. The double-cut side is for heavier work on spades, picks, axes, and hoes.

18

Axe and Hatchet Sharpening Stone,
MODEL JT-3,
NORTON, $3.50–3.75 **(19)**

Man-made "crystolon" bonded abrasive stone, 3 inches in diameter, ⅝ inch thick.

Sharp tools are always safer and easier to use, and this stone, which can be held in one hand, will help you keep the blades of axes and hatchets sharp. The stone has two surfaces — a coarser side for beginning the sharpening and getting rid of nicks, and a fine-textured side for the final finish. Keep in mind that a sharp axe should have a strong obtuse wedge-shaped edge; don't try for a knife edge. To sharpen, stroke with a circular motion and hold the stone at approximately 45 degrees from the axis of the head. Repeat the motion and constantly work in the same direction. (If you could see the motion, it would look like a spiral line.) Sharpen both sides of the axe with the coarse side, then with the fine side. This avoids burrs.

You'll want to use either the manufacturer's oil or a good quality of general-purpose oil with this stone. Whichever oil you decide to use, stick with it — changing oil type causes the stone to lose lubricity.

19

HAND SAWS

When buying a saw, its feel in your hand is the most important single consideration. Hold it at arm's length, twist it at different angles, and make sawing motions. Will you also be able to grip it well with gloves on? I'd rather use a small saw that felt right to my hand than a large one that felt awkward. Blade temper is critical because you want the saw to stay sharp as long as possible. Coatings such as Teflon seem to help a saw move more smoothly through sticky wood, but they aren't essential.

If you think most of your sawing will be through wood that is 6 inches in diameter or thicker, look for a saw with a mix of "raker" and cutting teeth. (The pattern is usually four cutter, two rakers.) The raking teeth are designed to draw dust out of the cut while you saw, so that it doesn't build up and make the going too rough.

If I could have just one tool for outdoor cutting of wood, it would be a large pruning saw. While not really designed for taking down big trees, they're the most versatile of the outdoor handsaws.

But before considering the designs and use of pruning, bow, and two-man saws, it's important to remember that cutting live wood is not the same as sawing kiln-dried lumber. When working with seasoned wood, I use a saw that cuts at the same thickness as its blade. If I used this saw on a tree, I would find that the sap and gum would soon bind it in the cut, causing it to buckle and, at least, cause frustration. Look at the teeth of the outdoor saw and you'll see they're offset from the blade, creating a cut that is wider than the blade. This makes the saw easier to use on fresh wood.

The curved pruning saw, especially with raked-back teeth, does more cutting when pulled toward you than when pushed away. This is good because you generally have more control over this half of the stroke, and when removing branches from a living tree, you want as precise a cut as possible. However, don't get the idea this saw can only be used for pruning fruit trees. The large ones in this section will handle wood up to about 10 inches in diameter. The pruning saw's slim blade fits between interfering branches and twigs, and it can be used to cut at just about any angle. It leaves a smooth cut that heals well, and since it has a conventional handle, it's easy to use with one hand. It's dangerous to use a chain saw on a ladder or in a tree, but a good pruning saw will go with you to where the job is.

Now, when the job happens to be turning long trunks and limbs into firewood, I much prefer the bow saw. While not as versatile as the pruning saw, the bow saw does the job of cutting downward through wood — rather than horizontally — well.

The modern bow saw evolved from the old wooden-framed cross buck with wire braces and a thick blade which used to be a fixture on every woodpile. The modern bow saw has a thinner, more efficient blade and can be worked with one or two hands; the bowed handle allows you to put more pressure into each stroke than you would with a pruning saw.

continued

Unfortunately, that same bowed handle gets in the way when you're trying to cut a branch from a tree while working in among other branches. Nor do you get the pressure advantage when you flip the saw on its side and try to cut down a tree. It will work in this position, but it can be awkward. Finally, the bow ultimately limits the thickness of wood a saw can cut.

Bow saws generally will cut wood ranging in diameter from 10 to 20 inches, assuming you flip the wood over and cut from both sides. If you're concerned that the saw you're considering purchasing might not make it through wood of a given thickness, measure the distance between the top of the blade and the inside of the handle. Take this measurement a few inches from either side of the blade so that you allow for travel of the saw through the log.

Bow saw blades are relatively thin and, if not properly tightened, will buckle. Before you buy a saw, check the mechanism for tightening the blade. I like ones that are adjustable so that you can set the desired tension. (You don't have to worry if a replacement blade is a fraction of an inch larger or smaller than expected.) But this mechanism must set and hold blade tension easily and firmly. To test the tension, snap your fingernail against the center of the blade. You should get a twanging sound.

The long, two-man crosscut saw, and shorter, one-man "bull" saw are quickly becoming anachronisms thanks to the proliferation of the chain saw. Still, there are those who would rather use muscles than motors, and when it comes to felling large trees, or cutting through thick logs, these saws are most efficient users of manpower. Of course, any good saw will do these jobs faster (and with less huffing and puffing) than an axe.

To use the two-man saw, you'll need a partner who is both willing and skillful. When you're trying to pull a thin blade some 6 feet long back and forth through a tree, it's very easy to buckle it. The basic trick is for each to pull in his turn. Don't push. Working together smoothly takes the coordination of a skilled rowing team in a racing shell.

The bull saw is a little easier to use. Its blade is a couple of feet shorter and it has a single handle of conventional design, making it possible for one-man use. (The model I've included can also be used as a two-man saw.)

Hand saws can be sharpened with triangular files designed for the job. To reset the teeth, you'll need saw sets, a special kind of pliers designed to bend the teeth out uniformly. If all this sounds complicated, it is. Obviously, some of us enjoy tools and love to care for them ourselves, taking pride in such work. I appreciate that, but I admit that I take my saws to the neighborhood sharpening shop. They have tools there that can do the job automatically and in a short time for a reasonable charge.

I did run into one problem recently. I wanted to have a curved pruning saw with raked-back teeth sharpened. The owner of the sharpening shop refused, because it didn't fit in his machine. He said to sharpen it by hand would cost more than buying a new saw. Such is progress!

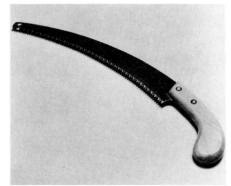

20

Pruning Saw, ORSA MODEL 7362, IMPORTED BY SKODCO, $8.25–9.50 (20)

Swedish alloy steel, heat-treated blade about 15 inches long; ¼-inch teeth; blade has long, slight curve, tapering from 1¾ inches wide at the base to ¾ inch wide at the tip; lacquered beech handle with 2 bolts and sleeves; hanging hole at blade tip for storage.

This small saw should be used primarily for pruning, but it comes in handy while clearing woodlots when you're faced with closely branched shrubs and tree thickets. It has straight, high toothing for cutting on the pull stroke.

21

Curved Pruning Saw, ORSA MODEL 7072, IMPORTED BY SKODCO, $20.00–22.00 (21)

Swedish alloy steel, heat-treated 24-inch blade tapering from 3⁹/₁₆ inches at the handle to 1 inch at the tip; handle of laminated wood with blade fastened to it by 3 bolts and sleeves.

This is a curved-blade saw featuring raker toothing with deep indentations for heavy-duty tree work. The teeth are straight on the forward part of the blade for starting cuts. It doesn't make as smooth a cut for easy healing of a tree as smaller types do, but does well on large pieces of wood.

Bow Saw, "SWIFTY," MODEL 331, SANDVIK, $5.50–6.00 **(22)**

21-inch blade; 7¼-inch clearance at center between blade and handle; frame bright orange Swedish steel; blade tension maintained with adjustable lever mechanism; "skip-tooth" pattern.

Sandvik has been selling this saw for years to Christmas-tree growers for quick harvesting of trees. The saw is intended for light pruning and landscape work around the house — not for fine pruning. It's also handy for cutting firewood.

The "skip-tooth" design means that the configurations are always different between the teeth, guaranteeing a fresh cut every time the tooth goes into the wood. The specially hardened blade is said to last up to five times longer than conventional blades. The blade is not meant to be sharpened; when it gets dull, throw it away and get a new one.

Bow Saw, MODEL 3914, SKODCO, $5.75–6.25 **(23)**

21-inch blade, on ¾-inch round tubular frame, with tension lever to ensure proper blade installation; blades made of Swedish heat-treated steel; 4 cutting teeth separated by one short, double-raker tooth.

The light weight of this saw makes it particularly useful for cutting firewood up to 5 inches in diameter. The saw is fast cutting; the blades are hardened, which keeps them sharper up to five times as long. This model is

available in lengths from 21 inches to 42 inches.

Bow Saw, MODEL 19-098, AMES, $9.50–11.00 **(24)**

36-inch blade, in chrome-plated tubular steel bow frame; frame parallel with the blade its entire length, giving a clearance of 10 inches; blade se-cured with adjustable wing nut; pattern of 4 cutting teeth, 2 rakers; plastic hand grip at one end of bow.

This saw will manage just about any firewood your fireplace or stove can handle, since it can cut through logs up to 20 inches thick. The design is available also in 21-inch, 24-inch, and 30-inch sizes.

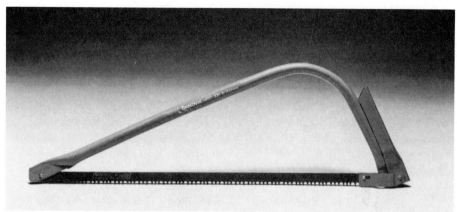

22

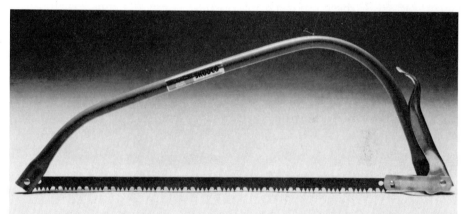

23

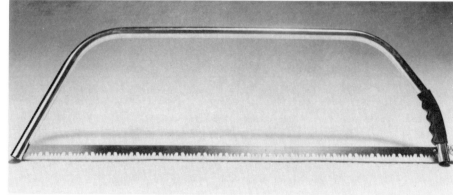

24

25

Bull Saw (ONE-MAN CROSSCUT SAW), MODEL P400, STANLEY TOOLS, $31.00–34.00 **(25)**

3 feet long, 5¾ inches at widest point tapering to 2¼ inches at end; 2 cutter, one raker tooth configuration; tempered steel; lacquered handle with large hand grip.

For many years, this fast-cutting tool was known as the one-man or bull saw. Use it for felling trees or for cutting up wood. The balance of the saw is very good for one-hand use when cutting vertically, or for two-hand use when making horizontal cuts. The adjustable handle can be pulled to the end to permit the use of two operators, like a miniversion of the larger two-man crosscut saw. When this adjustable handle is moved down near the regular handle, the bull saw serves as an excellent tool for cutting firewood on a saw buck.

Two-Man Crosscut Saw, MODEL 33A, JEMCO TOOL, $65.00–70.00 **(26)**

6-foot cutting blade, 5½ inches deep at the center tapering to 3¼ inches at each end; removable 11-inch-long wood handles at each end; combination cutting teeth and rakers.

The two-man crosscut saw has been around at least 100 years, and can be a powerhouse for cutting down large trees. (The size of the tree which can be cut depends on the strength of the operators, but 3-foot-diameter trees are possible.) The saw is less likely to bind if you are careful to start out at a straight angle, and pull, never push, this saw. It should be sharpened with a 12-inch bastard file; when filing the teeth, be sure to touch up the rakers lightly on each side.

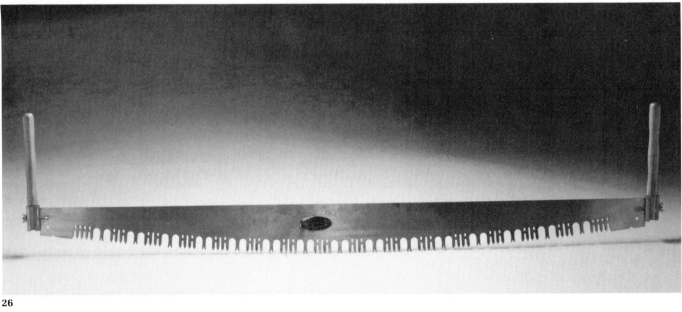

26

FELLING WEDGE

WOOD-HANDLING TOOLS

Felling Wedge, MODEL PN23565, OMARK INDUSTRIES, $2.75–3.25 **(27)**

Yellow plastic wedge, 5⅛ inches long and 2¾ inches wide at the thin edge; striking surface 1 inch wide and 1¾ inches long.

This lightweight wedge is meant to be used when cutting down trees, not splitting logs. When inserted in the cut, it can add impetus to the final felling strokes and encourage a tree to go in the desired direction. You'll also want to use it sometimes to hold a cut open to keep the saw from binding. Obviously, a metal wedge could serve the same purposes. The beauty of this plastic one is that if your saw blade strikes it accidentally, the wedge may be damaged, but not the saw.

Have you ever wondered if there are efficient ways to dislodge a fallen tree that doesn't make it to the ground? Or how to move logs to the saw buck without scraping your knuckles trying to get beneath them? There are, of course, and professional woodsmen have been using them for years. With the increase in wood burning, and with more people doing their own felling of trees and sawing of firewood, these specialized tools are now finding a place in the home workshop. We've included two such tools here. If you have a large woodlot, or plan to lay in a winter supply of firewood, you'll find them helpful.

Cant Dog (PEAVEY), SNOW & NEALLEY, $20.00–22.00 **(28)**

Wood handle 3½ feet long, tapers from about 1 inch at the top to 2½ inches in diameter at the shank where it supports a 4-inch center spike and free-swinging side hook.

If that tree you were felling didn't fall, a cant dog may come to your rescue. It's a handy tool for dislodging a hung-up tree, giving you some leverage and a little distance from the tree so you can get out of the way quickly if your efforts to dislodge are successful. The cant dog is also useful for rolling logs, and two can be used together as a handle to pick up logs if both the center spike and side hook are embedded.

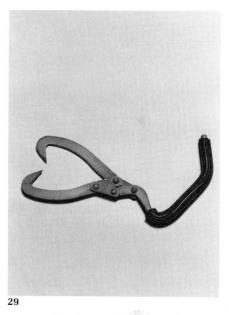

29

Lifting Tong, MODEL 34089, SANDVIK, $12.00–14.00 **(29)**

Black plastic tubing covers the 7-inch handle; ⅛-inch-thick flat steel tongs painted orange will open nearly 7 inches.

Double-pivot construction in a square or diamond pattern allows me to use this tool with one hand to pick up heavy, awkward wood. You'll be able to lift and carry logs more than 6 inches in diameter with these tongs. The pivot construction forces the teeth deep into the wood. A quick tap of the end of the handle against one of the tongs will release the tool. It can also be used as a hook to pull wood by holding one tong against the handle.

27

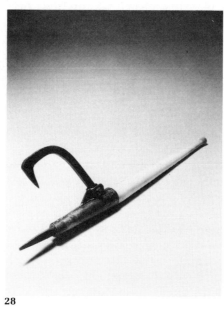

28

CHAIN SAWS AND SHARPENERS

Robert Frost describes the weight of an axe head "poised aloft," the spread of feet on firm ground and the "life of muscles rocking soft . . . in vernal heat." But our modern muscles aren't always as tough as they might be, nor do we always have enough time. With a chain saw, we can cut as much wood on a Saturday morning as it took my grandfather the weekend to accomplish.

Not everyone will find such a saw necessary, but if you have a large suburban or rural lot, or if you gather wood for a stove or fireplace, you'll find chain saws very useful. You don't need one of the giants. Something with a blade 12 to 16 inches long and in the middle price range ($175–250) will do just fine. After all, a 16-inch chain saw will take down a tree 32 inches in diameter, and if you're tackling something bigger than that, maybe you should be calling in the pros anyway.

Chain saws are dangerous if used carelessly. Before tackling any job with your own, a rented, or borrowed chain saw, be sure you have taken all safety precautions and are aware of any special safety features of the saw you're using. You need protection for your head, eyes, and ears. You must be extra careful about getting good boots, wearing clothes that fit snugly and don't flap loose, and using gloves that keep your hands warm, yet are flexible enough to leave you in complete control of the saw. Make sure everyone else is well clear of the tree you are felling, flying wood chips, a sudden backlash from the saw, and of course, any rotten branches that may shake loose. Clear away debris from where you will stand and be sure of your footing. Then, *and only then,* start your saw.

Your first decision in purchasing a saw — whether to buy an electric or gasoline motor — depends on how you intend to use the saw. For cutting wood within range of electricity, the electric saw has several advantages. It's quieter. That's a blessing to neighbors and saves you from very real damage to your hearing. There's no fussing with fuel, spark plugs, carburetors, rope starters, needle valves, or similar mechanical aspects. Just plug it in and squeeze the trigger. Remember, you need a heavy-duty (grounded), weatherproof extension cord of no more than 150 feet (check the manufacturer's recommendations for exact length limits). You can't drag such cords through brush, or over extremely rough ground, either. If most of your work will be around the yard, an electric saw will do the job. If you are cutting down a great deal of wood in the forest, you'll need a gasoline model. Gasoline saws come in a greater range of styles and prices.

As with the axe, think first of control. When you shop for a saw, pick several up and make a serious test of the weight and balance. Hold the saw in front of you at arm's length. Tilt it at different angles. Try the trigger grip to make sure it's comfortable and see if while holding the trigger you can easily work the plunger that oils the blade. You'll have to do this while the saw is cutting, and you don't want to have to change your grip to use it. On some saws oiling is automatic. In the gasoline version, check to see how the saw is placed for filling the tank. On some models, the saw must be held at an awkward angle to do this.

Some other features you might look for are:

1. a detachable nose guard that covers the front few inches of the blade. This prevents you from using that section of the saw, shortening its effective length, but it also removes the biggest chance of kickback (a saw jumping away from the wood toward your face) by covering the tip of the blade where such action usually originates.

2. chain brakes that stop the saw immediately when it binds or hits a foreign object. There are also brakes that stop the saw when your hand slips across the blade. Saws with these brakes have a shield in front of the handle which, when touched, stops the chain.

3. a highly visible color. A chain saw spends much of its active life sitting on the ground amidst bark, brush, and branches. So it's nice to be able to spot it when you want it, as well as when you want to simply avoid tripping over it.

4. a distinct separation of the cap to the oil reservoir from the cap to the gasoline tank (also, an indicator of some sort that lets you know how much oil is left in the reservoir without removing the cap).

Caring for the electric saws mostly involves keeping them dry and clean. The gas saws need the same attention that any small motor needs, with seasonal cleaning and tuning. Sharpening chain saws is a tricky, but essential, process. As with other saws, if in doubt, leave it to the people who make it their business. You can tell when a chain saw is dull by looking at the residue it leaves. A pile of fine sawdust means it's bruising its way through the wood. Chips and small strips of wood with a minimum of sawdust are what you can expect from a sharp saw. If you wish to do your own sharpening, however, do seek adequate directions. I've included in this book some instruments designed for professional woodsmen that will do the job.

Chain Saw, MODEL XEL, HOMELITE, $70.00–90.00 **(30)**

Red electric chain saw with 14-inch cutting blade; weighs 9.9 pounds; 1.5-horsepower, 11-amp engine with double-insulated housing; power tipped bar and chromed chain; push-button manual chain oiler, ball-bearing construction; built-in rear hand guard and rubber-coated wrap-around handle bar.

The Model XEL has many of the safety features found in Homelite's gasoline engine line. The blade tip is protected by a 2½ × 2½-inch hardened steel guard that reduces the danger of kickback, a major cause of chain saw accidents. There's a safety lock that must be depressed before the operating trigger can be used. You can reach the chain oil dispenser

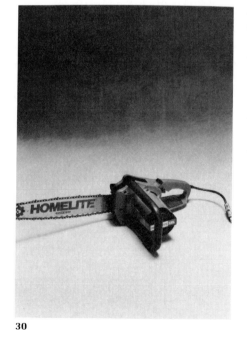
30

easily with your right thumb while the saw is in use.

This inexpensive electric chain saw is meant to be used for light pruning and trimming and sawing firewood logs no larger than 8 to 10 inches in diameter.

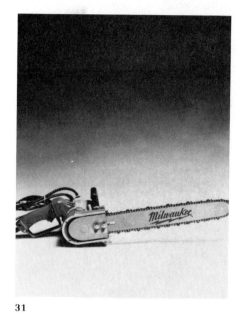
31

Chain Saw, MODEL 6211, MILWAUKEE ELECTRIC TOOL, $240.00–260.00 **(31)**

Electric chain saw with 16- or 20-inch blade; weighs 18½ pounds; 120-volt, 15-amp engine, all ball bearings; use on a circuit of at least 20 amps.

This saw was designed for the construction industry, but if you plan to do a lot of harvesting wood and cutting it up for the stove, you may appreciate its heavy-duty features. The saw cuts rapidly and the motor is quiet and starts quickly, even in freezing temperatures.

32

33

34

Chain Saw, MODEL S25DA-14, BEAIRD-POULAN, $170.00–190.00 **(32)**

Gasoline-powered saw with 14-inch cutting blade; green housing; total weight 8 pounds, 9 ounces; two-cycle, 2.3-cubic-inch engine; automatic chain oiler with manual override.

The light weight of this saw is a welcome change from some of its bigger brothers, and permits use in among the branches of trees sometimes difficult to reach with larger saws. The gasoline and the chain oil fills are separated in a desirably safe design; the automatic chain oiler helps prevent wear and tear on the engine.

Chain Saw, MODEL 015AV, STIHL, $215.00–235.00 **(33)**

Gasoline-powered saw with 10-, 12-, or 14-inch guide bar; red and white colors; antivibration system; power-head weight 9.6 pounds; available with electric ignition option.

Stihl saws are used extensively by commercial operators, yet the size and weight of this unit makes it a good model for homeowners. You can convert this in less than 5 minutes to use the engine to power a brush cutter, or a hedge trimmer (purchased separately). A safety switch guards against accidental starting. The upper

handle on both top and side is encased in nonslip rubber. A safety bar is designed to stop the chain instantly if the operator's hand slips forward of the handle toward the blade. Since the fill caps for gasoline and the chain oil are close to each other, be careful not to get these confused.

Chain Saw, MODEL 451EV, JONSEREDS, DISTRIBUTED BY TILTON EQUIPMENT, $330.00–360.00 **(34)**

Red, gasoline-powered saw with 16-inch blade; weighs 13.5 pounds; 44.3-cubic-centimeter engine with vertical cylinder; bar lengths 12 or 15 inches; heated handles with space for gloved hand.

The Jonsereds saw, used by professional loggers in Sweden, incorporates several safety features. The operating trigger can't be used until the safety switch has been released. There's a brake to stop the chain, should the operator's hand slip forward from the handle — the chain stops in less than $1/10$ of a second. The chain oil filler cap and gasoline cap are well separated to avoid confusion, and both can be filled while the saw is safely resting on its right side. The antivibration figures of this model are less than half the figures fixed by Swedish regulating agencies.

Chain Saw File, MODEL 82004, NICHOLSON FILE, $5.50–6.00 **(35)**

4-inch red plastic handle supports round file 5 inches long and $5/32$ inch in diameter, and a guide bar for assuring straight uniform sharpening strokes; other file diameters available from $1/8$ to $1/4$ inch.

This file and guide will make it possible to sharpen most chain saws by hand in the field. It does not joint or assure the uniform depth of the saw cutters, but it is a convenient tool that will fit into the pocket for the kind of minor improvements in the blade that can make any job go easier.

35

Saw Chain File Sharpening Guide,
"FILE-O-PLATE,"
CARLTON, $2.00–2.50 (36)

Metal plate about 1 inch wide, 2½ inches long, with perforations to fit over individual chain teeth.

The Carlton Company, manufacturers of saw chains, also makes an inexpensive plate that fits over the individual teeth on a saw chain to guide filing to a proper angle. It's possible to lower the depth gauges progressively as needed, which is important because saw chain stretch often is caused by a depth gauge that is too high, creating tension and stress on the chain and eventual breakage. By the way, the Carlton Company passes on this tip for telling if your saw needs sharpening: every saw chain is capable of cutting through a log 10 inches or less in diameter at the rate of more than 1 inch per second; if your saw doesn't do this, your chain needs sharpening.

36

37

Saw Chain Sharpener, "FILE-N-JOINT,"
MODEL G-106,
GRANBERG INDUSTRIES, $19.00–21.00 (37)

Metal precision chain sharpener with chain clamps, file holder and 9-inch guide rod.

The homeowner who wants to sharpen his own saw chain often goes about it the hard way. He decides to take the chain off the bar, files too much off the teeth, has trouble assembling the saw again, and vows that next time he will go to a professional. The "File-N-Joint," made by the largest American manufacturer of chain saw sharpeners, is designed to help out the occasional chain saw user. It attaches to the bar itself, provides the correct angle for the file — insuring proper depth — and makes it impossible to file off too much, as can happen when sharpening by eye. It works on all makes and sharpens chain from ¼- to ½-inch pitch. Keep in mind that a correctly sharpened chain will work more efficiently and last up to twice as long as a dull one.

38

Chain Saw Sharpener, "GRIND-N-JOINT," MODEL G-912,
GRANBERG INDUSTRIES, $29.00–32.00 (38)

Tool comes in an orange plastic case about 5 × 2 × 2 inches, with 8 feet of electric cord for attaching to 12-volt battery; depth gauge plate is adjustable to provide the proper depth for various types of chain saw cutter blades; grinding tool is about 1 inch long and ⅛ inch in diameter, and operates at speeds up to 24,000 revolutions per minute.

If you are really doing a lot of chain saw work, this tool will make field sharpening easier. You can run it off your 12-volt car battery, or a suitable portable unit. It's lightweight, safe, efficient, and comes with detailed instructions. Grandberg also makes a 110-volt heavy-duty grinder for the professional user.

LOG LIFTERS

If you have a lot of wood to cut, consider using a log lifter. It steadies the log while, at the same time, preventing the chain saw from digging into the ground or kicking back toward you. That's important, because chain saws that end up cutting soil rather than wood risk becoming dull or hitting a rock. There's a safety element as well. If you attempt to cut a log lying on the ground, it tends to close up as it's cut through — often causing the saw to kick back. If a log is placed in a lifter, the kickback is unlikely. With a log lifter, you can work alone because you don't need another person to hold the wood.

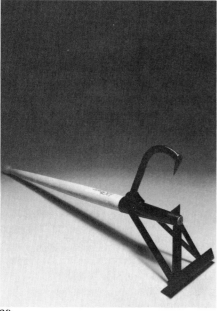

39

40

Log Lifter, "JAC-N-REST," BISHOP, $34.00–37.00 **(39)**

3½-foot northern hardwood handle attached to metal peavey; overall height 8 inches; weighs 9 pounds, 2 ounces.

Here's a log lifter that used to be made for Maine lumberjacks but is now aimed at the many homeowners heating with wood. To use it, hook the peavey end over the log's center, then place the log lifter in a vertical position. Put the swing hook on top of the log and pull the handle downward toward the ground.

When you're ready to cut, be sure to stand on the same side of the log as the handle, to keep the handle from

coming up and hitting you as you saw. The lifter holds logs up to 14 inches in diameter.

Log Lifter, "BETTER'N BEN'S LOG LIFTER," HAYES EQUIPMENT, $38.00–42.00 **(40)**

1¼-inch-diameter steel tubing with black rubber handle; overall height 16 inches, length 46 inches; weighs 10½ pounds.

This unit, made by the manufacturers of Better'n Ben's fireplace stoves, is made of strong steel tubing and gives sufficient leverage to lift logs with diameters of up to 18 inches. It's sturdy and hard to dislodge.

WOOD-SPLITTING TOOLS

Splitting Maul, MODEL 122-H, WOODINGS-VERONA, $23.00–26.00 **(41)**

6 pounds, with 3½-inch cutting blade and 8½-inch-high head with flat top for driving wedges; 36-inch-long handle slightly flared to reduce splitting.

While the axe you use for chopping down a tree can also be used to split firewood or fence rails, a better tool for this task is a splitting maul. Opposite the cutting edge is a flattened head designed for driving wedges. Since you'll always be swinging down with this tool, the extra weight (about half again as heavy as an axe) will add power to the stroke without being too much of a burden. The blade is fatter than an axe's, so it tends to do a better job of pushing wood apart along the grain. Using such a maul will save the keen cutting edge of your axe from striking the ground occasionally while splitting wood. This maul is available in an 8-pound model also.

41

42

43

44

Splitting Axe, "CHOPPER 1,"
CHOPPER INDUSTRIES, $35.00–39.00
(42)

*7-pound axe with a 5-inch cutting
face, 6½-inch-high head, and a handle 32 or 36 inches long; a movable
metal finger juts out from each side of
the blade at a point about 2½ inches
above the cutting edge.*

This is a new and unusual design that
works. The basic idea is for the two
metal fingers to be forced out (sideways) as the blade enters the wood.
This not only aids the splitting action,
but also prevents the blade from sink-
ing too deep in the wood and becoming stuck if the log doesn't split. If the
axe doesn't penetrate, it tends to
bounce a few inches and fall back on
the wood. This can eliminate a great
deal of use of wedges and mauls
while splitting wood.

Sledge, MODEL 84H,
WARREN TOOL, $21.00–23.00 **(43)**

*8-pound hammer with a 6½-inch-long
head that has a 4-square-inch striking
surface on each end; 32-inch-long
handle; also available in sizes from 2
to 20 pounds.*

Whether you're driving a wedge to
split wood or clearing your land of an
old foundation or some other eyesore,
the sledgehammer can make fast work
of the task. What I said about temper
in axe metal and even grain in handles applies to sledges also. A sledge
should see years of rough use, so it
has to be built well. You also want to
make sure you get a handle length
and weight that feel well balanced
and comfortable to you. Be sure to
wear safety goggles, or a face shield,
when using a sledge — when that
metal end hits anything, whether it's
wood, rock, or steel, there's a chance
that small chips are going to be sent
flying in all directions.

Wedge, MODEL 120, WARREN TOOL,
$7.50–8.50 **(44)**

*5-pound metal wedge painted red; 9
inches long, with head 1½ inches
wide at the thin edge; striking surface
measures 2⅜ inches; also comes in
weights from 3 to 8 pounds.*

A wedge is a help in splitting and it's
a good idea to have two or three
wedges of different sizes. This way, if
a small one becomes buried in the
wood and won't come out, a larger
one can be inserted to rescue it. Use a
splitting maul or sledgehammer to
drive the wedge into the wood —
never the back of your axe. Wear
safety goggles or a mask to protect
your face because when you have
metal striking against metal, as you
will when driving a wedge, there's always the chance of fragments flying
off from the wedge or hammer.

BRUSH-CLEARING TOOLS

If you're faced with a tangle of overgrown bushes, young trees, shrubs, and vines, you'll find your task easier with specialized brush-clearing tools.

For occasional lightweight work, a machete will do fine. It can be used to hack through small branches and vines with a one-hand stroke. Bush hooks are heavy-duty tools requiring a two-handed swing. They're sometimes used to clear the lower branches from trees or cut down saplings. The powered brush cutters will handle material up to 4 inches in diameter, and, while they'll make the work go faster, few homeowners have enough need for brush cutting to justify the expense of a fine power cutter. It's better to rent one for a weekend in most cases.

Whether you rent or buy, however, do apply an extra measure of safety to the use of any of these tools. It's good to remember that the machete is also viewed as a weapon, and although you'll be swinging it with just one arm, its long cutting edge and weight make it deadly. With both the powered and manual types of brush cutters, make sure people and pets are well clear. Be sure of your footing. When working with brush, you'll probably be on uneven ground with the residue of your efforts around you. It's also easy to snag a tool in motion on a rock, or a thicker tangle of limbs and brush than anticipated, and this could literally throw you.

When choosing a hand brush cutter, look for the keenness of well-tempered steel. You want an edge that will last, although the bush hook's edge need not be kept as sharp as an axe's. You also want a smooth, even-grained handle that you can grip with sureness.

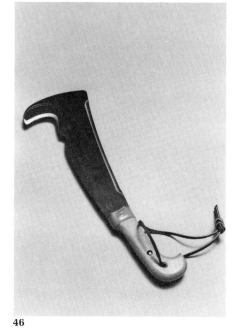

46

"Woodman's Pal," MODEL 481, OLEY TOOLING, $32.00–35.00 **(46)**

Unusual tool with a heavy metal blade about 12 inches long that flares to about 5 inches wide at the end.

This tool is a cross between a hatchet, machete, grubhoe, and trenching shovel. You can use it to split kindling, hack down small branches, dig out vines, or slash brush. Obviously, no multipurpose tool is going to do all these jobs as well as the individual tool designed for a single task, but for the person who has only occasional call to clear brush, or do many of the things that can be done with this tool, it is a handy compromise.

Machete, MODEL 128, IMPORTED FROM GUATEMALA BY COLLINS AXE, $8.80–10.00 **(45)**

Black plastic handle, with extension to keep fingers from slipping, holds 22-inch blade about 1½ inches wide near the handle and 2 inches wide near the tip; blade is about ¹/₁₆ inch thick; holding sheath available separately.

This tool is used for pruning small trees in the nursery and the growing tips of plantation-grown Christmas trees, but the homeowner will find it is most helpful in chopping through light brush, such as honeysuckle vines and brambles. It should be kept in a sheath or scabbard when not in use. A hole through the handle allows you to attach a leather or string wrist thong.

45

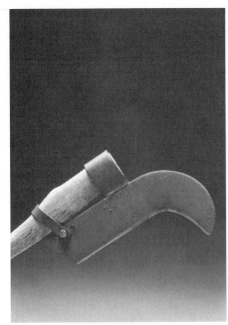

47

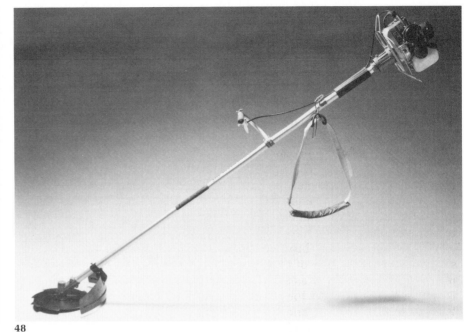

48

Bush Hook, MODEL 10, TRUE TEMPER, $20.50–22.00 **(47)**

Heavy, sharp cutting face about 11 inches long attached to 36-inch-long handle with 2 metal straps, one of which is adjustable; curving blade helps to keep the cutting edge away from the ground so it won't be dulled too quickly.

You need a lot of clear room and firm footing to swing a bush hook, but, if you have it, this tool will do a good job of removing brush and trees up to 1½ inches thick. Much of the work of this tool is in the power of the swing, not the sharpness of the cutting blade. Highway crews use these tools often, but unless you have a great deal of brush to clear, you're probably better off renting or borrowing one on the few occasions you need it.

Brush Cutter, "THE GREEN MACHINE," MODEL 3000, HMC, $320.00–340.00 **(48)**

(Base unit with trimmer); optional blades: saw blade 92130, $8.50–10.00; standard brush blade 92140, $12.00–13.00; cross brush blade 92180, $12.00–13.00. About 6 feet overall; 14-pound unit comes with string trimmer, blades are optional (see above); clutch housing with dual bearings; soft plastic handgrip on shaft; horizontal handgrip with adjustable throttle control; padded shoulder strap; approximately 1½-horsepower, 2-cycle, air-cooled cylinder engine.

"The Green Machine" is designed for the professional landscaper or large acreage owner who needs a strong unit for continuous work. The string trimmer has an automatic-feed head that cuts grass and light weeds. For cutting brush, switch to one of three blades, which takes only a minute to change. The saw blade, which you can hold over your head for tree pruning, should be used with a quick impact "karate" chop to remove limbs up to 3 inches. The standard brush blade cuts heavy weeds, such as burdock, or light brush. For very heavy

brush, such as buckthorn or choke cherry thickets, reach for the cross blade, 5 inches in diameter with an extended metal piece. It doesn't have to be sharpened as often as the standard blade, and once it gets dull, reverse it and use the other side. The tool kit, which comes with the unit, includes a file for sharpening.

Brush Cutter, MODEL FS-150,
STIHL, $390.00–430.00 **(49)**

Handles on bicycle-type bar; powered by the Stihl 015 gas chain saw engine; about 6 feet overall with 2 interchangeable 10-inch-diameter saw blades and a trimmer head; heavy-padded shoulder strap; rotary shield straps on to protect during storage; 17.6 pounds.

Saw blades will cut trees up to 4 inches in diameter and small brush. The target to be cut should be positioned against the left side of the guard to prevent kickback or loss of control. The nylon string cutter, using two 8-inch filaments, is good for general land clearing as well as for trimming around and under fences and around rock gardens and for clearing drainage ditches. The construction is heavyweight throughout and the tool will provide long, unstrained power.

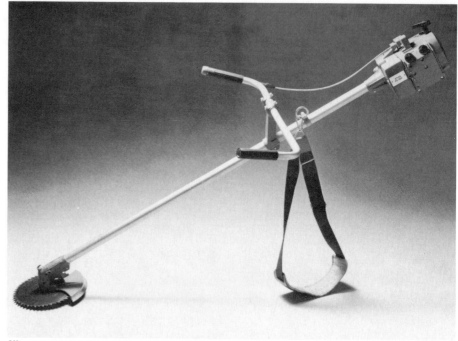

49

CLEARING STONES

Since stones don't come equipped with handles, it's nice to have sturdy tools that can help you pry them loose and remove them from a future lawn or garden site.

Picks, mattocks and crowbars all play their role in this process, as well as helping out with other land-clearing activities. Picks may have points on both ends of the head. They're good for breaking up hard, clayey soil, loosening a stubborn rock from its home in the ground, or smashing an old walkway or other paved surface.

Sometimes a pick is found on one end of a mattock head while the other end has a very heavy, dull blade. This blade is used for grubbing, that is, digging out roots. A mattock can also have a hoelike blade on one end and a more axelike blade on the other. Again, the blades are not sharp — they're not meant for chopping wood, but for digging around and cutting through roots. An axe or hatchet used for these jobs would quickly become dull.

The mattock, too, is useful for prying out small rocks, but larger rocks will probably require a crowbar and maybe some old timbers, which you can grease with used crankcase oil to help rocks slip more smoothly on them.

For rock work, I much prefer the bars with a chisellike end. Some crowbars have a more rounded end and these can slip too easily when used under a rock.

Crowbars are tough enough to take a pounding from a sledgehammer, and the sharpened end can be slipped in a crevice of a rock in an attempt to split it. Like other tools used in land-clearing operations, crowbars tend to spend much time flat on the ground. To make them easy to see, give them an occasional repainting with a bright orange or yellow.

Think about landscape possibilities for your stones. Some will find their way into walls or the rock garden, while other large ones may have a picturesque shape and weathered appearance that will make them an ideal landscape feature.

Crowbar, MODEL B518,
TRUE TEMPER, $26.00–30.00 **(50)**

18-pound, 60-inch-long wedge-point crowbar made of 1¼-inch steel stock.

This crowbar was originally used in industry for moving railroad cars or heavy equipment into place, but homeowners soon discovered its multiple virtues. It's hard to equal for moving heavy rocks while clearing a garden spot, or when rock garden stones too big to pick up need to be manipulated into position. If flagstones in the patio have shifted, use a crowbar to lift them up while replacing sand or soil underneath. It's also helpful for making an initial hole for tomato stakes or postholes. The high carbon steel composition means it is very strong and resists bending.

50

Clay Pick, MODEL 30-H,
WOODINGS-VERONA, $21.00–23.00 **(51)**

5-pound pick with a 21-inch-long head with a point at one end and a chisel blade, 1 inch wide, at the other; 36-inch-long handle.

The head on this tool is a little smaller and lighter than you're likely to see construction workers using, but that makes it a good choice for the home gardener. (Since a pick isn't the sort of thing you use frequently, it's better to have one that is a manageable size.) The handle on this tool is widest at the far end to prevent the head from flying loose. The pointed blade will do a fine job of breaking through tough spots, while the wedge end can be used both as a lever to pry loose small rocks and as a small cutting edge to chop roots.

51

Cutter Mattock, MODEL 05-103, EASCO TOOLS, $9.00–10.00 **(52)**

3-pound mattock with a hoelike cutter blade on one end and a more axelike blade on the other.

This is a good tool for digging out an old shrub, or simply chopping through hard-pan soil. You'll want to keep the blades sharp, although not with the keen edge you would put on an axe. The same company makes a 5-pound model (05-125) that has a pick at one end and a cutting blade at the other.

52

PREPARING AND PLANTING
THE GARDEN

Gardening begins with forks, spades, shovels, and trowels. These are the essential tools you'll need to prepare a seedbed and start planting. They aren't complicated or hard to find, but they are important, so I don't skimp on them.

A poor-quality fork will soon have its tines bent out of line and will be awkward to use. I want a shovel that will stand up to hard work without a broken handle, and I want a trowel that fits comfortably in my hand and won't bend in hard soil. That's why I buy the best-quality tool I can afford for those basic chores. I expect to use some of these tools the rest of my life. True, you might some day have to replace a broken handle, and, of course, you will sharpen and clean these tools regularly — but they should be just as useful in the year 2000 as they are in 1980. Don't be fooled by their simplicity. There are good ways and poor ways to make just about anything, and these tools are no exception.

I think there's a basic economy in buying a good tool to start with, and then taking care of it. This doesn't mean that you always have to choose the highest-priced ones, but it does mean that you should be aware that major tool manufacturers have several different lines of tools of varying quality and price. You can't simply make your decision by the name on the tool or the reputation of the manufacturer. You should also check to make sure you're buying from one of the better, if not the best, line of tools.

Since you'll be living with these tools for a long time, be careful to pick ones that match your capacity. A rake or shovel can have as personal a fit as a new coat. Make sure it's a comfortable one from the outset.

When you have the basic tools, there are a few accessories to give thought to. First on my list is a cold frame. It's a must for getting a jump on spring, hardening-off young seedlings, and extending the gardening season in the fall. Many people build their own frames, but there is also a fine commercial version available now, complete with automatic ventilation.

Many of the other tools and accessories in this chapter I wouldn't be without. They have made my gardening easier and more interesting. But if you're just starting out, start right. Go for the best quality you can afford in those tools you will need most and obtain others as time, inclination, and pocketbook permit.

FORKS

If you have a relatively small garden, you'll probably turn it over each spring by hand, and for this task, as well as several others, the critical tool is a short-handled fork.

Forks differ in the length, shape, and number of tines, according to their use. The ones with long, thin, rounded tines are meant for pitching hay or manure. They don't have the sturdiness for the heavy work of turning over soil. For this task, we look for a fork with 4 relatively flat, heavy, pointed tines.

There are several minor differences in style of such forks and some more important ones in the width of the head and length of tines. As with so many gardening tools, many of these differences arose not from whim, but from regional demands that varied with local soil conditions and the crops grown.

When you choose a fork, look first for a tool that fits you. The forks of one major manufacturer, for example, range in head width from 6 to 8 inches and in tine length from 8½ to 12 inches. The weights of these forks go from 2 pounds, 9 ounces to 4 pounds, 10 ounces. With the smaller, lightweight tool, the jobs will take longer (and perhaps you won't be able to dig quite so deep), but each forkful of soil will be easier to lift. I prefer a longer-tined fork because I want to turn over the soil to as great a depth as is reasonably possible; but if such a fork is going to wear you out quickly, the smaller one is better.

The main danger of buying a cheap fork is that the tines soon bend out of alignment, making the fork relatively useless. There's plenty of pressure put on these long metal rods, especially when a stone gets wedged between them. You want a fork made of fine-tempered steel that will snap back into place when temporarily bent out of line. As with other large hand tools, you also want to look for a sturdy handle of even grain, finished to a smoothness that will be kind to your hands.

Fork, MODEL 18-025, AMES, $16.50–18.00 **(1)**

4-tined fork with 30-inch "D"-shaped handle, 10¾-inch tines; 7⅛-inch-wide head (also available with 48-inch handle).

This top-of-the-line fork has an especially long (10-inch) chrome-plated steel ferrule that makes for a firm connection between head and handle. That "D" style is what Ames calls their "Armor-D" because the flame-toughened, northern ash handle extends right through the "D" to the top. In other words, you have a wooden "D" completely encased in a steel one for extra strength. You'll find this "Armor-D" on some other Ames tools, also.

1

Fork, "ENGLISH DIGGING FORK," MODEL EDS4D, TRUE TEMPER, $17.60–19.00 **(2)**

4 tines, 12 inches long, on 8-inch-wide head with 30-inch handle; Model EDSL has 48-inch handle.

Squeeze the spring-tempered, high-carbon steel tines on this fork toward one another and they'll spring back into place, as they should on a good fork. The square-shaped tines are a bonus for clay or stony soil. The handle is of fire-hardened northern ash and the steel ferrule has a glossy maroon finish.

2

SPADES

Spades usually have short, "D"-shaped handles with a strong, nearly flat metal blade, sharply edged. I use a spade for transplanting either balled or bare-rooted plants, because spades cut cleanly through the soil and the roots that must be severed, and also allow you to pick up soil from the bottom of the trench. Spades are also helpful for cutting woody weeds; cutting, lifting and tamping sod; slicing sod for shallow cable or pipe installations; prying stones and roots; edging planting beds; splitting small wood; driving stakes; cutting baling wires; and chopping ice. When buying a spade, look for an almost flat blade and good-quality steel.

Spades with short, beveled cutting edges work best. They can be kept sharp with a hand file, sharpening stone, or emery wheel (used slowly when wet so it will not destroy the temper of the metal).

narrow, deep trenching to install drainage tiles, pipes, conduits, and other underground utilities. It can also be used efficiently to dig small shrubs, trees, and perennial flowering plants.

Spade, JENKS & CATTEL MODEL 243, IMPORTED FROM ENGLAND BY GOOD-PROD SALES, $25.00–27.50 **(6)**

11½-inch blade, 7 inches wide, painted black; heavy-gauge steel with nylon-coated green tubular steel handle fitted with black poly "D" grip.

This top-quality English spade will lift plants of all types. The long polished socket is very strong and the tool handles well.

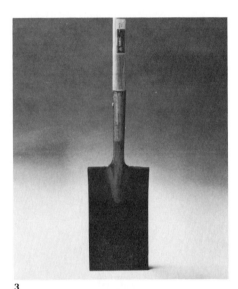

3

Spade, MODEL 15-631, AMES, $11.50–12.50 **(3)**

12-inch-long, serrated cutting blade, 7¼ inches wide; hollow back, with "D"-shaped handle 27 inches long.

This is a light spade that gets a little extra cutting power from the serrated edge. Note the long metal socket and the "Armor-D" handle.

Spade, MODEL DGS, TRUE TEMPER, $9.00–10.00 **(4)**

41-inch handle, 6⅛-inch-wide and 9½-inch-deep blade with a shallow curve to the edge; also available with 30-inch "D" handle (Model DGSD).

This light, hollow-back spade (3 pounds, 5 ounces) has a curved-over step for easy pushing into the ground with the foot. It's a good tool for edging and cultivating, as well as other tasks.

Spade, MODEL DS16, TRUE TEMPER, $21.50–24.00 **(5)**

Hot-taper-forged blade and socket formed from 1 steel bar; blade 16 inches long, 5½ inches wide at top, tapers to 4⅜ inches at bottom; "D"-shaped handle about 22 inches long, secured in shank with 2 strong rivets; ½-inch turned-forward edge on blade top.

This narrow, 5-pound spade with a gently rounded point is designed for

5

4

6

SHOVELS

In the last century, before much mechanized labor, some studies determined that a 21-pound load was about the right weight for a person to lift efficiently with a shovel. Load it up more and he could still lift it, but he would tire sooner. Load it up less and it was just a gift.

I suspect that many of us are somewhere below the 21-pound efficiency of the man building railroads in the 1850s, but the principle is the same. You choose a shovel that will hold the amount of dirt, snow, manure, grain, or whatever else, that you can lift efficiently. Large, heavy shovels are for strong people; if your muscles are more accustomed to lifting pencils, choose a lighter-weight shovel. For most garden shoveling, I like a long-handled, gently pointed shovel. It gives me good leverage, is kind to the back muscles, and its point makes cutting into the soil easier.

There are two basic methods for making a shovel and the major manufacturers offer shovels of both varieties.

The least expensive way is to stamp the shovel out of a flat piece of steel. A shovel of this sort must be reinforced by putting a crimp just below the socket. This results in a bulge, called a "frog," in front of the blade, and a hollow in the back — thus the term "hollow-back" shovel. The main disadvantage to this is a slightly weaker blade and a tendency for dirt to clog in the hollow. Still, these shovels are perfectly adequate for typical home use. However, if you want a heavy-duty "industrial" shovel, then turn to one that is rolled from a solid bar of high-carbon steel. This shovel has a 1-piece blade and socket without seams and welds — what is known as solid-shank construction.

A shovel needs to be kept clean, dry, and stored out of the weather.

Shovel, MODEL 12-017,
AMES, $17.50–19.00 **(7)**

Solid-shank steel shovel; 8¾ × 11½-inch blade; 47-inch northern ash handle.

Given proper care, this medium-weight shovel should last a lifetime. Its solid-shank construction means that blade, shank, and socket are forged from one solid bar of steel. In addition, the steel is thicker at points of maximum wear and stress. The handle is strong and slightly tapered, making it comfortable to use.

7

Shovel, "PEERLESS RAM,"
MODEL 13-059,
AMES, $12.20–13.50 **(8)**

47-inch handle with heavy steel serrated blade about 9 inches wide, 12 inches long; hollow back.

This medium-weight shovel has a deeper dish than many shovels on the market, enabling you to fill up and throw more soil than with a flatter shovel. The socket, about 9 inches long, is very securely riveted to the ash handle. The serrated edge covers about 4 inches of the blade width and makes it easier to cut through hard soil, sod, and roots.

8

Shovel, MODEL HGL,
TRUE TEMPER, $9.00 10.00   **(9)**

Ash handle, 42 inches long; blade 6 inches wide, 8½ inches deep with a rather sharp point; hollow back.

This lightweight (2 pounds, 8 ounces) shovel is designed for light digging, or for those who prefer to pace their efforts with a tool that doesn't demand too heavy a lift. It's available also with a 30-inch "D" handle.

9

SMALL TOOLS

Trowels are one of the few truly essential gardening tools, so don't skimp on them. Here's what I look for in a trowel:
- **solid, 1-piece construction so it won't break or bend;**
- **rust-protected metal, or, better yet, rustproof metal such as aluminum or stainless steel;**
- **a comfortable handle that feels easy on your hands;**
- **a brightly colored handle. Much as I like a natural wood finish, I'm forever trying to find where I last put my trowel in the garden.**

Trowels are most useful at transplanting time when it's handy to have two of different blade widths, depending on the size plant you're working with.

A trowel looks like a small shovel and sometimes you will want to hold and use it as you would any scoop. But to best use your trowel, grip it by closing your fist around it, as you would an ice pick, with the indented side of the blade facing you. Plunge it into the soil to the proper depth, and move it back and forth. The result is a quickly made, clean hole into which you can place the roots of the young plant.

Some of the sets of small tools on these pages include a small fork that is useful for transplanting larger plants in a garden or cold frame, as well as for rooting out the most stubborn weeds. You'll also see a bulb planter, another tool I consider especially useful.

I take these small hand tools seriously and make sure they get all the care of the larger ones. It's too easy to leave them lying about the garden with soil caked on them, letting them eventually become damaged or lost. They should be cleaned and stored, just as you would an axe, saw, or other tool.

10

Trowel, "NO-BLIST'R,"
RAY SANDERS, $5.00–6.00   **(10)**

1-piece, rustproof aluminum alloy construction; 5½-inch blade; 5¼-inch curved handle with bright red plastic grip.

No photograph can do justice to this trowel because only by picking it up and working with it can you appreciate its beauty. It is an honest, no-frills implement designed to serve long and well. The broad and shallow blade can be cleaned in an instant because there are no indentations or hidden pockets to catch and hold dirt.

Trowel, "ALL-PRO," MODEL 200, WILCOX ALL-PRO TOOLS & SUPPLY, $4.00–4.50 **(11)**

1-piece, heavy-gauge steel construction, plated for rust resistance; 14-inch-long, 3-inch-wide blade comes to a sharp point; red plastic handgrip.

If you're looking for a tough trowel to do those rugged digging jobs, such as rooting out dandelions, this is the one. It's part of a line of trowels designed not just for gardeners, but for campers, hunters, and fishermen who need a tool to dig out (or in) tent stakes, trench around the perimeter of tents, dig a small firepit, or carry out similar chores in soils far harder than those of most gardens and lawns. For the gardener, they'll do all the routine work of other trowels, plus take on harder jobs, such as digging holes in sod to naturalize bulbs, dividing plants where the roots have formed a thick mass (useful both indoors and out), or even chopping ice from steps and eaves.

11

Trowel, MODEL 19-821, AMES, $2.80–3.25 **(12)**

Chrome-plated steel, 12 inches long; 6-inch blade about 3 inches wide, strongly riveted to shank and held in handle with ferrule; blue plastic grip with finger indentations and hole for hanging.

Although not of 1-piece construction, this tool is well made and rugged. Ames makes a similar trowel, a little narrower (2½ inches wide) with marks on it indicating the depth to 4 inches. These marks are helpful, especially when planting bulbs where specific depth is important.

SMALL TOOLS

12

Trowel, SPEAR & JACKSON MODEL 4005, IMPORTED FROM ENGLAND BY GOOD-PROD SALES, $6.75–7.50 **(13)**

Stainless-steel, mirror-finish blade with walnut handle held securely by a set screw; 9 inches long, 1¾ inches wide.

Narrower than the standard trowel, this one has a clearly marked, pre-measured blade (up to 5 inches) that is good for planting seedlings or bulbs.

14

13

Trowel Set, "GRIPMASTER," MODEL 3064, IMPORTED FROM ENGLAND BY GREEN GARDE, $15.00–16.50 **(14)**

3 tools made from 1-piece, high-tensile aluminum alloy; each is about 9 to 10 inches long; handles have thumb depression on top and "trigger" on bottom; the 4-tined fork and the blade of the trowel are both 2½ inches wide, the blade of the "planter" (narrow trowel) is 1½ inches wide; soft plastic wall case; five-year guarantee.

Not only are these English tools sturdy and rustproof, they have an unusual handle grip designed by a lady suffering from arthritis of the wrist. She wanted a tool that both she and other gardeners, whether disabled or not, could use with ease. She came

up with a smooth, ½-inch protrusion (the trigger) on the bottom of the handle, placed within easy grasp of your index finger, which gives you more leverage with the tool. The smaller trowel is especially handy for transplanting smaller vegetables and flowers, as well as some bulbs. In case you don't want the whole set, the tools are available individually. The highly polished finish makes them easy to spot in the garden.

15

Fine-Point Trowel, MODEL W-478, WILKINSON SWORD, $6.00–7.00 **(15)**

Stainless-steel trowel, 9 inches long; 1½ ounce weight; offset handle fitted with gray lightweight plastic grip.

This tool is designed for small, delicate gardening tasks such as transplanting from flats to individual containers or for small bulb work. The offset head helps keep the hand above the soil surface, making it easier to work the soil. The tool may also be used for sowing fine seeds with a tap of the fingertip on the handle, or for indoor houseplant cultivation. Wilkinson makes a similar model (W-476) with a larger blade for use in damp or heavy soil.

16

Metal Can Shear, A. M. LEONARD, INC., $11.00–12.00 **(16)**

Zinc-plated metal shear; 26-inch-long handle with 2 grips at the top; total length, 29 inches; weight, 4 pounds.

If you've ever tried to free a shrub from its nursery can while doing minimum damage to its roots and to your hands, take a look at this tool created for professional nurserymen. You stand over the nursery can and, in one quick motion, slice downward through the metal. A few cuts and the plant is free, while you keep a safe distance from the can's edges. Homeowners with large lots to landscape might find this a handy tool.

Bulb Planter, MODEL 19-462, AMES, $8.00–9.00 **(17)**

Steel handle 26 inches long with an 8-inch crossbar at top; handle is riveted to a flat blade about 8 inches wide at the top, then rolled to form a 5-inch cylinder about 2¼ inches in diameter.

This bulb planter has two advantages over the smaller varieties. First, you can use it standing up. (Of course, you'll have to bend over to plant the bulb.) And second, you can apply your full weight to it to cut through tough soil or sod. If you apply a slight twisting motion as you press down on this, it will cut better. In most loams, this will pull out a plug of soil, but if your soil is sandy or rocky, you'll run into problems using it or any similar bulb planter.

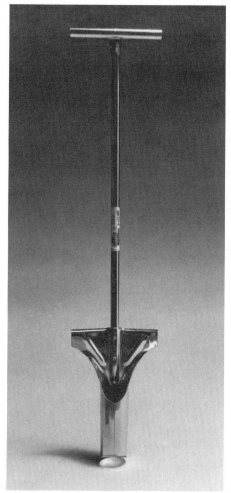

17

Bulb Planter, MODEL TBPD,
TRUE TEMPER, $3.70–4.25 **(18)**

Thin, polished metal, tapered round blade, 2½ inches wide, cutting depth about 4½ inches; wood handle; overall length 9½ inches.

This tool will cut a hole in the ground for planting bulbs, seedlings, vegetables, and flowers. The beveled core makes a round hole 2¼ inches in diameter and up to 4 inches deep. It works best in reasonably moist loam; in sandy, dry soil, a garden trowel will do a better job.

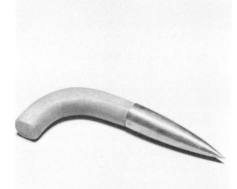

19

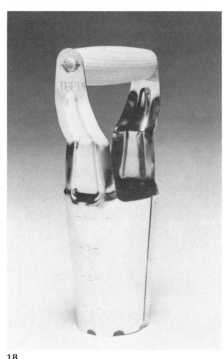

18

Dibble, MODEL 218,
C. S. OSBORNE, $9.75–10.50 **(19)**

Bent hardwood handle, approximately 3 inches long; ¼-inch-diameter iron point, 5 inches long.

I use a dibble whenever I have a number of transplants to set out. Just poke it down in the soil and place your plants in the hole it makes. Be sure to firm the soil and water the transplant so that the soil isn't compacted. It's especially good for setting out long-rooted plants such as onions or leeks. Keep it dry and oiled because the untreated iron will eventually rust.

20

Folding Shovel, MODEL 15-924,
AMES, $7.20–8.00 **(20)**

36¼ × 8⅝-inch, 3-way green metal folding campers' shovel; steel handle; vinyl grip.

This tool is similar to the Army trenching tool I use on *Crockett's Victory Garden.* I find it invaluable for transplanting plants that are too large for a trowel and too small for a spade, as well as for planting small shrubs, perennials, and, of course, for making trenches. During winter, I keep one in my car for moving snow.

MATTOCK HOE

Mattock Hoe, "DIG-EZY,"
MODEL 18-395,
AMES, $10.00–16.00 **(21)**

Wood handle, 54 inches long, holds a 13-inch metal head, ⅛ inch thick, with 2 cutting edges; one cutting blade is 3½ inches wide, and the other is 1¾ inches wide; blade held to handle with heavy pin closed in by a steel ferrule.

Here's a long-handled, lightweight tool designed more for heavy garden work and rooting out stubborn weeds than the mattocks used for land clearing I mentioned in the previous chapter. This tool has more than a 4-foot reach and allows you to stand upright while using it. It really is a hybrid between hoe and mattock, having more cutting power than the hoe, but less than the mattock.

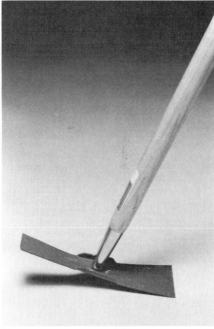

21

CARRIERS

Have you ever stopped to think of how many different objects there are to haul around the garden and yard? — flats of seedlings in the spring, dead leaves in the fall, compost, manure, mulches, fertilizer, stones, soil, firewood, and, of course, your harvest. That's why I consider a wheelbarrow or good-quality cart an essential garden tool.

Although there are dozens of types, your basic choice boils down to the traditional wheelbarrow, with its single wheel up front, and the more boxy garden cart. I use the wheelbarrow for many of my chores, since I find that most of my hauling involves loose loads that are easy to put into a wheelbarrow and dump out. I also find the single wheel makes the wheelbarrow more maneuverable. Here in New England, I'm frequently maneuvering where the ground is covered with rocks (or plants) and space is at a premium. You can get the wheelbarrow through less than ½ foot of room on the ground.

On the other hand, the cart is more stable than the wheelbarrow. Several designs have a wide, flat base that makes them particularly good for that tiresome chore of hauling trash cans from the garage to the roadside on pickup day. They also put less strain on your back and arms.

So which one should you buy? Let the primary use you have in mind, your own physical condition, and personal preference dictate the decision. What's most important is not whether you get a wheelbarrow or a cart, but that you get a sturdy machine that will stand up to rough terrain and weather conditions. I've seen flimsy carts rust out in less than a season, or end up with broken wheels. Select a unit with sturdy wheels and reliable bearings, and oil them regularly. If you buy a steel hauler, make sure the steel is of heavy gauge and well protected from rust. Keep it that way with an occasional fresh coat of paint, catching small spots with a touch-up spray paint when they appear. No cart or wheelbarrow should be left outside all the time, but I'm realistic enough to know that most of them will spend lots of time exposed to rain and snow.

Wheelbarrow, MODEL 34,
RADIO STEEL & MANUFACTURING,
$60.00–66.00 **(22)**

Metal wheelbarrow of traditional contractor's design with hardwood handles; seamless construction; 4-cubic-foot capacity; 36½ × 27½ × 7½–inch tray; 16 × 4–inch pneumatic tire on 8 × 4–inch wheel with oilless bearings.

Extra braces on the legs and countersunk bolts contribute to the sturdiness of this heavy-duty wheelbarrow, which is easily kept clean because of its smooth exterior. This type of wheelbarrow shows its finest points when hauling soil, compost, rocks, or other loose material that is readily loaded and unloaded. You'll appreciate the 4-inch-wide wheel when going over soft ground or rough terrain — where the ground might be littered with small rocks and pieces of wood — or when maneuvering between garden rows.

22

Wheelbarrow, "BALLBARROW,"
MODEL 250,
BALLBARROW, $50.00–55.00 **(23)**

Tough body of green polyethylene with a 3-cubic-foot capacity; orange pneumatic wheel 10 inches in diameter inflated to 3 psi; rustproof handles and frame.

The "Ballbarrow" is new to the U.S., but is a popular gardening aid in England. The plastic finish won't dent or crack under normal use, and, of course, it won't rust. It weighs less than 18 pounds, which is about half the weight of a conventional metal wheelbarrow of similar capacity. The smooth interior is easy to keep clean and the manufacturer says that even cement doesn't stick to it.

The wide ball and large legs mean it's less likely to tip over accidentally when carrying an awkward load, but the main advantage of the ball is that it provides smooth maneuvering over soft lawns, mud, rocky surfaces, and garden soil.

23

24

Cart, MODEL 76,
RADIO STEEL & MANUFACTURING,
$50.00–55.00 **(24)**

Metal cart painted green with 5½-cu-bic-foot-capacity tray measuring 35¾ × 21¾ × 10 inches; semipneu-matic tires are 16 × 1.5 inches.

The flat, angled front of this cart can be placed level with the ground so that it's easy to shovel, rake, or sweep loads into or out of it. The large spoked wheels bear most of the load, since they're near the center of the cart. The bed is flat, and the tops of the sides are rounded so there are no sharp edges. The cart can carry loads up to 200 pounds over all but the roughest terrain with maximum stability.

25

Yard Cart, MODEL 16,
JACKSON MANUFACTURING,
$79.00–89.00 **(25)**

All steel, welded red metal cart with 4½-cubic-foot capacity; measures 42 × 23¾ × 10½ inches; baked enamel finish; weight 62.25 pounds; 16-inch chrome-plated bicycle-type, puncture-proof wheels.

This well-balanced yard cart's bicycle-type wheels make it easy to move around. The slanted front is shaped similar to a dustpan, allowing you to scoop out contents rapidly, as well as being narrow enough to go through a standard-width doorway. Use it when transplanting plants or for moving batches of compost or leaves.

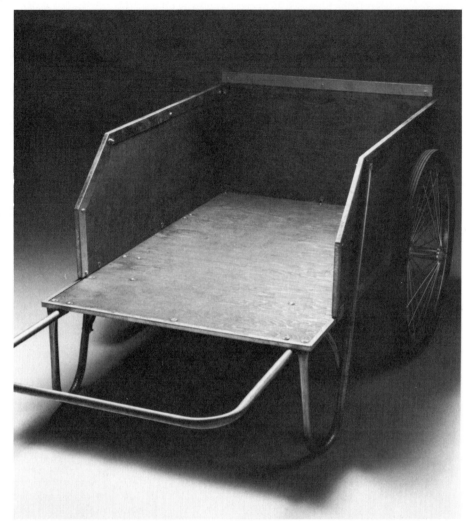

26

Cart, MODEL 26,
GARDEN WAY RESEARCH,
$130.00–145.00 (mail order only)
(26)

More than 13-cubic-foot capacity in a cart with inside dimensions of 31 × 47½ × 16 inches; frame of galvanized steel and zinc-plated metal, body of ½-inch exterior plywood stained for weather resistance; pneumatic tires 26 inches in diameter.

The wheels on this cart have 32 steel spokes that are more than twice the diameter of ordinary bicycle wheel spokes and about 4 times as strong. The double ball bearings at each end of the hub are prelubricated and should be oiled only once a year. (These same wheels are used in racing surreys.) You'll find that its flat bed makes carrying objects such as trash cans easier. Where you can usually fit just 1 can into carts or wheelbarrows with slanted sides, in this cart, you can fit 5. The handle telescopes 16 inches to adjust to the user's preference for length, and the front panel is a little higher than the sides so you can place a wide load on top of the sides without its slipping forward. The stain is soaked in, not painted on, and the back extends past the sides to provide an extra platform for carrying wide loads. The large high wheels and rear stands make it possible to straddle a garden row. There are two smaller models and any of the models can be bought in kit form where you supply the plywood.

Cart, "THE TOTE MACHINE,"
SLATER PRODUCTS, $100.00–110.00
(27)

Steel frame (51 × 25 × 22 inches) with ½-inch high-density polyethylene bucket measuring 33 × 11 × 28; 16-inch spoked wheels.

Here's a 3-pronged attack on the carrying problem. The basic machine is a flatbed dolly that nicely carries a 4-cubic-foot bale of peat moss, for example. For a variety of heavy loads, you'll want to use the smooth, easy to clean, polyethylene bucket that snaps into place and has a capacity of over 5 cubic feet. For lawn cleanup of light material such as leaves, there's a bag holder that installs higher up on the handle and allows you to fill and haul a large (30 × 48–inch) garden bag. Accessories include an extension bar which snaps into the front of the dolly for hauling logs or balancing bulky loads, tie-down straps for awkward loads, and a sifter which fits onto the bucket for compost and soil mixes.

27

ROTARY TILLER

Rotary Tiller, 6 HP "TROY-BILT
HORSE,"
GARDEN WAY RESEARCH,
$600.00–800.00   **(28)**

*Rear-tined rotary tiller, 20 inches
wide; 6 HP Tecumseh-Lauson engine,
manual or optional electric starting;
power-driven wheels; 2 tine speeds; 4
forward speeds, reverse for tines and
wheels; 8-position depth regulator to
8 inches deep; 4.80 × 8 tubeless tires;
gear driven transmission. Comes with
tines for all-purpose work; some options include cultivating tines for
shallow cultivation; pointed pick
tines for heavy clay, gumbo, or hard-
pan soils; a hiller/furrower; a
dozer/snow blade; and a protective
bumper. Troy-Bilt makes a less expensive 15-inch-wide "Pony" model
with a 5 HP engine that is suitable for
smaller gardens, and 7 and 8 HP versions. (Price varies with motor and
start options. You can buy direct from
the factory and there are off-season
discounts.)*

A rotary tiller is a godsend when it
comes time to prepare the soil for
planting, or to cultivate between
growing crops. I insist on using a
rear-tined tiller with the tines
mounted behind the engine and
wheels. A front-end tiller, with the
tines in front of the wheels, may be
cheaper than a machine like this
"Troy-Bilt Horse," but to my mind it's
a poor investment at any price. Not
only will a front-end tiller drag you
roughly around the garden, tiring you
quickly, but the very soil it is meant
to loosen is compacted again by the
wheels and your feet following it. In a
rear-tined tiller, the front-mounted engine makes for good counterbalance
with the working area at the rear. The
wheels rather than the tines pull (or
push) the machine around the garden.
Wheel speeds on the "Troy-Bilt
Horse" range from about .7 mph to
1.7 mph, depending on the gear in
use. Tine speed will be 5.5 to 13.5
times faster, again depending on the

28

choice of gears. You walk beside, not
behind the tiller, operating it with one
hand on the handlebar. A heavy steel
hood keeps the dirt from being
thrown up at you and also helps break
up any chunks the revolving tines
missed. There's a hinged section on
the back of the hood to smooth the
freshly tilled soil.

A tiller shouldn't be a once-a-year
tool. I use mine in the spring to turn
in a crop of rye planted to enrich the
soil, and later on in the summer, set
at a shallow depth, as a cultivator. In
the fall, I bring it out to turn in manure, compost, and garden residues.
You'll also find it excellent for preparing a lawn for seeding.

Note: In the past two years, Troy-
Bilt has started to establish a dealer
network and now has 150 dealers
around the country. Still, most people
buy directly from the factory. Troy-

Bilt provides a toll-free, 24-hour parts
"hot-line," consultation service, and a
detailed, well-illustrated owner's
manual (the one for the "Horse"
model is 184 pages). They suggest
that if there is a problem, you fix it
yourself, or take it to a lawn mower
shop, along with the manual. If this
arrangement makes you uncomfortable, I suggest you look at other tillers
with rear-mounted tines, sold by a
dealer in your vicinity with a reputation for reliable repair service.

If these tillers are too expensive for
your budget, consider renting one at
least once a year for the otherwise
back-breaking chore of soil preparation.

LAWN & GARDEN TRACTORS

With the trend toward large vegetable gardens, those new, lighter-weight tractors designed for the homeowner can look very attractive. They'll plow, harrow, and till the soil, remove snow, and make the chore of carrying wood, hay, manure, leaves, compost, trash, or whatever, much easier. Besides, for the weekend gardener they can be fun to use.

I've looked at many of the new smaller lawn and garden tractors. Most are well built, perform garden tasks with ease, and have all kinds of fascinating accessories — and carry a price tag comparable with a subcompact American car. I think that unless you have a very large acreage or mini-farm, you would be better advised to rent a tractor for the very few times one might be essential.

I'm content with a rototiller for turning over the garden, a standard mower for the lawn, a snow blower for the driveway, and a solid wheelbarrow to do all the carting chores. That may seem like a long list, but in terms of price and maintenance, it's nowhere near the price of a garden tractor costing between $2,500 and $6,000.

You may decide that a garden tractor makes good sense for you. Before you buy, ask yourself how much you will use the tractor. My definition of need is something over 300 hours a year. If I can honestly say the tractor will be put to that much use, I can justify it. If I were going to buy one, as a luxury or a need, here's how I'd go about it: first, write major manufacturers and ask for detailed literature on their products. I'd want to study and compare this material in the quiet of my home. The subtle pressure of shopping in a dealer's showroom can overwhelm the best of intentions. Having a good idea of what's available, I'd then look for a nearby reliable dealer with a good reputation for service. Such a dealer is essential and can be the deciding factor on which brand you choose.

Finally, check the following points:

• Can one person handle the task of installing and removing accessories? (Some of these can weigh over 200 pounds.)
• Is the vehicle geared well for the tasks I have in mind? (Horsepower isn't everything. Proper gearing can make a 16 horsepower tractor do a better job than an 18 horsepower one on specific tasks.)
• What's hidden beneath the styling? (Yes, glamour has come to the garden tractor world.) Check the engine, steering, clutch system, transmission, and drive methods.
• Can I test it? You test drive a car, so why not test drive a tractor on your home turf? It may be hard to believe, but a $4,000 tractor can do a poor job of lawn mowing, for example.

SOIL TESTING

If there's one key to successful gardening, it's proper soil. But what is proper soil and how do we know how your soil ranks?

That's where soil testing enters the picture. You don't have to become a chemist to test your soil, but you do have to follow some commonsense rules. As a gardener, your concern for soil covers two basic characteristics: structure and chemical content. Structure is something you'll eventually learn to judge with hand and eye. For chemical content, you'll want to either make some tests yourself, or prepare a proper soil sample so a laboratory can make a test for you.

The most important chemical test for the home gardener is the one to determine the acidity or alkalinity of the soil. This is measured on a scale of 0 to 14, with 7 being the neutral point. The pH scale is geometric, so the acidity of a pH5 soil is ten times that of a pH6, while the acidity of a pH4 soil is 100 times as great as pH6. This means that what might appear to be a relatively small deviation from the neutral point is actually quite large. When we say that vegetables like soil with a pH between 6.5 and 6.8, we mean they like a slightly acid (sour) soil. If your soil is more acid than this, as it is in most of the Northeast, then you'll want to make it a little more alkaline (sweeten it) by adding some lime. If your soil is too alkaline, then you'll want to add sulfur or aluminum sulfate.

Most gardeners find it sufficient to take a simple pH field test each fall and spring at several locations in the garden. Lime should be put on in the fall and a pH test will tell you which areas need it most. Lime put on in the spring won't be available to your plants immediately, but it will help some during the growing season.

Testing the acidity of soil is a relatively simple process and can be done with a fair degree of accuracy using the products in this section. The test kits listed here can help you determine the presence of nitrogen, phosphorus, and potassium, the three major elements plants need. The best way to get a thorough soil analysis, however, is to send a sample of your soil to a professional testing station. These are run by state and county agricultural extension services, land grant college experimental stations, agricultural/vocational schools, or private companies.

When taking a soil sample, select a specific area and inform those doing the analysis what you plan to grow. For example, you may dig up one sample from the perennial bed, another from the vegetable garden, and another from the fruit orchard. Provide more than one sample for large areas which are likely to have varying soil conditions. Wait until your soil is reasonably dry before digging a sample.

Here's the procedure for preparing a proper soil sample:

1. Take a large sheet of white paper and a clean, unrusted garden trowel.

2. Scoop out a section of soil shaped like an ice-cream cone by digging vertically with the trowel about 6 inches deep. Discard this.

3. Move the trowel back about ½ inch from the edge of the hole you just made. Make a second downward cut so you get a vertical cross

continued

pH Soil Tester, "PAPER DISPENSER PHYDRION," MODEL 151, MICRO ESSENTIAL LABORATORY, $3.00–3.50 (29)

2 rolls of sensitive papers about ¼ inch wide in a small plastic container about 2 inches in diameter with rounded corners; each side of the container has a color chart with 6 colors indicating the acidity of the soil from pH4 through pH9 — the range of most garden soils.

This is a quick way for testing the acidity of soils as well as materials in the field, garden, or home. Remove a small strip of paper (up to 2 or 3 inches) from the dispenser and place it in firm contact with the soil, solution, or other material to be tested. Within 10 minutes, the paper will have changed color and it can then be compared with the colors on the chart on the dispenser. The acidity of the soil for some garden plants is essential. This kit will give a quick and reasonably accurate reading of the soil acidity.

29

section of soil about ½ inch thick that includes material from the surface to about 6 inches deep.

4. Place the soil on the paper and spread it out a little. Do not, at any time, touch the soil with your hands. Repeat this process in 4 other locations scattered evenly about the area you're testing.

5. Place each new sample on top of the last, then mix them all together. Take a small portion of this mixed sample (enough to fill a baby food jar is sufficient) into your home and let it dry for several days. Sift the soil to remove any large particles and put it in a jar. Now you're ready to test it yourself or send it to a laboratory. (If you send in moist soil, the testers just have to dry it, which makes extra work for them and delays the results.)

This procedure yields the best results in any soil test. As you will see from the individual product descriptions in this section, there is no need to be this elaborate if you're only checking for a pH reading.

Finally, remember no soil test is perfect. Even the results from professionals should be viewed as guidelines, not the final word. A continuous soil improvement program should be part of any gardener's standard routine.

pH Soil Test Kit, MODEL ST-T, LAMOTTE CHEMICAL PRODUCTS, $3.00–3.30 **(30)**

Plastic carrying case about the size of a deck of cards holds 2 porcelain test plates, a color chart, and a plastic bottle of indicator solution sufficient for 100 tests; 59-page soil handbook included.

This simple field test kit gives an accurate pH reading in about 1 minute. The porcelain plate has a keyhole-shaped depression in it. In the larger, dime-sized end of this "keyhole" depression, place a small sample of the soil to be tested. Put a few drops of indicator fluid on this soil and wait a minute for it to mix. Then tilt the porcelain plate so that some of the fluid runs down the channel to the much smaller depression at the other end. Examine the color of the liquid and compare it to the color chart to determine soil pH. This kit can be used without first drying the soil (although you don't want to test soil right after a rain) and it is much easier than collecting samples and bringing them into the house for more elaborate tests. The handbook is a helpful guide to making other tests and contains a wealth of basic soil information.

30

Soil Test Kit, MODEL D, SUDBURY LABORATORY, $10.00–11.00 **(31)**

Clear plastic case about 4 × 8 × 1½ inches contains 5 ½-ounce bottles of chemicals and 4 color-coded test

tubes to make approximately 70 tests for nitrogen, phosphorus, potash, and acidity; instruction pamphlet, color chart, and pure tin stirring rod for phosphorus test included.

If you wish to make more elaborate tests for the most important garden chemicals, this test kit will give you reasonably accurate results. First, follow the procedure for taking a soil sample outlined in the introduction to this section. The manufacturer gives detailed instructions for mixing the correct amount of chemicals with the soil sample in one of the test tubes supplied. You mix the soil and solution, then wait several minutes for it to settle. Once the soil has gone completely to the bottom of the test tube, compare the color of the liquid in the tube with the colors on the test chart. (It's best to do this in daylight rather than artificial light, which might distort the colors.) The instructions translate the results into percentages of a given fertilizer you must add. Say, for example, you test for phosphorus and the color of the liquid compares with strip "B" on the color chart; the manufacturer recommends using a fertilizer with 4 percent phosphorus content. Sudbury also makes several more elaborate kits.

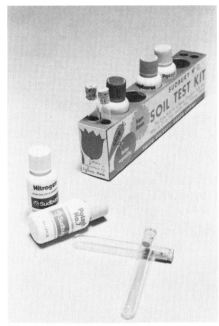

31

LINE LEVEL

Line Level, MODEL 42-187,
STANLEY TOOLS, $2.00–2.50 **(32)**

*3-inch aluminum tube holds a spirit
level and has hooks on either end for
hanging on a taut string.*

Want to make sure your new patio
will be level? Set a specific pitch to
some garden drainage pipes? Even the
grade of your lawn or driveway? Just
string a taut line between two stakes,
then make sure that line is level with
this handy little device. Hang the
level on the line and raise or lower
one end until the spirit bubble sits
precisely in the center. You can measure
down from the line to set either a
constant or sloping grade. You may
want to drive stakes into the ground
beneath the line and mark them at the
desired level. Then all you have to do
is grade to the marks.

32

RAKES

**A good steel garden rake with a long handle and a head about 15
inches wide is indispensable for the final preparation of a seedbed,
whether it's part of the vegetable and flower garden or the lawn.**

Use the side with the teeth on it for breaking up small soil clods
and pulling out the worst of the stones and weeds. Flip it over and the
smooth metal back allows you to do a final flat grading of the bed.

There are two basic choices in metal rakes. The "level head" has a
flat head above the teeth, which attaches directly to the handle. The
"bow" type usually has the teeth bent back a little to a gently rounded
head (still useful for doing that final smoothing of the soil) and is
joined to the handle by a metal bow. Both do the job. The "bow"
shape gives a little springlike action to the raking that some people
like. You'll also find one special wood rake here for more gentle preparation
of the seedbed.

Garden Rake, MODEL T 14,
TRUE TEMPER, $11.60–13.00 **(33)**

*5½-foot handle, 14¾-inch-wide head
with 14 2¾-inch tapered teeth; flat
head design.*

True Temper has "good," "better,"
and "best" lines of rakes. This is their
"best." It has a 1-piece forged steel
head, copper finish, and sturdy, maroon
metal ferrule.

Rake, MODEL B 15,
TRUE TEMPER, $12.00–13.00 **(34)**

*Bow-style rake with 5-foot handle, 15-
inch-wide head and 15 curved 3-inch-
long teeth.*

This is a top-of-the-line rake with
forged steel head, and copper finish.
A similar model, the B 12, has a 12-
inch head and 4½-foot handle, and
some gardeners may find this tool a
little lighter and easier to use.

33

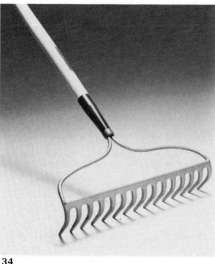

34

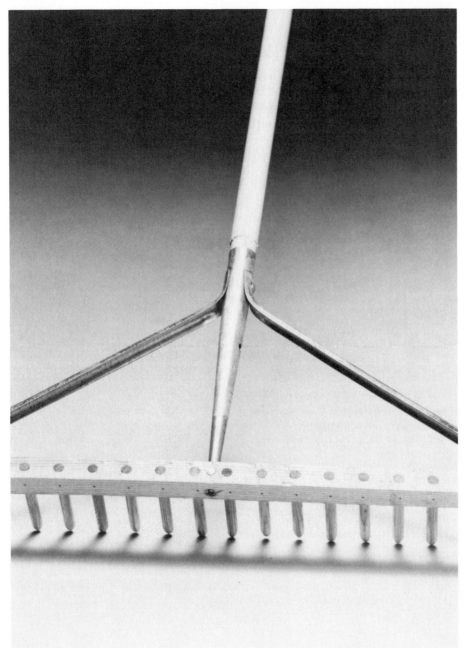

35

Lawn Roller, MODEL BB 140,
BALLBARROW, $45.00–50.00 **(36)**

Revolving drum of polyethylene on nylon bearings is 14 inches in diameter and 24 inches wide; empty weight is 15 pounds; capacity up to 200 pounds.

Before sowing grass seed or planting ground covers, you'll want to firm loose soil, and the best way to do that is with a roller. Most gardeners have very infrequent use for this tool, so they rent one. The good points of this unit are it doesn't rust, it is easy to fill, and its light weight makes it easier to store than metal types. (You can even hang it on a wall with the roller high out of the way.) You can vary the weight by adding water; when filled all the way, it weighs 200 pounds. To judge the proper weight for rolling soil, I look at my footprints as I walk behind the roller. If there are none, the soil is being packed too hard. If all parts of my track show, the soil is too loose. But if my heel marks show and there is almost no track from the sole of my shoe, then the soil is just about right.

Grading Rake, MODEL 60,
RUGG MANUFACTURING, $8.20–9.00
(35)

28-inch hardwood head with 24 ash teeth; head secured to a 63-inch handle with socket and 2 galvanized bracing arms.

This special tool achieves a smooth, floating finish for garden or lawn on freshly tilled soil before seed is applied. It's easier to move this wood rake gently over the soft soil than a steel one. The top of the hardwood head can also be used as a smoothing tool.

36

SEEDERS AND SPREADERS

Grass seeds are among the finest of seeds, and they are difficult to broadcast evenly — especially if there is any wind. This isn't critical for a winter rye, a green manure crop, but no one wants a lawn coming up in a ragged fashion after all the effort that goes into preparing the soil. There are two basic kinds of tools that can help you here: the broadcast spreader and the drop spreader.

Both of these devices are designed to sow grass seeds as well as apply some fertilizers and weed controllers. (Before you apply lime with any of these devices, be sure to check manufacturers' directions carefully to find what the individual model can do.) The difference is the manner in which they do it. The broadcast spreader distributes a lot of material, putting it out fairly quickly and distributing it fairly evenly. So it's a good choice for covering very large areas at a time. The basic principle is to "throw" the material out in an even pattern in all directions at once.

For seeding the lawn, though, I prefer the drop spreader, which has a very directed flow. It's slower, because it covers an area only about as wide as the spreader. Here's how I seed a new lawn with it. First, I figure my seed need at about 1½ to 2 ounces per square yard. Then I divide the total needed for a given area into 2 equal parts. I put the first amount in the spreader and walk back and forth, overlapping my previous path a little each time. If you don't do this, your lawn will end up looking like a checkerboard because seeds don't fall near the wheels. When the first batch of seeds is all gone, I load up the spreader again and go over the same area at right angles to the path I traveled before.

This sowing should be done in calm weather, when the soil is just dry enough not to stick to your shoes. Cover the seeds with a thin layer of soil, not more than ⅛ inch deep, by going over the area gently with a rake.

just the setting, just loosen a wing nut and slide a wire in place.

Get the hang of using the spreader before putting seeds or fertilizer in the bag. Just walk at a comfortable pace, turning the crank about one revolution each time your right foot goes down. After you feel comfortable with it, load it, begin cranking, and then pull back the wooden handle that opens the slot letting seeds fall through. It will snap into place and stay there until you release it by pushing a wire catch with your thumb. Close while still cranking. The manufacturer advises frequent oiling of the gears.

37

Hand Spreader, "CYCLONE SEED SOWER", MODEL 1A1, CYCLONE SEEDER, $19.00–21.00 **(37)**

Lightweight wood base, 6¼ inches wide, 15 inches long, has canvas bag (12½ inches deep) stapled to perimeter of board and extending above it to hold seeds; on bottom of board are gears, a slot (with adjustable opening) to dispense seeds, and 6½-inch square plastic platform with 4 ¾-inch-high vertical ridges; metal crank handle with wooden knob extends about 7 inches below board.

The description above is far more complex than the device. The basic idea is to feed a measured amount of seeds or pelleted fertilizer continuously to the plastic platform, which is spun by the handle. As seeds drop onto it, centrifugal force throws them out in all directions, covering an area up to 30 feet wide. The wooden platform is curved at one end so it rests comfortably against your hip. The bag has an adjustable shoulder strap.

Before using this, consult the chart stapled to the bottom of the board. It tells you the spread of different types of grass seeds and fertilizers, the number of pounds needed per acre, and the proper setting of the opening that lets the seed fall through. To ad-

38

39

40

Broadcast Spreader, MODEL B1, CYCLONE SEEDER, $40.00–45.00 **(38)**

Circular red enamel hopper about 12 inches in diameter, 14 inches tall; handle and portions of frame constructed of enameled tubular steel 1 inch in diameter; shutoff control located at center of "T" bar handle; moves on 2 8-inch-diameter wheels; 5-gallon capacity; weighs 20 pounds.

This push spreader operates essentially on the same basic principle as the hand-carried spreader in the previous description. As you push this unit, materials are applied in a swath from 4 to 10 feet wide. For uniform spreading, keep the unit level; I get best results by covering the area 2 times in cross directions.

Be sure to clean and oil immediately after use.

Cyclone also offers several other models including B.B.S., which has a stainless steel hopper for resistance to corrosion, and B.P.1, with an adjustable tractor hitch.

Drop Spreader, MODEL PF1, O. M. SCOTT & SONS, $35.00–38.00 **(39)**

18-gauge rolled metal unit with baked-on epoxy powder coating; hopper capacity is 28.5 pounds, or 1,760 cubic inches; application width is 21 inches; rubber tires on 10-inch steel wheels.

This drop spreader and the following model operate on a gravity force-feed principle. Material is equally distributed by a finned agitator to evenly spaced openings along the width of the unit. As this spreader is designed for use only with Scott products, there is no information for setting the control dial for use with other manufacturers' products. Scott recommends that you not lime with it, as lime frequently cakes up and bends the agitator fins. Try to wash it out and let it dry after every use.

Drop Spreader, MODEL 50, CENTRAL QUALITY INDUSTRIES, $34.00–38.00 **(40)**

Heavy-gauge steel body with rolled edges; baked enamel finish; built-in lawn marker; 10-inch wheels with semipneumatic tires; rust-resistant removable spray shutter and feed plate; 80-pound capacity; tested setting booklet.

This top-of-the-line spreader will make a 20-inch swath of lawn seed, fertilizer, or weed control mixture with little effort. It comes with a booklet with tested settings for several manufacturers' products, and a lawn marker for greater accuracy.

LAWN NETTING

Lawn Net, "EROSIONET,"
SACKNER PRODUCTS, $95.00 **(41)**

½-inch-square-mesh net of twisted paper cord comes in rolls 45 inches wide and 250 yards long; can be held down by wire staples 4 to 6 inches long.

A new lawn has to be kept moist while the seed is germinating and the seedlings are tiny. One way to do this without worrying about the seeds floating away is to protect it with this fine-mesh netting. The lawn will eventually grow through it and the net will decompose, becoming part of the soil. This is especially useful on large plots on the sides of slopes.

You can also protect small areas of freshly planted grass with a thin layer of burlap, cheesecloth, muslin, hay, or straw. A large area can be covered with chopped straw, which will eventually decompose. To keep it in place, use a large net. Sackner makes "Mulchnet" of the same material as the "Erosionet," but with a mesh size of 2 × ½ inches, which is meant to be put on top of straw to hold it in place.

As the manufacturer only sells this product in 250-yard rolls, you might want to get together with some of your neighbors to purchase it.

41

SOD PLANTER

Sod Planter, MODEL SP,
YOUNG INDUSTRIES, $9.00–10.00 **(42)**

Metal tool about 33 inches long with a 2-inch-square cutter and extractor at the base; 2 small webbed plastic-handled handgrips at the top of the "T" handle; plunger can be operated with either hand; wide foot piece about 7 inches long permits easy insertion into the soil by hand and foot pressure.

Gardeners who have lawns of zoysia, dichondra, or St. Augustine grass will find this a handy tool for transplanting. (It was designed by a California gardener for just this purpose.) Cut the planting hole by pushing down on the foot step, discard the core, pick up a 2-inch square of sod with the planter, and insert it into the planting area. Make sure the sod is flush with the top and sides of the planting hole.

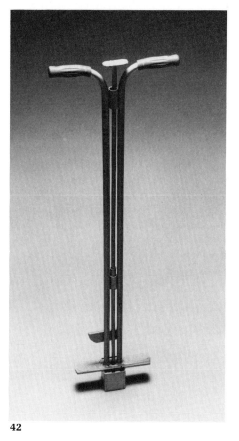

42

TAMPER

Tamper, MODEL 308 005,
UNION FORK & HOE, $17.00–19.00 **(43)**

Metal plate, 8 inches square, with reinforcing ridges; wooden handle 43 inches long.

This is the tool to use if you're installing a walk, driveway, or patio. It's also used for gently firming new grass sod in place. The idea is to turn loose, puffy soil or gravel into a firm, even base. When using it, let the weight of the tool apply the force. The tamper is a necessary tool for these jobs, but chances are your need for it will be relatively infrequent, so consider renting one.

43

THERMOMETERS

Like people, plants are very sensitive to changing temperatures. Seeds won't germinate if the temperature is too high – or too low – and while many plants can survive cold weather, nearly all stop growing when the temperature drops.

This is why I find thermometers a very useful garden accessory. They can tell you when the soil has warmed enough to plant many crops safely, how well an insulating blanket is protecting a cold frame, when to open a greenhouse vent, and the location of micro-climates in the yard and greenhouse.

All of these tasks and several others can be carried out with a simple outdoor thermometer. (Be cautious about buying just any inexpensive thermometer, and make sure it's designed for exterior use; many indoor types have been calibrated around the 72-degree mark, but not to the freezing point so important to gardeners.)

The most useful departure from these standard instruments is the maximum-minimum thermometer. I like using the U-shaped tube ones, though they might take a little getting accustomed to since the two scales go in opposite directions. They will tell you the current temperature as well as the highest and lowest temperature reached since they were last set. Since gardeners are usually concerned about these extremes and can't always plan to be on hand to spot-check temperature readings, these are a real boon. I frequently leave one in my cold frame, one in the greenhouse, and one outdoors.

The soil thermometer is a more specialized instrument. You can check soil temperatures simply by burying an outdoor thermometer, waiting ½ hour, and noting the reading. What I like about the metal soil thermometer included here is that its dial scale faces upward, making it easy to read when placed in the soil. Since it's metal, you don't have to worry too much about breaking the probe against a stone.

Any thermometer should be shaded from direct sunlight if you want an accurate reading; an outdoor thermometer should be mounted at least 4 feet from a heated building. I prefer liquid thermometers over the spring-dial types generally, because they seem to be more accurate.

Although some liquid thermometers have the scale inscribed or painted on the tube, in most cases the scale is on a case behind the tube, making the way the tube is secured to the case important. On inexpensive thermometers, this might be a relatively weak staple arrangement that works loose so the tube slips and the thermometer becomes inaccurate.

Outdoor Thermometer, MODEL 403
PENN,
AIRGUIDE INSTRUMENT, $9.00–10.00
(44)

Gray enamel finish with white numerals on metal case; 11¼ inches high, 2½ inches wide; ⅛-inch-thick metal bracket with 2 screw holes for mounting on wall or post; swivels 360 degrees in bracket; registers from −60° to +120° Fahrenheit in 2-degree increments; includes Celsius scale; red liquid indicator fluid.

This is an easy-to-read, durable thermometer which should withstand extremes of temperature in the outdoor environment, as well as the humidity of a greenhouse or cold frame. Mount it just outside your window and it can be read from indoors, or mount it on a post in the garden, sheltered from direct sun, for a more accurate idea of exactly what temperatures your garden plants are being subjected to. Airguide also makes a maximum-minimum thermometer with magnet reset (Model 416; $16.00–17.00).

Outdoor Thermometer, MAXIMUM-MINIMUM MODEL 5458,
TAYLOR INSTRUMENTS,
$17.00–19.00   **(45)**

Gray plastic case is 10½ inches long, 2¼ inches wide; scale reads in 2-degree increments from −40° to +130° Fahrenheit in white letters on black background; attaches to wall or post through keyhole-type screws in top and bottom; pocket at top holds magnet which is used to reset.

The mercury in the U-shaped tubes pushes a tiny black indicator barb upward. When the mercury falls, the barb stays in place. On one side of the U-shaped tube, the highest point reached indicates maximum temperature. But the instrument is so constructed that on the other side of the "U" tube, the highest point reached is the minimum temperature. The temperature at any given instant can be read on either side, or you can look at the bottom of the black indicators to find out the highest and lowest points reached since the thermometer was

last reset. To reset the thermometer, the small magnet supplied is drawn along the outside of the tube, pulling the indicator down so it touches the mercury column. (This sometimes takes several strokes.) It's a good idea to put a string around the magnet and tie it to the thermometer so it doesn't get lost. (There's a hole in the magnet for this, and replacement magnets are available from the manufacturer, but of course any small magnet will do the job.) Taylor's 5460 ($15.00–16.00) reads both in Fahrenheit and Celsius and has a pushbutton-type reset mechanism rather than a separate magnet.

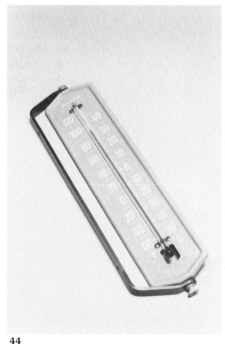

44

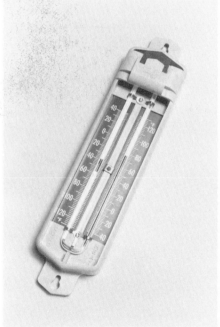

45

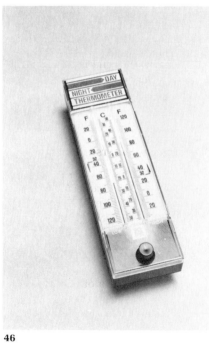

46

47

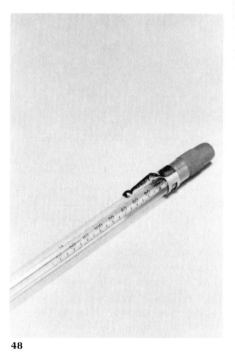

48

Thermometer, MODEL DN-76D, LAB SYSTEMS, $19.00–21.00 **(46)**

Black plastic case about 1 inch thick, 2¼ inches wide, 8 inches high; white face with black figures; both Fahrenheit and Celsius scales; U-shaped with mercury indicators and ½-inch blue needles to register the highest and lowest temperatures since the last reset; resetting done by a black button at the base of the unit.

This all-weather, waterproof thermometer tells not only the present temperatures in both Fahrenheit and Celsius scales, but also minimum and maximum temperatures reached since the last reading. It has a range of −40° to +120° Fahrenheit. To reset, just turn the knob. It comes with an adjustable mounting bracket.

Soil Thermometer, MODEL 5911-12, TAYLOR INSTRUMENTS, $9.00–10.00 **(47)**

2¾-inch-diameter dial-type thermometer, stainless steel case, with sealed, moisture-proof dial; stem is 6 inches long, ¼ inch in diameter; scale in 2-degree increments from 20° to 220° Fahrenheit.

This rugged thermometer has enough range to test soil temperatures for seed starting as well as to check on the progress of any compost or garden soil you may be sterilizing. The most temperature-sensitive area of the stem starts about ¼ inch above the tip, so insert this thermometer at least ½ inch to get a soil reading.

Pocket Test Thermometer, CATALOG NO. 60-B175463, IMPORTED FROM ENGLAND BY E. C. GEIGER, $5.00–5.50 **(48)**

6½-inch tubular glass thermometer with red temperature-sensitive fluid; scales read from freezing point to just above the boiling point; clear plastic case with clip to attach to pocket.

You can "wear" this little thermometer in your pocket like a ballpoint pen. It's handy for taking temperature measurements in air, liquids, and soft soil. As there is approximately 1 inch of scale length for 60 degrees, don't expect a precision reading; however, it is certainly accurate enough for typical garden needs. I found it especially useful for checking temperatures in indoor seed-starting flats and pots. (Other soil thermometers made larger holes and tended to tip over in the light soils and shallow containers, disturbing the seedlings.) Be careful taking measurements in soil outside, as it would be easy to break the tube against a buried rock.

RAIN GAUGES

Is your garden getting enough water? The only way to be sure is to watch your plants, but sometimes they wait too long to tell you. That's why a rain gauge is the handiest weather instrument for a gardener, after a thermometer.

Many people are satisfied with using a flat-bottomed tin can or glass to determine rainfall, and for gross amounts of water (particularly when applied by a sprinkler), this works fine. But many times, rain comes to us in a series of small showers and what we are most interested in is not just the fall for any given day, but the accumulation over a week or month. (A rough rule of thumb is that a minimum of 1 inch per week is needed for the lawn and garden to grow properly. If nature doesn't provide it, you should.)

Rain gauges are tapered according to a strict formula so that a small amount of rain fills a fairly large space in the gauge. (This is why a 12-inch gauge measures just 5 inches of rain.) This large, vertical column of water is then easy to read against a properly calibrated scale. It's possible, for example, with some inexpensive gauges to read as little as 1/100 inch of rain.

It's a good idea to mount your rain gauge on a post at eye height, making sure it is level. Try to keep it at least as far away from an obstruction (building or tree) as the height of that obstruction. (Small bushes, a few feet high, can be near the gauge as they'll act as a windbreak and probably lead to more accurate readings.) And always keep the gauges clean. Frozen water can break most gauges, so be sure to empty yours after each rain, and don't use it in the spring and fall when a freeze is imminent. The portable gauge that you can stick in the ground is best if you plan to be using it for measuring water from a sprinkler.

mixed with an equal amount of bleach. Leave this in the bottom of the gauge for 15 minutes, then rinse clean.) This is a sturdy, reliable gauge that should satisfy the most scientific gardener's desire for accurate information.

Rain Gauge, "CLEAR-VU,"
MODEL 2702,
TAYLOR INSTRUMENTS, $3.50–4.00
(50)

Rectangular-shaped collector measures from .1 inch (2 millimeters) to 5 inches (127 millimeters); 12½ inches long; collector opening is 2¼ × 1¼ inches; clear plastic with scale in black numerals.

The rectangular form of this instrument makes it easy to read, as well as clean. (Use a mild soap, water, and a bottle brush.) The base comes to a rounded point so it can be stuck in the ground, or you can use the two keyhole-type openings in it to mount it by screws to a post. With this type of keyhole opening it can be removed without unscrewing.

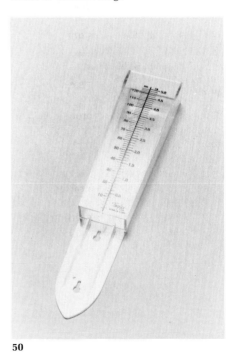

50

Rain Gauge, "TRU-CHEK,"
TRU-CHEK RAIN GAUGE DIVISION,
EDWARDS MANUFACTURING,
$4.00–4.50   **(49)**

Wedge-shaped instrument measures from .01 to 6 inches of rain on a scale 12 inches long; top opening is 2.5 × 2.3 inches; clear plastic construction with metal bracket to mount to post.

If you want to get precise about rainfall, this is the instrument. Even at the top of the scale, where it's the smallest, there are 20 divisions for a single inch. This tapers to a fine wedge at the base, which enables it to measure a very small amount of rainfall. (The drawback to this shape is that it's easy for dust and insects to accumulate in the bottom. To clean it, the manufacturer suggests using ¼ cup of water

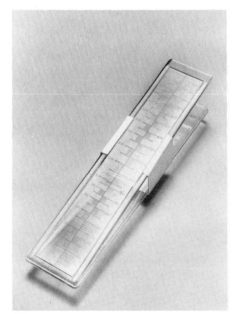

49

RECORD-KEEPING

Gardening is a very personal hobby allowing us to learn by growing and grow by learning. One way to enhance this whole process is to keep systematic records.

Such records are useful on both a short- and long-term basis. Do you know when you usually get the last heavy frost? You can look at a special map for that information, but many of us live in mini-climates on the side of a mountain, near a large lake, or in some other area for which the general references that give frost dates by region are only rough approximations. How much rain fell this week? The answer to that will help you decide how much extra water to give your crops, but if that rain fell in several small showers, you probably won't have the answers unless you've kept daily records. Do keep records. Over a period of time, you'll find yourself becoming much more sensitive to weather changes, and that in itself will make you a better gardener.

For these types of records you can get a gardener's journal (there are several published each year) or you can use any loose-leaf or bound notebook. In fact, many people just get a wall calendar with large squares for each date and write their gardening information there. You'll want to keep track of when you start seeds, move them to a cold frame, and plant them outdoors. You'll want to note when flowers or vegetables and fruit mature in your garden and how the various new varieties performed. Did you mulch your potatoes last year? What was the yield? As good as the year before when you didn't mulch them?

In addition to the types of records you can keep by date, you'll also want to have a garden plan. This doesn't have to be an elaborate, drawn-to-scale affair on graph paper (although that's nice to have) — it can be just an approximation on any sheet of paper telling you what you planted where, so that the next season you can be sure not to duplicate it. That way you won't be inviting the bugs back for a second helping by planting their favorite meal right where they wintered over.

Finally, if you want to be quite detailed about it, try keeping a 3 × 5 file card on each variety of flower or vegetable you grow, noting all the meaningful dates in the plant's life cycle, the yield, and any relevant comments about pests and weather conditions.

They say that experience is the best teacher, but if you don't remember those experiences, there's not much you can learn, so write it down. You'll be a better gardener for it and enjoy the hobby more.

SEED-STARTING

When the dreariness of winter is upon us here in New England, I get the jump on spring by starting flowers and vegetables indoors. That's fine, you might say, for someone with a greenhouse and all the accessory equipment. Yes, it is, but it's also easy for just about any gardener today, thanks to sterile starting mediums, a host of excellent containers, fluorescent lights, and cold frames that open and close automatically. I'd like to tell you a little more about the things that are available to make indoor seed-starting for today's gardener practically foolproof.

Start with those soil or sterile mediums. You have a choice of vermiculite, sphagnum moss, or any of several commercial mixes that make use of these, plus perlite and, in some cases, a small dose of fertilizer. These are clean, lightweight, easy to use, and they eliminate the biggest headache of seed-starting indoors, the damping-off fungus. This fungus can knock off whole flats of seedlings in soil that isn't sterile and for years has frustrated gardeners who saw their young plants emerge, then suddenly bend over and die. (See my Indoor Gardening chapter for a discussion of soil.)

If you want to keep seed-starting fuss to an absolute minimum, try an expandable peat pellet (such as Jiffy 7 or Jiffy 9) or one of those

Some of the essential equipment needed for growing seeds indoors.

Sifting milled sphagnum moss over newly sown seeds.

flat-topped peat pyramids called "Kys Kubes." In either case, no container is needed, although you'll probably want a waterproof tray to hold the cubes or pellets. If you're using the cubes, just water them, then plant the seeds. The peat pellets come in the form of hard, flat wafers, about 2 inches in diameter. When you pour warm water on them, they expand in just a few minutes to about 2 inches high. This isn't large enough for tomatoes and other fast-growing plants, but it is for many annual flowers and vegetables. The Jiffy 7 type stays together by virtue of a nylon net around it. Since this is not biodegradable, it tends to stay in the garden and some gardeners find it irritating. The Jiffy 9 is a bit smaller pellet that is held together by an internal gel. The secret to using this successfully is to let the pellets set for about 3 to 4 hours after expanding. This gives the gel time to harden. If you try to pick up the pellet just after it has expanded, it may break in your hand.

The virtue of peat pots is that the pot is made of the same fibrous material so beneficial to the health of your garden soil. Plant roots can penetrate the soft pot sides and there is virtually no transplant shock when they are put, pot and all, in the garden.

Ordinary plastic pots, sold primarily for houseplants, are also fine. Collect several of the 2-inch, 3-inch, and 4-inch sizes. These have many advantages: plants don't dry out quickly in them (always a danger with seedlings); the soil stays warmer than it would in peat pots; they are reusable as long as you wash and soak them for 10 minutes in a solution of 1 part bleach to 10 parts water; and they cost only slightly more than peat pots do, which can be used just once. Polystyrene pots and flats have similar advantages.

In looking for other types of containers to hold a soilless mix or other seed-starting medium, I am partial to any individual container over a flat. Flats are fine for the commercial gardener with thousands of seedlings to raise, but plants grown in flats have their roots entangled with one another and when transplanting time comes, there's always a shock to the plant. The hobbyist has fewer plants to care for and can spare more individual attention. Individual containers need not be fancy; people use cut-off quart milk cartons for tomatoes and peppers, for example, and I have an acquaintance who collects used Styrofoam coffee cups at his office. He rinses them clean, punches a hole in the bottom for drainage, and has all the containers he could possibly use.

Once your seeds have germinated, light will be your main concern. In most homes, even the light of a south window is inadequate to develop truly healthy seedlings that aren't tall and spindly. A greenhouse, or window greenhouse, is one obvious solution, but is beyond the means of many gardeners. A simpler solution that does the job about as well is the normal fluorescent light. All you need is a very basic setup, described in the chapter on Indoor Gardening. A pair of "cool white" fluorescents, or one "cool white" and one "warm white," will light about 6 square feet. That's enough space for more than 200 seedlings in 2-inch pots. Put the plants so their leaves are just an inch or two below the lights and burn the lights 16 to 18 hours a day.

Finally, you'll want a cold frame, which is easy to build yourself.

A plastic bag helps hold in moisture.

The tricky part is keeping a close eye on it to ventilate it properly when it gets too warm. Many gardeners simply aren't around all day to carry out this process. The solution is an automatic ventilating frame (you'll see one in this chapter) or a frame of traditional construction that uses one of these automatic, temperature-actuated opening devices. (Two such devices are included in the chapter on Indoor Gardening.)

Cold frames have many year-round uses, but most gardeners get one first to harden-off young seedlings. Any plants started in the greenhouse, or indoors, need about a two-week transitional period in the cold frame where they slowly adapt to full sunlight, wind, and cold night temperatures. Then they're ready for full exposure in the garden.

There are two other ways to get an early start with seeds. One is to turn your cold frame into a hot bed. The electric soil heating cable and thermostat in this chapter are the key elements in that process. The other is to use cloches (you'll find some of those here too) in the garden to let the sun heat up the soil in advance and thus allow you to plant right in a garden row. A cloche really acts like a mini-greenhouse or cold frame set over a selected area of garden. It protects plants from frost and keeps the worst of the chill off. However, as with cold frames and greenhouses, it must be ventilated, or removed entirely on particularly sunny days.

All of these things add up to a chance for any gardener, with a relatively small investment of time and effort, to get a real jump on spring.

Seed Flat, MODEL 100-608, MOLDED FIBER GLASS TRAY, $4.00–4.50 **(51)**

Fiberglass tray, 20½ × 12¾ ×2¼ inches; channels about ⅛ inch deep run along sides and down center to provide drainage; tray rests on outside of these channels, allowing air to circulate beneath it.

If you're tired of flimsy, plastic flats that bend and crack from the weight of pots in one end, or give out after a single season, here's a flat of easy-to-clean, nonrot fiberglass. This flat can be filled with starting medium and seeds planted directly in it, although you must be careful not to overwater since there are no drainage holes. Its prime use, however, will be to hold small pots or flats of seeds. The drainage channels allow excess water to run to the bottom of the tray so seedlings won't be drowned, and you can water plants in it without fear of harming the surface beneath.

51

Seedling Flat, "AP PROPAMATIC,"
MODEL P 24-40,
IMPORTED FROM ENGLAND BY GREEN
GARDE, $9.00–10.00 **(52)**

Polystyrene water tray 15 × 9½ × 2⅜ inches; flat plant platform that sits on tray; capillary mat to cover plant platform; plant pack with 40 1½-inch-square, 2-inch-deep compartments that sits on capillary mat; 2-inch-high clear plastic cover.

This is a true A-to-Z plant-starting system that leaves little to human error. Here's how it works: fill the water reservoir nearly full with water, adding a few drops of liquid plant food. Put the tray over the water compartment. Soak the capillary matting, then place it on the tray with the end extending into the water reservoir. Fill the compartments with seed-starting medium and plant two or three seeds in each compartment. Place the tray on the capillary mat and cover with the clear plastic cover. If excess moisture gathers on the cover, wipe it dry. If it continues to gather, prop the cover open a little to allow the air to circulate. Once the seeds have germinated, remove the cover and move the flat to a greenhouse, south window, or under artificial lights. Check the water reservoir every few days and when it's low, add water in the slot at the end, along with some liquid plant food. When seedlings are large enough to transplant, they may be removed by flipping the tray over. You'll notice there are a series of soft spikes on the bottom that match perfectly the holes in the bottom of the planting compartment. These can be used to push out the plants, or you can use your finger. Once plants are removed, wash the unit thoroughly. *One added hint:* use an indelible marker to letter the 5 rows on one end A through E, and number the rows down a side 1 through 8 — that way you can plant different types of seeds in each compartment, keeping a scoreboard of what's where.

If you find clipping off seedlings a waste, germinate your seeds in a separate pot and move young seedlings to the seedling flat, which takes care of the most critical problem that claims the life of too many young plants — a lack of water. This same system can be purchased with different sized containers and replacement containers are available. It should give several years of service if used carefully.

Seed Flat, "TODD PLANTER FLAT,"
MODEL 150,
SPEEDLING, $2.50–3.00 **(53)**

13½ × 26½–inch seed flat of expandable polystyrene with 128 pyramid-shaped compartments, 1½ inches square at the top, and 2½ inches deep.

Here's a new shape in seed starters that results in a root ball shaped like an upside-down pyramid, an easy shape to transplant. There is a hole, about ¼ inch square, at the bottom of each cell that provides drainage, and, if the flat is raised off the shelf at the corners, the roots that extend through these holes will be "air pruned" in a gentle, natural fashion. The seedlings come out of their compartments easily and don't stick to the sides of the flat.

The polystyrene is tough, and thick enough to keep seedlings warm as they develop roots, but it won't last forever, so careful treatment is important if you want to use this flat repeatedly. To sterilize the flat for reuse, soak it in a solution of 1 part household bleach to 10 parts water for at least 10 minutes.

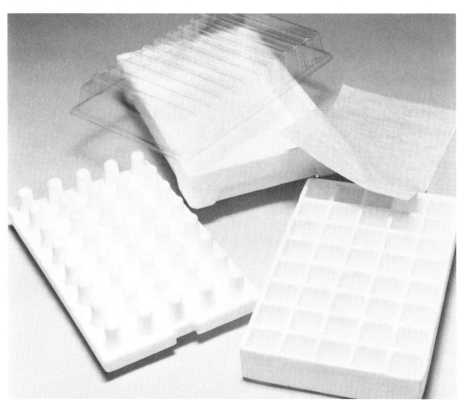

52

53

The flat is available in 10 different sizes: the smallest gives 595 ½-inch-square cells just 1 inch high, the largest, 18 4-inch-square cells, 4 inches high.

54

Automatic Watering Tray, "PLANT MINDER,"

IMPORTED FROM ENGLAND BY BRAMEN, $9.00–10.00 **(54)**

White plastic tray measuring 8 × 20 × 1½ inches; capillary mat sits on top with end dipped in the tray's water reservoir; plastic film cover for mat included.

This could be used for 3 or 4 houseplants, but it is especially useful (because of its small size) for starting a few seeds. It will hold 40 Jiffy 9s, for example, and keep them moist for more than a week without watering. There's nothing complex here. Just fill the tray with water, put on the cover, lay down the capillary matting and wet it, then cover with the plastic film. Cut a small hole in the plastic film where the plants are to sit. The film will keep down algae growth on the mat and will also lessen evaporation. If you don't see these as problems, just place your plants directly

on the mat. This is a nice size to slip under a pair of 20-watt fluorescent tubes if you only want to start a modest number of plants from seed. A larger size is also available.

Heating Mat and Thermostat,

PRO-GROW SUPPLY, $30.00–33.00 (mat), $19.00–22.00 (thermostat) **(55)**

Heating wire is sealed between 2 layers of rubber to make a 22-inch-square mat with 5-foot cord; uses 100 watts; thermostat, which can handle 2 mats, measures 2 × 3 × 4½ inches, also with 5-foot cord; mat plugs into receptacle in back of thermostat plug; temperature is marked off in 10-degree increments from 40° to 100° Fahrenheit on thermostat.

The gentle bottom heat provided by this mat will create excellent germination conditions for seeds or rootings

from cuttings. The manufacturer suggests that the flats be set between ⅛ and ¼ inch above the mat by using wooden lathing or something similar. Under unusual conditions, this mat can heat above 150 degrees, so use with care.

The thermostat settings are approximate. To get a precise temperature, push the thermostat bulb into the soil of the seed flats at the depth the seeds are planted and parallel to the mat, then check with a soil thermometer at the same depth and adjust accordingly. While you shouldn't run this under water, don't worry about moisture from the seed flats or mist propagating system damaging the mat. But be careful not to get the cords, plugs, or thermostat wet, and only operate the mat when flat. Never roll or fold it over when it's in operation. Do not use the mat without the thermostat.

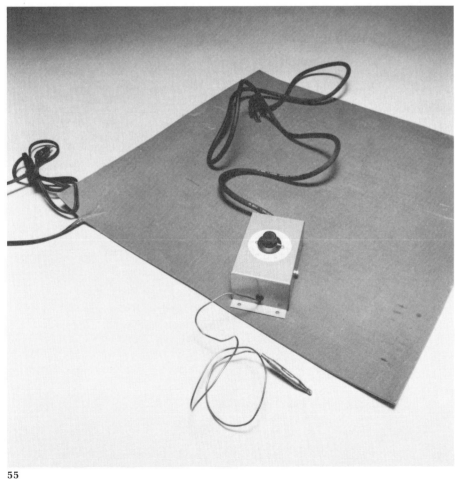

55

Soil Cable, HEATING CABLE 73002,
THERMOSTAT HSC6,
GENERAL ELECTRIC, $35.00 (cable),
$53.00 (thermostat) **(56)**

*Lead-armored heating cable 30 feet
long; 120 volts, 200 watts. Thermostat
in 5 × 4 × 4–inch aluminum weatherproof box; 15 amperes, 120 volts, adjustable from 30° to 120° Fahrenheit;
30-inch capillary tube and temperature sensing bulb; 3-foot, 3-wire power
cord.*

Gardeners use heating cables to raise
the temperature of the soil in a propagating flat, greenhouse bench, or hot
bed. You'll find several inexpensive
cables on the market and they're generally pretty reliable. The short ones
(6 to 12 feet) are suitable for heating a
flat to start seeds or root cuttings.
Since they aren't protected from anything except moisture, use them with
care. The GE cable shown here is
more expensive, but is also more durable and is recommended for any
permanent installation, such as a
greenhouse bench or a hot bed.

The main feature of this cable is
the lead shield around it. This is
grounded and connected to the third
pin on the plug. Grounding is an important safety feature because when a
cable is buried a few inches deep in a
hot bed, there's always the chance
that the gardener will run a sharp
trowel or other instrument through it.
If he's lucky, the only result will be
sparks and a broken cable, but there's
enough current involved to prove fatal
if the gardener happens to provide the
best path to electrical ground. The
lead-shielded cable makes it more difficult to cut through to the wire in the
first place, and chances are that if this
does happen, the trowel will be in
contact with the lead shield and thus
the current will take that path to
ground.

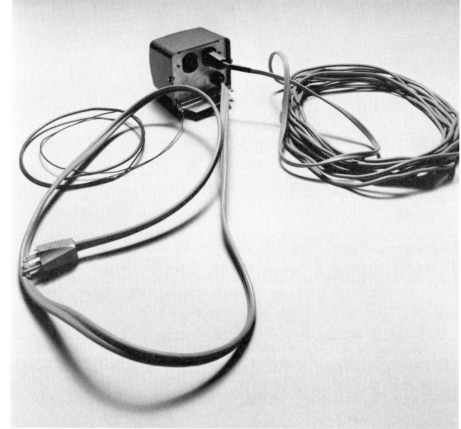

56

In either case, it's wise to shield
the cable with a layer of hardware
cloth. (Even if it's galvanized, this
will eventually rust, and won't provide permanent protection.)

The less expensive cables have a
thermostat built in, usually in a clear,
sealed plastic bubble right near the
end of the cable. This should be buried in the soil at the same depth as
the cable and set for a specific temperature, usually about 74 degrees.

With this GE unit, the thermostat is
separate. It's designed to be mounted
somewhere near the soil, like on the
back of a cold frame. The temperature
sensing bulb should be buried in the
soil at about the same depth as the cable (approximately 6 inches) before
adjusting the thermostat to the desired
temperature. You may, for example,
want just to keep the soil from freezing during part of the year, while at
another time, you may want it at 60 or
70 degrees to germinate certain seeds.

You'll find the lead cable is easier
to lay down because it stays where
you put it.

Deciding how much cable you
need depends on the lowest expected
outside temperature and the desired
soil temperature. For example, with
an outside temperature of 20 degrees,
and a desired soil temperature of 70
degrees, this cable is sufficient to heat
20 square feet. These cables are also
available in 60- and 120-foot lengths.
(Other companies make shorter cables.) Read the manufacturers' directions for the size cable needed for
your area, and follow the procedures
carefully. No cable should ever cross
over itself, or a hot spot will develop
which might eventually short the cable. Since cables seldom get above
140° Fahrenheit, there's no harm in
setting them on most surfaces, but be
careful not to put any unusual strain
or wear on the cable.

SEED PLANTERS

Planting seeds, especially tiny ones, can be a trying experience demanding patience. Seeds vary so much in size, shape, and texture that it's nearly impossible to come up with a gadget that's reasonably priced and really helpful for all kinds of planting. Quite elaborate systems abound on the market. To plant small seeds, I usually end up tapping the side of the packet or pouring them onto a 3 × 5 file card I've folded to create a V-shaped groove. But if you prefer a little more help, try these seed planters.

Seed Planter, "SEED SOWER," PARKS, $.75–1.00 (57)

Clear plastic tube about 6 inches long, 1 inch in diameter; one end is sealed with a red plastic plug, opposite end is open and cut at an oblique angle.

Take the plug out, fill this sower up, then gently tap. Seeds of nearly all sizes, including those of larger vegetables, can be handled by this simple, inexpensive device.

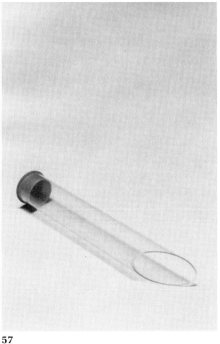

57

Seed Planter, "TINY TIM," NICOL & ASSOCIATES, $3.00–3.50 (58)

Chunky plastic tube, 4 inches long and 1 inch wide, resembling a hypodermic needle; spring-loaded plunger at the top for releasing seeds.

This isn't a "must" tool, but if you find it difficult to plant small seeds evenly, this will help. It holds about one package of seeds and you can adjust the size of the spout opening by twisting it. It can handle the following seeds: flowers — pansy, geranium, petunia, portulaca, salvia, sweet william, alyssum, aster, phlox; vegetables — lettuce, tomato, carrot, turnip, rutabaga, radish, cabbage, parsley, dill.

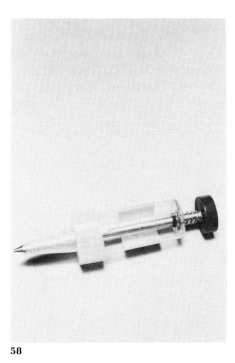

58

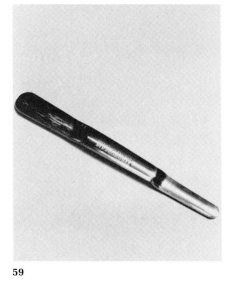

59

Widger, "STRONGBEAM," IMPORTED FROM ENGLAND BY ALLEN SIMPSON MARKETING & DESIGN, $1.75–2.00 (59)

7-inch-long stainless steel implement, concave (like a very narrow shoe horn), ¾ inch wide at the top and half that at the bottom.

What is it? The English call it a "widger," but don't rush to your dictionary, because I doubt you'll find it there. It's useful for planting small, hard-to-handle seeds, or transplanting tiny seedlings from the pot in which they've germinated to a flat or individual containers. To use it as a seeder, just put some seeds in the concave portion near one end. Hold it firmly in one hand a few inches above the planting medium and tap lightly with the other hand. You'll find this is really quite an easy way to get small seeds to roll off one at a time. When getting out the young seedlings, it's just a matter of sticking the end in the dirt below the seedling, prying upward, then grasping the seedling by a leaf and pulling gently. (Don't grab the stems.) You'll also find this useful for loosening the crust around the base of a potted plant, or sliding down the inside edge of a pot to loosen a plant before transplanting it. You can also use it for a light dusting of fertilizer around a potted plant. That's a widger.

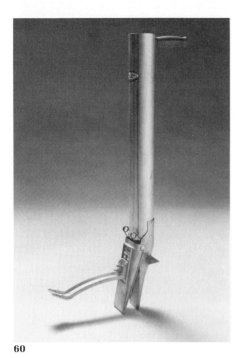

60

Potato Planter, "SPADE POTATO PLANTER," MODEL 7000, EARTHWAY PRODUCTS, $20.00–22.00 **(60)**

Aluminum tube, 3 inches in diameter, 33 inches long, with red plastic handle at top and foot rest at bottom; bottom mechanism is die-cast zinc, so it won't rust; angled leg at bottom adjusts for planting depth from 1 to 6 inches.

This is an unusual tool that will come in handy if you plant many potatoes. Just set the leg at the bottom for the desired planting depth, then tighten the wing nut. Drop a seed potato piece into the tube and step down on the foot rest, forcing the spade portion into the ground. Now rock the device forward and a door opens, depositing the potato portion. Withdraw it from the soil and the door springs shut. Move on to the next spot, dragging your foot as you go to knock the soil back into the hole and cover the potato just planted. Once you get the feel for it, you can plant a lot of potatoes quickly with this device. I usually sling a canvas bag over my shoulder to hold my seed potatoes.

TRANSPARENT COVERS FOR CLOCHES, COLD FRAMES, AND GREENHOUSES

Whether you're building a simple cloche, a more complex cold frame, or a home greenhouse, you'll want a transparent covering material that is safe, easy to use, and durable.

Here's a review of the most commonly used materials with a note on the advantages and disadvantages of each. All will let in sunlight sufficient to grow plants. All are reasonably strong. The major difference between them lies in cost and durability, and here there's a pretty direct relationship. By and large, when you pay a premium price, you're buying extra years of service.

Polyethylene: This flexible film, usually sold in thicknesses of either 4 or 6 mil., costs between 1 and 5 cents per square foot and usually lasts just a single season. As with all plastics, its main enemy is the ultraviolet rays of the sun. A better, ultraviolet-stabilized polyethylene, such as Monsanto 602, costs about twice as much and gives 2, possibly 3 years' use.

This cheap, quick covering is sometimes used for temporary shelter or "storm windowing" either inside or outside a glass greenhouse or cold frame. Commercial growers make Quonset hut–style greenhouses of pipe and two layers of polyethylene, forcing air between the layers to create an insulated air space. Polyethylene is available from greenhouse supply companies in rolls up to 100 feet wide. These long, wide sheets are good for providing a continuous cover with no air leakage, a problem in structures covered by glass or any material cut into several small sheets.

Vinyl: This heavier, flexible film, usually between 4 and 12 mil. thick, will last anywhere from 1 to 5 years. Its cost varies from about 3 to 25 cents a square foot. Because it's clearer than polyethylene, many people find it more attractive. Unfortunately, it is also somewhat electrostatic and tends to attract dust. Vinyls are popular for cold frames, window greenhouses, and similar small units.

Fiberglass: This is a catchall term for panels of glass and acrylic (the acrylic content is quite low). About 20 to 40 mil. thick, it is usually sold by weights between 4 and 8 ounces per square foot. (The heavier panels will stand up better against the weather.) The cost varies from 20 to 55 cents per square foot.

Durability varies, so be sure you know what you're buying. A standard, clear fiberglass panel may last as little as 4 years, while a premium panel with a layer of Dupont's "Tedlar" film bonded to its surface will last at least 20 years without significant degradation.

A cold frame with a top of translucent corrugated fiberglass.

These panels are commonly available in flat sheets either 2 or 4 feet wide and up to 50 feet long, or in corrugated panels either 26 or 52 inches wide and commonly available in lengths up to about 30 feet. The stronger corrugated panels are usually used in roofs, where they'll do a better job with snow loads. They are meant to be overlapped on 2- or 4-foot centers.

Although there is a fire-retardant variety, most fiberglass will burn — and quickly. However, it is very tough, which makes it desirable as a roofing material where hail or vandalism may be a problem. (A stone or baseball will probably just bounce off it.) At worst, the fiberglass will tear, not shatter.

This is one feature I like about all the transparent covers I've mentioned so far. I try to build all structures that are close to the ground out of shatterproof material. With a glass cold frame cover, for example, I'd be worried that a child might stumble and put an arm through it. With fiberglass and the films, I don't have to worry.

Acrylic: This is a premium covering material with a premium price. It won't last any longer than glass and the cost is in the neighborhood of $1.00 to $2.50 a square foot, depending on the thickness. It's commonly sold in thicknesses of $1/10$ inch, $1/8$

inch, and ¼ inch, and sheets about 4 feet wide and several feet long. It is perfectly clear, can be bent into graceful curves, and is about 10 times as impact-resistant as glass. But it scratches easily, so be careful about the cleaners you use on it; and because it expands and contracts with the temperature, it must be held down in channels with a flexible glazing compound.

Despite the price and some of the other drawbacks, acrylic is useful for small greenhouses and cold frames because it comes in large sheets that can be applied to keep air leakage at a minimum. Its toughness and durability are also desirable.

Glass: *It's been used in greenhouses for centuries and it will continue to be used. A single thickness (⅛ inch) costs about 45 cents a square foot, and double-strength glass goes for about 55 cents a square foot. I recommend the double strength for garden use.*

Although glass is brittle and easily shattered, no one questions its durability. Glass 43 years old has been tested and found to have about the same light transmittance as new glass. Its main drawback from an energy standpoint is that it comes in small panes and no matter how tightly you try to seal the panes, there will always be some air leakage, which means heat loss. But the clearness of glass makes it blend with home architecture; many choose it for greenhouses because they feel fiberglass or the various films look artificial.

I still prefer glass in a greenhouse, though I've used fiberglass for the cold frame lids, as well as for making cloches.

There are several new energy-saving materials on the market. Keep an eye on these new materials, and if you feel adventuresome, by all means try them. But remember, many of them haven't been out long enough for the intensive testing needed to be sure how long they will last. Here are two new products you might want to investigate; both utilize a double layer with a dead-air space between. The first is Tuffak-Twinwal, a double-walled, hollow-channeled polycarbonate sheet about ¼ inch thick, made by Rohm and Haas, Independence Mall West, Philadelphia, PA 19105. The other product, Sunwall, from Kalwall Corporation, 88 Pine Street, Manchester, NH 03103, utilizes two pieces of fiberglass bonded together in an aluminum frame with ½-inch dead-air space between.

CLOCHES

A cloche is very similar to a cold frame, but with one important difference. You move plants to a cold frame, but you move the cloche to the plants.

Using a cloche, you can start tender plants in your garden several weeks ahead of schedule. Just plant them in the soil, then cover them with the cloche. It protects plants from harsh spring winds, the worst of the cold at night, and frost. A cloche is simplicity itself. It's just a clear cover that you can slip over a row of plants. Europeans have been using them for years, but cloches have only recently come into favor in this country.

There's a plan for making one in *Crockett's Victory Garden,* but it's so simple I think you can get the idea from a few words here. All you do is take a single piece of 26-inch-wide corrugated fiberglass and bend it in the shape of a Quonset hut. Now form a stiff wire in the same shape and place it over the fiberglass. To help the wire hold its shape, attach another wire across its base. (If you think of the first wire as a bow, this would be the bow string.) Let the ends of the first wire extend down a few inches below the bottom of the fiberglass so you can poke them into the ground to anchor the cloche.

In this section, you'll find some ready-made cloches, some material to use in making your own, and a couple of devices American gardeners have been using for years to create miniature, 1-plant "greenhouses."

You'll find all of these items especially useful for plants that don't like to be transplanted. Do remember, however, that they trap the sun's heat. The ends of the cloche can be closed at night, but they should be open during the day and on some sunny days, you'll want to remove the cloche completely, lest you bake your plants before you ever harvest them.

Cloche, "SONNENHUT," IMPORTED FROM SWITZERLAND BY GOOD-PROD SALES, $5.00–6.00 (for package of 10) **(61)**

Cone-shaped plastic with alternating clear and green stripes measuring 7 inches across the base and 8½ inches high; top opening is 1 inch wide; small tabs in sides with holes in them for pegging to ground with wire or dowel.

These give single plants some protection from frost, heavy winds, hard rains, insects, and birds, until they have a chance to become well established, or the weather becomes milder. You also might want to use them to protect a fall crop of spinach, lettuce, or some similarly low-growing plant from an early frost. The alternating green and white stripes let in some sun, but not too much. They're sturdy enough for several seasons of use.

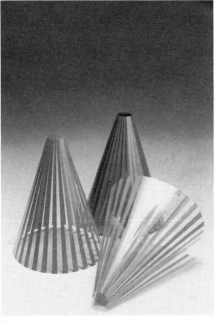

61

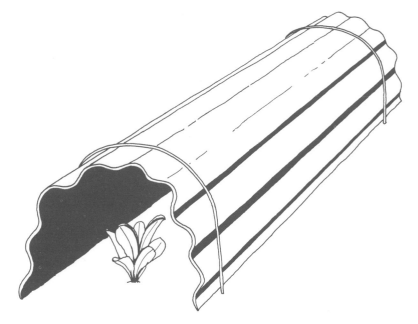

62

63

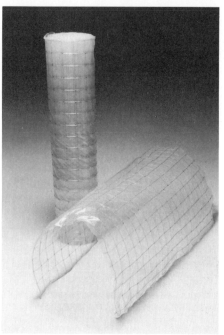

64

Cloche, SOLAR CAPS, $1.00–1.20 each **(62)**

4-sided pyramid of thick translucent white plastic, about 8 inches square at the base and about 9 inches tall; rounded point is closed.

A gardener in Wisconsin who needed protection against the high winds and cold nights of his northern spring designed and has started manufacturing these cloches. The weight and tapered pyramid shape help keep the cloche sturdy during winds, while translucent plastic material allows young seedlings to receive light while avoiding excessive heat buildups. Make sure you remove the cloches for a while during the warm part of the day to allow for good air circulation and to harden-off the plants gradually. And, (an added bonus!) rabbits don't bother to gnaw through the heavy plastic.

Cloche, "HOTKAPS," MODEL F-13, GERMAIN'S, $2.70–3.30 (for package of 20) **(63)**

Treated paper cloche with wire "setter" to put in ground; measures 6 inches high and 11 inches in diameter at base.

Here's an inexpensive cloche used by commercial growers to protect young tender plants in the spring. Each package comes with 20 paper cloches, or "Hotkaps," with a rim on the bottom which should be anchored down by soil. Although at first glance the "Hotkap" looks as though the wind would easily dislodge it, the tapered design helps prevent this from happening. Be careful, and the "Hotkaps" should last more than one season. Larger sizes up to 9½ inches high are available as well as "Hotents" up to 12 inches high, 18 × 14 inches at the base.

Cloche, "INSTANT GREENHOUSE," MODEL 212010, GILBERT AND BENNETT, $8.00–9.00 **(64)**

Galvanized wire with 2-inch-square mesh and 4 mil. polyethylene laminated between wires; comes in roll 36 inches wide and 25 feet long.

Here's a quick route to a cloche. Cut this material in 2-foot sections, bend like a Quonset hut, cut out square sections to cover each end, and you have a 3-foot-long cloche. You'll also find this material has other uses. For example, covering a cold frame lid with polyethylene frequently leads to problems with sagging. The wire in this adds enough stiffness to avoid that problem. The longevity of this product depends on how much sun exposure you give it. (Sunlight is the major enemy of polyethylene.) Left out in the open, it will probably last only one season, but cared for and used only when needed, you may get several seasons' work out of it. If you make cloches from it, store them in a dry, dark area when not in use.

COLD FRAME

65

Cloche, "GUARD 'N GRO,"
HARRISON-HOGE INDUSTRIES,
$23.00–26.00 **(65)**

Rigid polypropylene material measuring 42 × 18 × 21 inches; 2 end panels to seal off unit; galvanized-wire fastening rods for anchoring to ground; weighs under 5 pounds; folds flat for easy storage.

This unit was originally manufactured in California where gardeners used it to conserve moisture during droughts and to protect plants from drying winds and excessive sunlight. It creates a warm, moist, miniature greenhouse environment. The plastic center tentlike structure is firmly held in place with galvanized rods and has end panels for protection. The unit can be joined with connectors to create a protected row of any length you wish. Individual units cover 2 16 × 18-inch flats or 10 to 20 flowerpots. As well as protecting against cold in northern climates, it's useful for starting softwood cuttings, perennials in late summer, or for intensive gardening.

The cloche is easy to assemble without tools, and, carefully handled, should last for several seasons, as the plastic is treated with an ultraviolet inhibitor to prevent deterioration from the sun's rays.

Cold Frame, "VENT O'MATIC,"
MODEL 1200,
DALEN PRODUCTS, $55.00–60.00 **(66)**

Redwood and acrylic cold frame, 48 inches long, 36 inches wide, 11 inches high, with sun-powered vent system that opens when interior temperature is about 72° Fahrenheit, and closes at about 68° Fahrenheit.

I consider a cold frame an essential piece of gardening equipment, not only for hardening-off plants started indoors, but for a host of other garden projects year round — such as protecting late crops from frost, giving houseplants a summer vacation, starting cuttings, and forcing bulbs. For years, cold frames had one problem: they trap a relatively small volume of air, then heat up and cool off quickly. This isn't too bad for the experienced grower who's around all day and can open his frames at 10:00 A.M. when the sun gets strong and close them again at 11:30 when some unexpected clouds come over and a cool northwest wind develops. But for the hobbyist who has a job to go to, it's a real problem. This frame solves that dilemma with its automatic vent system. (You can purchase the vent separately. See the chapter on Indoor Gardening.)

The way this works is simplicity itself. There's a temperature-sensitive fluid in a cylinder and when it heats up, it expands enough to push a piston out of the cylinder. This is hooked to the cold frame cover, raising it. A spring pulls it closed when the cool fluid contracts. The ⅛-inch-thick acrylic sideboards are a little thin, but the material is sturdy and, with care, will last a long time. And they let in more light than wooden sides can — a boon to seedlings.

While there's an 8-inch acrylic extension kit ($20.00–22.00) that gives this cold frame more height, there's another simple way around this. Just set the cold frame over a hole about 6 inches deep. Put in some pebbles and sand for drainage and you've got a taller growing area at just about no expense. Of course, this means the frame has to stay put, which limits its versatility.

This frame (in kit form) takes an hour or two to assemble with a screwdriver and pliers. The instructions are detailed and easy to follow.

If this is more cold frame than you think you need, Dalen has another smaller model, as well as plans for building your own unit using one of their automatic ventilators. I think you'll find that you'll soon outgrow the 12 square feet of growing space this frame supplies. We built a 16-square-foot cold frame in the Victory Garden, then another, and another. . . .

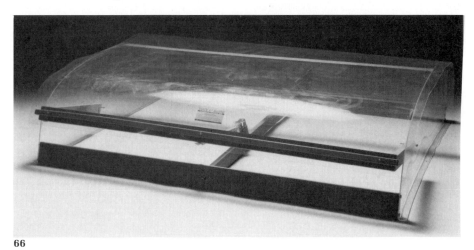

66

PLANTING AIDS

To me there are several indispensable aids for planting. One is the garden line. In the Victory Garden, I've just taken a couple of 14-inch wood stakes, pointed them for easy insertion in the soil, and added a baler to one, upon which we can wrap up to 50 feet of nylon line. However, you don't have to make your own. Here are two inexpensive commercial models that will hold a good garden line. You'll also find my own favorite planting aid, a 4-foot board which makes furrows for seeds and is notched to help me properly space young plants.

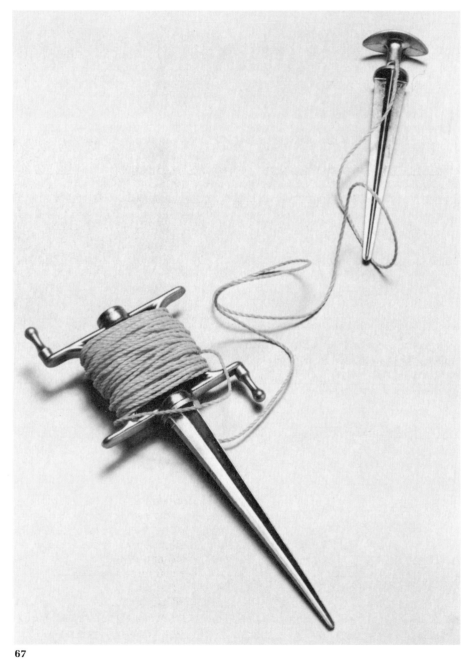

67

Planting Line, "LAN-BAR,"
IMPORTED FROM ENGLAND BY GOOD-
PROD SALES, $7.00–8.00 **(67)**

2 metal stakes, one 8¼ inches long, the other 10¼ inches, both veined near the base to help them hold their place in soil; 50 feet of ⅛-inch orange nylon line; windlass-type line holder.

The line winds or unwinds easily from the windlass which holds up to 200 feet. And the bright color adds to visibility, always a nice feature with a garden tool. Be sure to sear or tape line ends so they don't unravel.

Planting Line, "STRAIGHT-ROW,"
L. L. SHROYER ENTERPRISES,
$7.00–8.00 **(68)**

2 15½-inch cast aluminum stakes with 100 feet of nylon cord; cord winds on cleatlike projections on sides of stakes; each stake is marked with a 12-inch rule that will help determine planting depth and spacing.

Planting Board, BIRCH MEADOW
FARMS, $9.00–10.00 **(69)**

Redwood, 4 feet long, ⅝ inch thick, 4½ inches wide; holes at each end for hanging in storage; one edge is notched every 6 inches, the other is beveled.

I designed this planting board myself to help shape a garden in several ways. After the soil is smoothed and ready for planting seeds, the planting board's beveled edge carves a straight furrow of the required depth. The other edge of the board helps you space young plants at healthy distances from one another. (When plants are small, it's easy to forget how much room they will need.) You'll thank yourself later if you trust to a measured guide. The board is also handy for leveling off short garden rows.

Warren Hoe, MODEL W7H,
TRUE TEMPER, $10.50–12.00 **(70)**

Pointed hoe; about 6¼ × 4¼-inch blade; handle 4⅓ feet.

This specialized hoe, designed by a

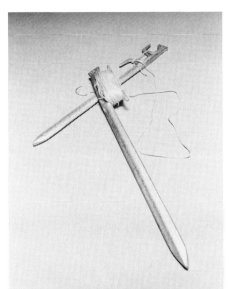

68

70

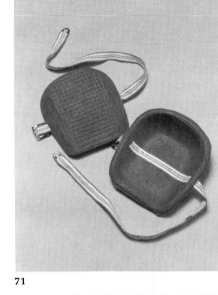

71

69

Mr. Warren of Michigan back in 1870, can be used for more than just hoeing. If you're sowing seeds, use the pointed tip to make furrows for larger seeds and then flip the hoe over and use the 2 ears at the other end of the blade to fill in the soil over the seeds. It can dig deeply for planting bulbs and dahlias. The Warren hoe cuts out weeds and is useful for hilling-up the soil around tomatoes, celery, potatoes, and other plants.

Kneepads, LIGHTWEIGHT MODEL, JUDSEN RUBBER WORKS, $3.00–3.50 **(71)**

Red rubber with small indistinct grid on the working surface of the pad; 12-inch strap with buckle that fastens behind the knee joint; straps are continuous and have been vulcanized to the body of the pad; weight is ¾ pound per pair.

When you're kneeling for extended periods of time planting bulbs, weeding, or setting out transplants, kneepads will protect your knee joints from severe cold or dampness. Because they can't relieve the knee from the strain of continual bending and carrying the body weight, remember to stand up to straighten and rest your legs frequently when you're gardening. Judsen also makes a larger model with an additional 1-inch sponge rubber pad on the inside.

Garden Aid, "GARDEN HELPER," DALEN PRODUCTS, $29.00–34.00 **(72)**

½-inch-thick wood base, 7 × 28 inches, holds kneeling cushion covered with brown vinyl; on each side are 2 18-inch-high supports bridged by a 1-inch-diameter dowel; vinyl pockets and tool compartment at one end; removable plastic bucket, 4 × 6 × 6 inches at other end.

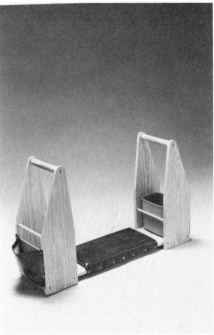

72

Here's an aid for gardeners who find kneeling and especially standing up and bending down uncomfortable. The handgrips make kneeling or rising easier, and the pad puts you down near the soil level, but on a clean, soft surface. The pocket on the side can hold seed packets, small tools, or similar items, while the plastic bucket is useful for carrying fertilizer or small amounts of vegetables.

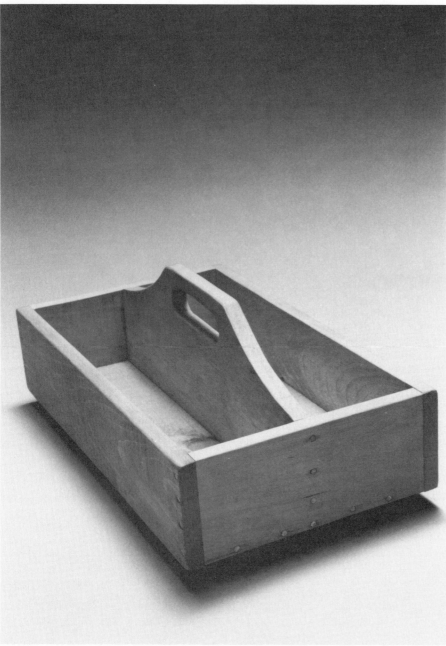

73

Labels, 10 STYLES,
PAW PAW EVERLAST LABEL, typical
price: 10 for $1.65 **(74)**

Soft, gray, thin zinc plate with marking area 1 × 3½ inches, either has wires attached for sticking in the ground, or can be tied to a plant.

This small, family-owned business began in 1962 as a hobby, and they take pride in providing fast service. These top-quality labels will last many years. You'll want to get the manufacturer's brochure to decide on what style you want, because some are better for shrubs, while others are ideal for various kinds of flowers, vegetables, and houseplants. Most of the styles are designed to be inserted in the ground and the label portion tilts back slightly so it's easy to read from above. The labels can be marked with a black crayon or black carbon pencil.

These zinc labels are fine for keeping track of bulbs, perennials, and many other plants. For annual flowers and vegetables, I prefer a simple, less expensive wood label. Plastic is durable and inexpensive also, but if the label gets lost or broken, plastic is not biodegradable.

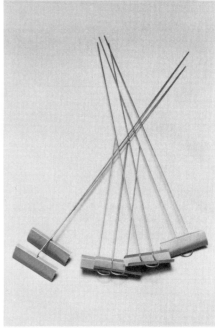

74

Carry All, MEDIUM SIZE,
SHELBURNE FARMS, $15.00–16.00
(73)

Nailed pine box measuring 17¾ × 10½ × 3½ inches, divided by a center board handle into 2 interior compartments; 4 pounds; unfinished; painted country green or natural oil finish available for small extra charge.

This carrying box, handmade on a dairy farm near Burlington, Vermont, is based on a traditional Vermont design meant to keep storage areas and workbenches less cluttered. It is also a great consolidator for garden equipment: small tools, seed packets, shears, gloves, string, plant ties, etc. The box is also available in small (13¾ × 10 × 2¾ inches) and large (18 × 13 × 4 inches) sizes.

GRAFTING TOOLS

Grafting is an ancient and fascinating horticultural art that requires more knowledge and skill than it does tools. This is not to say the amateur should shy away from it. Quite the contrary, the beginner can have success with joining together everything from cactuses to fruit trees. Just make sure you understand the few basic principles involved before you start your graft.

The basic idea of a graft is to get a clean cut at the proper angle, bring together the new portion (scion) and the plant it's to be grafted to (root stock), join the growing (cambium) layers together, and seal the wound until the plants have joined and formed their own natural protection.

The first thing you'll want for this job is a fine, sharp knife. You may also want a special tool designed to split and hold apart the root stock for insertion of the scion. Finally, I prefer to use a good grafting wax to seal the connection, protecting it from moisture and disease.

Although it may be tempting to use these sharp tools for other tasks, that's sacrilege to the true grafter, who takes pride in keeping his knife clean, honed, and oiled for one purpose — making those superb cuts that all but guarantee a successful graft.

Grafting Knife, MODEL 175RB, SCHRADE, $8.50–10.00 **(75)**

Blade 2¼ inches long, stainless steel; closes into brass-lined handle.

The oval handle fits the fingers comfortably during use and the blade remains open securely. It sharpens easily on an oilstone and it will last for many horticultural operations.

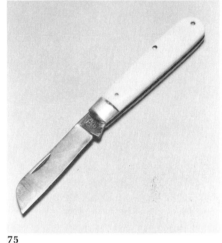

75

Grafting Knife, MODEL 2181, TRUE FRIENDS, $20.50–22.00 **(76)**

2-bladed cutlery steel quality grafting knife with opener, 8 inches long, 2¾-inch cutting area; blade hand-honed.

This handy grafting knife comes with 2 blades: one concave, 2¼ inches long, the other convex, about 1½ inches long. The brass opener is used to open the bark when inserting the scion grafts into the stock. Given ordinary care, this knife will last for years.

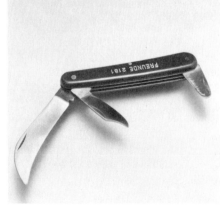

76

77

78

Grafting Tool, COLEMAN TREE PRUNERS, $4.00–5.00 **(77)**

Steel shank, ½ inch wide at base flares into a 2¼-inch slightly convex, curved splitting blade; 1-inch holding hook.

This tool is simple, strong, and light enough to carry in the jacket pocket. One end of the shank can be pounded with a hammer to make the grafting split in the stock. The holding hook helps keep open the split while inserting the scion. Its orange color will reduce the possibility of loss if it's dropped.

Grafting Tool, WALTER E. CLARK & SON, $10.50–12.00 **(78)**

Steel rod, ¼ × ⅜ inches, is curved into a hand hold and hanging hook at one end, and a 1¾-inch holding hook at the other; welded to the middle of the tool is a splitting blade that is about 4 inches long, slightly concave, and about 1 inch wide; painted flat black.

The concave blade is interesting because it will span more than a 4-inch branch for opening, and the outer edges will help hold the bark and cambium in, toward the wood, instead of pushing it outward and possibly tearing it. Be careful when driving this tool its full 1½-inch depth because the welding beads are left rough and could tear the plant tissue.

Grafting Wax,
WALTER E. CLARK & SON, $2.10–2.50 (for ½ pound) *(no photo)*

The traditional wax that has been used successfully for grafting by several generations.

This wax will be used to cover all exposed wood, and much of the scion, during the joining period. Your hands must be coated with tallow or oil if the wax is hand-warmed, a process that can make handling the scions and tools awkward. I prefer the other method, which is to heat the wax in a double boiler. This can be done outdoors with a charcoal grill, canned heat, and similar units. Trowbridge wax will last, protectively, on the plant until it is pushed off by the new plant tissue growth.

Wound Dressing, "TREEKOTE,"
WALTER E. CLARK & SON, $2.10 2.25 (for 1-pound brush-top can) *(no photo)*

Screwtop can with applicator brush; thick dressing for protecting grafted plant tissue, and also wounds caused by injuries or pruning.

This long-lasting coat will protect all surfaces from drying out. Thin the material with water when using it on small delicate grafts that could be injured by forcing a thick coating against them. It can also be mixed with sand and cement for filling small wound cavities. Its only limitations are that it must be applied above freezing temperatures, and the surfaces must be dry.

COMPOSTER

Composter, "ACCELERATOR 18,"
ROTOCROP USA, $58.00–62.00 **(79)**

*Green plastic cylinder, 34 inches in
diameter and 36 inches high; cover
hinged to flip back for loading; sides
are several vertical panels which slide
up individually to get finished compost out.*

I can't say enough about compost. It is
the best thing you can put on your
garden, so I consider a compost pile a
must. It need not be elaborate — I use
a simple, unrestricted heap at my
home. In the Victory Garden we've
built bins, as described in *Crockett's
Victory Garden*. This makes for a ti-
dier system and it is tidiness that is
the main virtue of the Rotocrop.

The green color blends in with the
landscape, the plastic is plenty durable, there are holes to let air in, and
a cover keeps out rain and pests. All
of these points are important either to
making compost, or to keeping the
pile from becoming a nuisance or eyesore in an urban or suburban garden.
In trying this unit, I found that it
must be mounted perfectly level, or
the side panels become difficult to
raise.

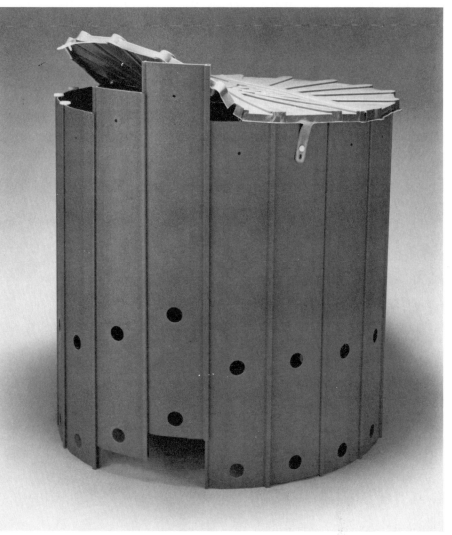

79

MAINTAINING THE GARDEN AND LANDSCAPE

I'm not going to say maintaining the garden and lawn is always fun, but I don't think it has to be the tiresome chore that some gardeners seem to feel it is.

What it really comes down to is that I find it hard to be bored or unhappy when I'm spending time among well-grown flowers, vegetables, lawns, and shrubs. Even when the chore is painstaking weeding around young onion plants, I take a genuine pleasure in seeing that January's seeds are now suitable salad additions.

Beyond this I look on maintaining operations as a sort of insurance policy, protecting the time I've invested in preparing the soil and planting, making sure that my labor will add up to a good harvest. On a sunny afternoon in August, however, with several rows of weeds to hoe, a lawn to mow, or borders to be trimmed, the rewards of such labor may seem very distant. I cut down on lengthy maintenance time by taking 15 minutes a day to pull weeds at twilight or during the cool freshness of early morning. It sure beats hours of cultivating on a hot Saturday afternoon!

I check my tools regularly to make sure they're sharp and clean. Many of the tools I've selected for this chapter are quite basic, but because most of us did not grow up on farms where tool knowledge was passed on, even the simplest tool can appear confusing. That's why I tell you how they're supposed to be used.

Mass marketing has reached the gardening business too, and we are all tempted by gadgets that look interesting but then prove useless. Manufacturers now tend to offer just a limited number of designs, omitting other more useful ones because no one asks for them or they're expensive to produce. Such is the case with hand cultivators. I admit that some of the small cultivating tools in this chapter may be a little difficult to find because they're not part of the sets that usually appear on discount store shelves. But it's worth a search of garden centers or specialty tool catalogs to find them.

Along with proper tools, there are also other techniques to ease your maintenance time. Many gardeners are enthusiastic about mulching, and consider it the easiest, most sure-fire method for beating the weeds. My enthusiasm for mulches is not so all-encompassing. I've found that when selectively used, mulches can indeed be a boon, but I am not ready to throw indoor/outdoor carpeting over the entire garden, as some gardeners have done. There's no doubt that mulching eliminates much watering and weeding, but because local environmental conditions vary, what works in one area will not necessarily work in another.

The current trend is to add power to nearly every aspect of gardening and landscape maintenance; for the most part, it is a good trend. I'm certainly thankful for the power lawn mower, which has undergone some interesting improvements since its invention. The new nylon cord trimmers are also useful time savers, but like anything else, this trend can be carried too far. Power hedge trimmers, for example, work fine on just about any shrub, but many bushes would look much nicer if pruned carefully by hand. The key consideration with a power tool is not only if it will do the job quicker and easier, but also if it will do as good a job as hand tools will. And remember, power tools aren't toys — they should be used with caution and care.

Weed killers present us with a more subtle problem. I favor devices that apply weed killers in small doses to finely targeted areas. Though weed killers help improve a lawn, the best weed control is to water, fertilize, and cut the grass properly. Well-grown grass chokes out weeds. If you decide to use a weed killer on your lawn, don't use the lawn clippings as a mulch in the garden, or add them to your compost heap, or you'll be killing desirable plants as well as weeds.

Finally, you might want to consider intensive gardening methods. These involve a lot of work at first — constructing the raised beds, turning the soil over to a depth of 2 feet, and enriching with plenty of organic matter and fertilizer. But once the beds are built, plants can be grown close together in them in such a way as to make cultivating, watering, and weeding chores much easier. You've seen how plants flourish in raised beds at the Victory Garden. This exciting method of gardening holds particular promise for crowded urban and suburban areas, and is certainly worth investigating.

GARDEN GLOVES

Garden Gloves, MODEL 06055, WOLVERINE, $5.50–6.00 **(1)**

Gray leather glove with short cuff and back of striped fabric; leather strip across back of knuckles; elastic strap on back to prevent them from accidentally falling off.

I rarely wear gloves while gardening, but I do like them when using heavy tools. Many gardeners prefer lightweight, cotton gloves for warm-weather work. If you are looking for cotton gloves, try to find a pair that has been reinforced in the palms and other stress points, or they won't last too long.

But for heavy gardening chores, these gloves offer plenty of protection. Strong soft leather protects your hands from the rough tools and objects that could blister or injure them. A leather tab extends down from the palm for additional protection for the front of the wrist. The palm's flannel lining provides some extra protection as well as a little warmth. This is one of many good gardening and work gloves in this line. There are also several goat and pigskin gloves suited for light work, such as Model 05315, an unlined ladies' pigskin work glove.

1

GARDEN BOOTS

Boots, MODEL 16-80-1071-00, B. F. GOODRICH, $15.00–17.00 **(2)**

Rubber boots, sizes 6 to 14; brown sole with nonskid pattern.

When the lawn is wet, the garden muddy, or you are about to wash the car, reach for the boots below. They're easy to slip in and out of and they will keep your feet dry. Another handy waterproof pair is Goodrich Model 16-22-1065-00 (right), an over-shoe type that fastens with 4 buckles and keeps your shoes as well as your feet dry.

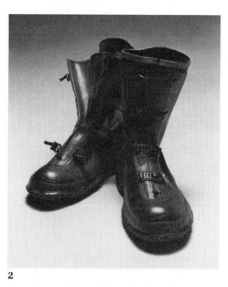

2

2

HOES

I can't imagine a vegetable or flower gardener working without a hoe, for it's an essential tool in the constant battle against weeds. Most gardeners can get by just fine with 2 hoes: a broad-bladed one used to hill around potatoes, dig furrows around other plants, and do some heavy weeding; plus one of the scuffle types for weeding between rows.

The broad-bladed hoe must be tilted nearly flat for weeding, so that its face will be drawn toward you just below ground level, cutting off the roots of weeds. This can be a tiring operation, especially when the rows are long and the sun is hot. The head of a scuffle hoe, on the other hand, lies flat on the ground. Don't push soil with it, but rather use in a back and forth motion so the blade cuts at or just below ground level to chop off and turn over weeds. (This action also loosens and aerates the soil.) Take a close look at some of the special designs for hoeing extra close to plants in both the broad-bladed and scuffle hoes and find one that fits your specific need.

Because a hoe is a cutting tool that is constantly being dragged or pushed through dirt, it needs frequent sharpening. (There's more information on sharpening in "Clearing the Land.") Choose a hoe of good-quality steel that will hold an edge as long as possible. And look for a solid connection between blade and handle. There's a lot of pressure on this point, especially when using the broad-bladed type to push or pull soil. Don't be confused by the many regional styles on the market. Pick a style of hoe that's comfortable to use and suited to your soil. Southern gardeners often prefer larger hoes to penetrate the heavy soil of that region, while in certain areas of California, custom and soil conditions dictate the use of an even broader-bladed hoe.

Finally, take care of your hoe. Clean and oil it, and at the end of the season sand any nicks in the handle that might lead to splinters or blisters the next year. Don't leave it lying in the garden. Not only does this invite rust and weathering of the wood, but you're also courting a black eye or a broken nose if you step on it.

3

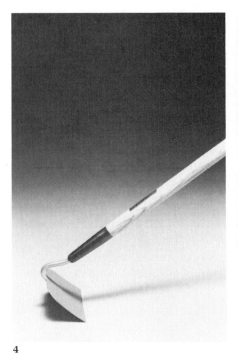

4

Hoe, MODEL 18-473,
AMES, $10.00–11.00 **(3)**

*Garden pattern hoe with 6¼ × 4¼-
inch blade; blade, shank and socket
are 1 piece of forged steel, fastened to
the handle with 2 rivets; weight,
about 2 pounds.*

Nearly every major tool manufacturer
will have a hoe similar to this all-purpose garden hoe with the size, weight,
and shape used for average garden
loam. It will do a good job of cutting
weeds, chopping into relatively tough
soil, or preparing furrows or saucers
around newly planted shrubs.

Hoe, MODEL PC75,
TRUE TEMPER, $11.00–12.00 **(4)**

*Regular pattern "cotton hoe" with 5-
foot wood handle, gooseneck shank,
and 7 × 5-inch aluminum finished
blade; metallic blue ferrule; weight,
about 3 pounds.*

This heavy hoe is designed for use in
clay soils typically found in the
South. It is good for heavy work in
preparing the soil, but the extra
weight may be a bit much for routine
cultivating chores. True Temper also
makes the "Southern Meadow hoe"
(Model PSM08), designed for heavy
soils, but with a slightly lighter
weight.

5

Hoe, MODEL A,
SCOVIL HOE, $10.00–11.00 **(5)**

*"American Pattern" style; 6 × 4½-
inch steel blade painted flat black attaches to 4½-foot handle through eye
in blade; weight, about 2 pounds.*

The "eye" type of construction is similar to that used for attaching the head
of a grub hoe. This means the handle
is largest at the blade end so that the
blade can't slip off. A spiral nail
through the socket and handle rein-
forces the hold. Scovil makes several
regional hoe styles such as the large
"Italian Grape Pattern" used on the
West Coast.

Hoe, MODEL LY5,
TRUE TEMPER, $10.00–11.00 **(6)**

*"Floral hoe," with 4-foot handle and
5 × 3¾-inch blade; weighs slightly
more than 1 lb.*

This hoe is designed for light weeding and is especially good for small
hands. Children will find this easier
to use than standard hoes.

6

Hoe, MODEL 18-411,
AMES, $9.20–10.00 **(7)**

*"Square Top Onion Hoe"; 7 × 1¾–
inch blade attached to 4-foot, 4-inch
handle.*

This hoe weighs a little more than a
pound and is traditionally used for
the kind of in-tight cultivating required around closely spaced plants
such as onions. Both the sides and
bottom edge are sharpened.

Scuffle Hoe, MODEL 18-663,
AMES, $7.30–8.00 **(8)**

*Wooden handle, 4½ feet long, holds
6 × 1-inch blade in a galvanized
hanger attached to the handle with 2
bolts.*

Ames calls this an "action hoe" because the blade moves about ½ inch
as it is being pushed or pulled, alter-
ing the cutting angle and thus cutting
off weeds a little better than a hoe
with a fixed angle would. As with
other scuffle hoes, you will use this
most of the time to cut off weeds at or
just below the surface. However, the
turned-up ends of the cutting blade
will permit turning it over on a corner
or side and cutting deeper into the
soil, or trimming an edge on a border.

Scuffle Hoe, MODEL 33,
GOSERUD PRODUCTS, $6.25–7.00 **(9)**

*Diamond-shaped blade about 6½
inches long and 2 inches wide in the
center, tapering to about ½ inch at
each end; blade is welded to a short,
gooseneck shank which is attached to
the wooden handle with a ferrule and
rivet.*

All 4 edges are sharp on this tool and
the shape allows you to get close to
and in between small plants. It also is
a good tool for cultivating under a
bark or rock mulch.

7

9

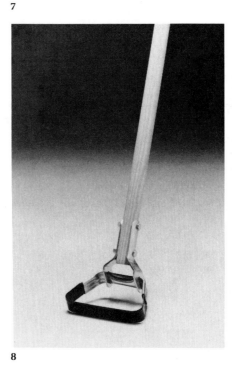

8

10

Scuffle Hoe, CATALOG NO. N-5370, IMPORTED FROM ENGLAND BY BROOKSTONE, $14.00–15.40 **(10)**

Tubular aluminum shaft covered with vinyl, about 4½ feet long, with black plastic handgrip; 6 × 4–inch blade, sharpened on all edges.

This English hoe is as versatile as it is handsome. The notch in the front is handy for removing suckers on roses or rooting out stubborn weeds, while the rear blade is useful when reaching behind a plant or bush to get at weeds that might escape some other tool. The "hang" of the hoe is so comfortable it can be used with one hand, and the manufacturer suggests that even someone in a wheelchair could use it.

Scuffle Hoe, "SWOE" MODEL 470, WILKINSON SWORD, $18.00–22.00 **(11)**

1-piece stainless steel blade, about 2 inches wide tapering to 1 inch; shank fits into ferrule at base of an aluminum handle; slightly curved handle at the tip with plastic handgrip.

All 3 edges of the blade are sharpened on this well-balanced tool, so it will cut forward, backward, or sideways. In style and design, this is an aristocrat among hoes.

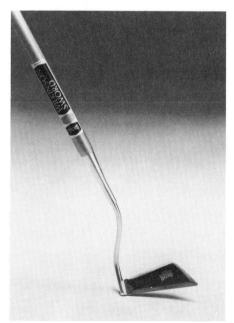

11

SMALL CULTIVATING TOOLS

Plants want to breathe, drink, and have plenty of elbow room, which is impossible if they're crowded by weeds — so you should get into the habit of cultivating your garden regularly.

Cultivators are designed both to loosen the soil for maximum air and moisture circulation as well as to eliminate weeds. Cultivators are usually pronged or tined tools that stir up the first ½ inch or so of soil, turning it over and exposing weed roots to the sun. (Do not cultivate deeply, and be careful when near the roots of desirable plants.) Some of them, such as the "Cape Cod Weeder," have small blades so they cut weeds like a miniature hoe.

The cultivators included here are one-handed tools meant for work close to plants. As with other small garden tools, I like hand cultivators to be easily visible because they frequently are left lying about the garden and tend to blend in with the soil. If you buy one with a clear, wooden, or dull handle, paint a bright stripe on it, or put on a few pieces of reflecting tape at a point where it won't interfere with your handgrip. Of course, you should develop the habit of keeping these small tools in one place, such as a basket or workbox that you can carry about the garden.

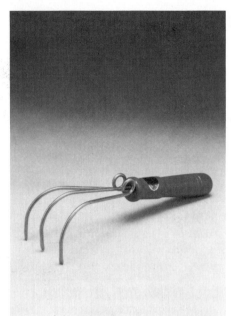

12

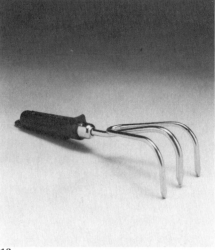

13

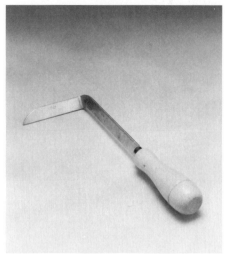

15

14

Cultivator, "MAGIC WEEDER,"
MECHANICAL APPLICATIONS,
$3.50–4.00 **(12)**

*Bright red wooden handle holds 3
metal tines; overall length, 9¾ inches;
tool width, 3 inches; weight about 3½
ounces.*

If you have room in your tool rack for
just one hand weeder, let it be this
one. The slender, curved, spring steel
tines move individually to loosen soil
to a depth of as much as 2 inches. If
you only need to scratch the soil's
surface, the beveled tips of these tines
will show the utmost respect for
tender seedlings and shallow, fragile
roots. Be sure to clean and dry this
handy ally in the war on weeds: its
"magical" powers don't include im-
munity to the ravages of rust. It also
comes in long-handled versions.

Cultivator, MODEL 19-826,
AMES, $2.80–3.20 **(13)**

*Rigid, 3-pronged cultivator, 11 inches
long, with chrome-plated metal tines,
blue plastic handgrip, and hanging
tab.*

Its sturdy construction and comfortable grip make this a pleasant tool to
use. The bright chrome finish makes it
easy to spot against garden soil.

Cultivator, MODEL SC4,
TRUE TEMPER, $11.40–13.00 **(14)**

*4 tines about 4 inches long curve
down at right angles from a 4-foot,
4-inch wooden handle; head is 5
inches wide.*

Use this tool for stand-up cultivating
between rows and around plants, but
be careful not to go too deep or get
too close to the plants. You just want
to loosen the top of the soil, letting in
some air and exposing the roots of
young weeds to the sun. You'll also
use this tool for breaking up hard-
packed soil, or for the first step in
preparing a new garden.

Cultivator, "CAPE COD WEEDER,"
BROCKTON CUTTING DIE & MACHINE,
$2.80–3.00 **(15)**

*An L-shaped hand cultivator 10
inches long with 3-inch pointed cutting blade; grip is 3½ inches long
with natural wood finish.*

This easy-to-use weeder cuts like a
hoe, but lets you get in much closer to
plants for delicate work that a hoe
can't do. Its shape allows it to get under the foliage of even very low-growing plants to cut weeds off right at the
surface. A little more convenient for
right-handed people, this tool can certainly be used by anyone. I also find it
handy for odd jobs such as digging
small holes for transplants or bulbs.

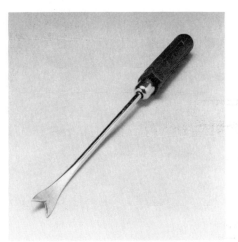

16

Cultivator, MODEL 19-825, AMES, $2.80–3.20 **(16)**

Chrome-plated, metal-pronged weeder, 14 inches long; plastic handgrip and hanging tab.

Many gardeners know this as an asparagus knife. It is also excellent for cutting deeply under the soil surface to pry out heavy tap roots of plants such as dandelions, thistle, or dock. You'll find it a good tool for cutting deep roots with a minimum disturbance to the surface of the soil.

Cultivator, MODEL GP-701, TURNER ASHBY, $4.00–4.50 **(17)**

Highly visible, yellow plastic handle, hollow at the top to hold extension handle if desired, holds a small metal blade about 2 inches wide, with large serrations on one side.

This thinning tool is the smallest of 3 similar weeders made by Turner Ashby. These weeders differ from other cultivators because they're pulling, not cutting, tools. Position the blade about 1 inch below the surface near the base of a weed. Then, keeping the weeder parallel with the surface, draw it toward you, snagging the weed in the notches and hauling it out, roots and all. Since it's not a cutting instrument, you don't have to be concerned about sharpening it. I find this model particularly useful for delicate weeding and thinning tasks near other plants.

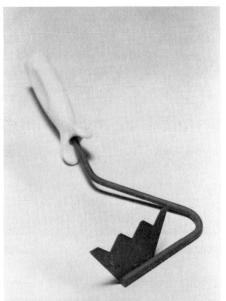

17

18

Cultivator, MODEL 1002, IMPORTED FROM NEW ZEALAND BY HARDWARE & INDUSTRIAL TOOL, $8.50–9.00 **(18)**

Green plastic handgrip on 12-inch zinc handle; 2 axles, 1 inch long, angle back from lower handle and each holds a 5-tine, 5-inch-diameter tiller coated with orange plastic.

Pushing or pulling the tool scuffs the tines through the soil with a tilling action that destroys small weeds as it

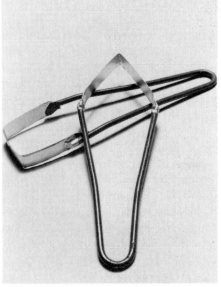

19

aerates, cultivates, and blends. Used on the back of sod, it removes the soil particles quickly. This strong, lightweight tool is good for use in small gardens, window boxes, large pots and other planters. This model also comes in long-handled, stand-up versions with either 2 or 4 tiller wheels, for general garden use.

Cultivator, MANUFACTURED FOR D. V. BURRELL SEED GROWERS, $1.60–2.00 **(19)**

2-inch, "U"-shaped wire handles; triangular-shaped spring steel blade about 3 inches long; both sides of the blades are sharpened and the blades are welded to the handles; weighs 4 ounces.

Here's a practical, inexpensive, and simple weeder used by commercial growers in the West. It's designed to slip just below the soil's surface to cut off weeds, loosen the soil, and to thin onions, carrots, and other small plants. The cultivator also comes in a square-shaped blade design.

WHEELED CULTIVATORS

If you'd rather roll through your cultivating jobs than push and pull a hoe, the wheeled cultivator is for you. Don't expect it to take all the effort out of cultivating, however, for you'll still have to apply plenty of muscle.

These simple, rugged tools have been made in practically the same form for decades. Little can go wrong with them, except rust, which can be kept to a minimum with proper care. (Wash, dry, and wipe parts with an oily rag after use.)

The longer your garden rows, the more practical these units become, for once you develop some momentum, they're easier to use. In short rows, the stopping and turning and starting up again can be bothersome. Though a wheeled cultivator won't do the job a good rotary tiller will, it is far less expensive, more maneuverable. and can work in a narrow row.

21

Wheeled Cultivator, "RO-HO,"
ROWE ENTERPRISES, $30.00–33.00
(20)

Rotary drum 9½ inches wide; 8 blades, each with a set of 5 hoe points; angled right or left on alternating blades; accessory of scuffle knife blade and 5 longer tines.

This looks something like a small, old-fashioned lawn mower, but it's a versatile cultivator invented in 1928 by Alvin V. Rowe, grandfather of the current president of the company. Since that time, nearly half a million of these have been sold. It takes considerable effort to push all those cultivating blades through the garden, but it does a good job of cutting weeds and shallow cultivating. You can use it 3 ways. For shallow cultivating, the 40 points on the rotating blades may be used alone. For efficient weed cutting, use the scuffle hoe knife, which can be adjusted to cut up to 1 inch deep.

Finally, for deeper cultivation, lock the scuffle knife up out of the way and use the cultivator "shovels" or tines to follow the 40 smaller blades.

20

Wheeled Cultivator, MODEL 17,
PLANET JR. DIVISION OF PIPER
INDUSTRIES, $63.00–70.00 **(21)**

Metal construction; plate holds a weeding knife, 3 cultivator tines, or a right-hand turning plow; 2 hardwood handles; 14-inch-diameter metal wheel.

For more than half a century, this man-powered cultivator has been marketed under the Planet Jr. name. It is a simple tool that takes some real muscle power to use. You have a choice of attaching the plow (handy for furrowing before planting), a weeding knife, or 3 cultivator teeth. All attach quite quickly with a single bolt (the cultivator teeth are attached individually) to the platform behind the wheel. The spacing of the cultivator teeth is adjustable.

MULCHES

Mulching is one simple way to attack watering and weeding, the two toughest maintenance chores.

A mulch is merely a barrier between the soil and air and light. It can insulate the soil against overheating in the summer or freezing in the winter. A mulch preserves moisture by slowing surface evaporation and allowing rains to trickle through. By shutting out the light, it keeps weed growth to a minimum. In fact, some gardeners use a heavy organic mulch to eliminate entirely preparing the soil, watering, and weeding. It stays on their gardens year-round. At planting time, they pull it back, scratch a few holes in the soft soil, and drop in their seeds. Northern gardeners may find that a perpetual mulch layer doesn't allow the ground to warm up soon enough in the spring.

All this sounds ideal, but mulches have their drawbacks, one of the main ones being that they provide perfect hiding places for slugs. One year, I grew 3 potato crops: the first the traditional way, one under a plastic mulch, and the other under a hay mulch. The yield from the "traditional" planting was far greater. The slugs ruined much of the mulched crops. But I do admit there was far less work in the mulched areas.

I recommend careful mulching for various kinds of protection around selected plants. A mulch on a large container plant will keep the soil from overheating in the summer; mulches around tomatoes are necessary for water conservation and will help keep the fruit of unstaked plants clean. I also use mulches for winter protection, putting them on perennials and herbaceous plants after the ground has frozen to break the constant freeze-thaw cycle that damages these plants. For evergreens such as rhododendrons, I put on a thick mulch before the ground freezes.

Mulches come in organic and inorganic forms. What you use will depend largely on availability, your concern for looks, and your willingness to cope with a new crop of weeds that can be the residue of a hay mulch, for example. If you use an organic mulch, sprinkle a little nitrate of soda on it to add nitrogen. Otherwise, your plants will suffer a temporary loss of nitrogen to the bacteria that will be busy breaking down the mulch. Here are some popular mulching materials.

Organic mulches:

Tomato plants surrounded by a hay mulch.

- **Grass clippings:** *Use no more than a 2-inch layer, as these tend to mat and become slippery and smelly.*
- **Hay, or spoiled hay:** *This is fine around fruit trees and other plants, but does leave a residue of weed seeds for the next season.*
- **Salt marsh hay:** *This is an excellent mulch, but is usually expensive and hard to find. It contains no weed seeds since it comes from a saline environment.*

Shredded bark mulch works well around shrubs.

Black plastic mulch holds warmth and moisture around zucchini plants.

- **Seaweed:** *There's no seed problem with seaweed, but some thin types tend to compact. Try to get a mixture that includes some rockweeds and perhaps some straw.*
- **Shredded bark or wood chips:** *This is a good, long-lasting mulch for perennial plants and shrubs. It also makes a good-looking path.*
- **Buckwheat hulls:** *They're fine textured, so they may blow away when dry.*
- **Cocoa shells:** *These have a fine texture and a pleasant fragrance when fresh. They're not good in footpath areas because they're slippery when wet.*
- **Corncobs:** *They can be used ground or whole. The ground ones have a relatively short life span, but will do the job.*
- **Leaves:** *A problem with leaves is that they tend to compact and form a thick mat. Oak leaves may last as long as three years, yet all form a rich humus.*
- **Sawdust:** *Many gardeners prefer to use it only after it has been aged and is well-weathered. Fresh sawdust tends to draw nitrogen from the soil.*
- **Newspaper:** *Newspapers aren't your most handsome mulch, but several layers put down and wet immediately can be effective. Position with stones so they don't blow away.*
- **Peat moss:** *Peat will cake and can repel water when dry. It also tends to blow away.*
- **Tobacco leaves and stems:** *These make a short-term, odorous mulch, which may repel small animals for a while.*
- **Spent hops, peanut hulls:** *If you can locate these, they make a good, short-term mulch.*

Inorganic mulches:

- **Aluminum foil:** *Its light reflections are said to confuse some insects, particularly aphids, but it tends to keep the soil cold.*
- **Gravel or stone chips:** *Put down a layer of black plastic beneath these mulches to keep weeds from poking through. (Slit the plastic in several spots to let moisture through.) Be careful when mowing near these with a rotary lawn mower as they can become dangerous missiles when hurled by the blades.*
- **Perlite, vermiculite:** *These natural products are rather expensive as mulches, and light, so they're easily blown away.*
- **Black plastic:** *A plastic mulch will last for several years if you wrap it up every year, but tends to overheat and dry out the soil, except in areas such as the Pacific Northwest where summers are cool.*
- **Roofing paper:** *This is useful for low-traffic areas, although it becomes brittle and will crack if walked upon frequently.*

I think mulches are worth experimenting with, but they're not a cure-all. Used with care, they'll improve conditions in your garden and lighten your workload.

GROUND COVER

Mulch, "GROUND COVER,"
STAPLE HOME AND GARDEN PRODUCTS,
$1.40–1.75 (no photo)

Black cloth in roll, 22 inches wide by 30 feet.

You wouldn't expect to see cloth used as a mulch, but this soft, porous cloth is an interesting alternative to black plastic because it is biodegradable. Spread among plants, it will keep weeds down to a minimum and help hold soil moisture. Or set it down before you begin to garden, cutting slits in it for plants as you would with a plastic film mulch. If you leave it on over the winter, it becomes brittle and quickly is incorporated into the soil.

SOD LIFTER

Sod Lifter, MODEL 1,
TRUE TEMPER, $27.00–30.00   **(22)**

Forged steel 9 × 5–inch blade, 18-inch bent steel shank, 32-inch wooden "D"-style handle.

Have a bare spot in the lawn that needs some quick repair? This tool allows you to dig and lift sods, doing little damage to them so they can be used elsewhere. You won't find use for it often, but if you're doing something like digging a new garden or planting several trees, you may want to use it to remove the sod and transfer it to another area of your property. The unusual shape of the metal part of the handle makes it simple to get this tool 1 to 2 inches under the sod and lift it up in usable pieces. Though this well-balanced tool calls for a certain amount of back-bending work, it's possible to develop an easy rhythmical motion to make the work go smoothly.

22

WEED CONTROLLER

Herbicide Applicator, "KILLER KANE,"
MODEL 102, RINGER, $4.50–5.00   **(23)**

Plastic tube, 1½ × 33 inches. Tube base can be rotated to control amount of weed killer applied.

I am a firm believer in spot weed removal, and this unit makes it easy. Drop a weed-killing tablet in the tube, fill with water as instructed by the manufacturer, and you're ready to go after dandelions and other broad-leafed weeds in your yard. (There's a separate tablet used for crabgrass.) Place the tube over the weed and depress it slightly to release the chemical. Be very careful with weed killers, making sure they aren't somehow carried over to desirable plants in the garden. I like this type of applicator better than the various sprayers because you have enough control to make sure the chemicals are applied to a small area only.

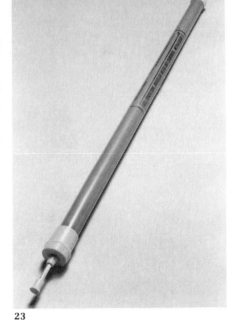

23

EDGERS

You can keep a clean, sharp edge along flower borders, walks, and patios with a good spade and grass clippers, but the job can be made easier with tools designed especially for this purpose.

To create a nice sharp edge, I like the semicircular edger. This tool doesn't cut grass, though, so I use the shears and rotary edger to give the edge that final manicured look. Though you can trim around steps, buildings, and borders with small shears, I'd rather save them for close work around trees and irregular-shaped paving stones. On a long, straight path or driveway, I use rotary trimmers and shears because they eliminate tiresome bending and do just as neat a job as small shears.

Edger, MODEL 040F,
TRUE TEMPER, $11.00–12.50 **(24)**

Semicircular blade, 9 × 4¾ inches; blade, shank and socket are 1 piece; wooden handle is 4 feet long; blade has turned-over top edge.

To use this tool correctly, insert the blade in the ground at a slight angle; put your foot on the turned-over edge, pushing down to cut through the sod. Use this also for lifting out the cut sod and slicing much of the soil from it.

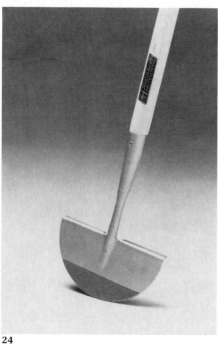

24

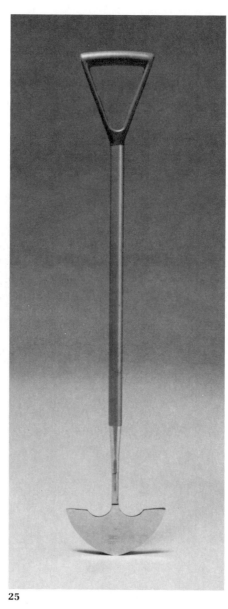

25

Edger, MODEL 468, WILKINSON SWORD, $30.00–33.00 **(25)**

Mirror-finished, semicircular, stainless steel blade about 8 × 4 inches is riveted to steel shank inserted in an aluminum tube about 3 feet long; top of the handle is "D" shaped and made of polypropylene.

This beautiful tool can be used like a long-handled knife to trim and cut edges. However, the flat surface at the edges of the top of the blade is only about 2 inches long, so you would have to be wearing very heavy-soled shoes to step on this tool with any comfort. It's fine for light trimming of grass edges.

Edger, MODEL W427, WILKINSON SWORD, $31.00–34.00 **(26)**

Cutting blades, 7½ inches long, of chromed steel are attached to tubular steel handles with shock-absorbing grips; overall length is 3 feet.

These are like big hedge shears, only they're designed to be operated with the blades on the ground and the user standing upright. Use them for trimming borders, edges, or along fence posts and buildings.

Edger, MODEL 99-D,
GOSERUD, $11.50–13.00 **(27)**

Rotary edger with tubular steel handle, vinyl grip, carbon-steel cutting blades, and double rubber wheels; overall length, 54 inches.

If you have a lot of edging to do along paved surfaces, here's a tool designed to cut grass and turf projecting over walks and driveways. Push the wheel on the pavement and the star-shaped cutter edges your grass.

EDGINGS

In many instances, it's important for the appearance of a garden, as well as the peace of mind of the gardener, to keep a clear dividing line between the lawn and certain other areas, such as a stone path, flower bed, or mulched area under a tree.

To help do this, there are many handy edging materials. Several of these are made of either plastic or aluminum and are simply solid, flexible shields designed to be put in the ground like a small fence. When seeking such a shield, look for durability (some plastics are easily destroyed by the sun) and an effective anchoring system. The idea of these edgings is to keep underground roots from spreading, so be sure to have the top of the edge right at ground level. You don't want it high enough for people to step on it, trip over it, or cut it with a lawn mower. A conventional half-moon edger, or better yet, a sharp spade, is a handy tool to use when installing these, for you must cut a slit in the ground for the edging material.

Several other materials such as brick, stone, concrete blocks (the 4-inch-wide types are less cumbersome), and cedar pegs can accomplish the same thing and are more attractive. In areas with freezing weather, just about any edging material is going to get tossed around by the frost, so one of your first tasks in the spring is to make sure the edging material is in good shape.

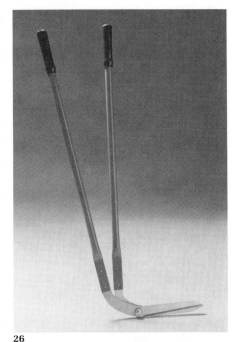

26

27

Edging, "EASY EDGE,"
WARP BROTHERS, $9.90–12.00 **(28)**

Semi-rigid, black polyethylene plastic, 5 inches wide, 20 feet long, rounded at the top, with a ½-inch projection at the bottom to resist vertical movement; about ⅛-inch thick at the top; tapers to about ¹/₁₆ inch at bottom.

The soft, rounded top sits about ½ inch above soil level, where the lawn mower won't hurt it and it won't hurt you if you accidentally step on it. Install it in a prepared slit, 4½ inches deep, making sure that soil is filled over the bottom lip to help keep edge secure. Ends of adjoining sections can be inserted into each other for a solid joint without the need of separate pegs or pieces. It's flexible enough to be used to circle a tree, yet rigid enough to make a smooth, straight border. The same firm also makes a 9-inch-by-40-foot flat plastic shield designed to be set on top of the ground, just under a fence, to prevent grass and weeds from growing there.

28

29

EARTH AUGER

Earth Auger, 18-INCH MODEL,
JOHNSON INDUSTRIAL SUPPLY,
$5.40–6.40 **(30)**

There is about 12 inches of auger screw welded to the rod in 3 places; designed to fit any ¼-inch or larger drill chuck; makes 1¼-inch-diameter hole up to 18 inches deep; also available in 24-inch length.

You're not going to strike oil with this auger, but you will be able to drill holes quickly and easily for inserting insecticides around building foundations or fertilizer around trees. In fact, it could even be used for drilling holes for planting bulbs, or installing small stakes or electrical wiring. When feeding a tree, draw an imaginary circle out at the drip line (the area where the branches extend to), and drill holes on the perimeter of this circle at 2-foot intervals. Fill every other hole with gravel so the sides won't fall in, then use them for watering. Use the remaining holes for fertilizer. While this tool will work in all soil, stony soil will wear it down rather quickly. The long point warns you when you hit a large rock, but many small rock particles will take their toll on the blade.

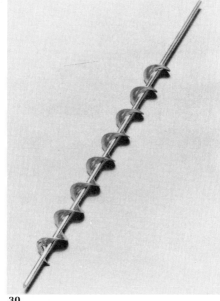

30

Border Edging, MODEL 1,
HORTISCAPE, $.60–.70 (per foot) **(29)**

Linear polyethylene edging, ⁵/₃₂ × 4⅝ inches in 20-foot strips; treated for resistance to chemicals; comes with stabilizers to anchor the edging against frost heaves; usually available in 100-foot quantities.

Lawn-care professionals prefer heavy-duty edging such as this, which comes in both standard (⁵/₃₂ inch) and heavy-duty (⁵/₁₆ inch) thicknesses. Its color blends in with most backgrounds and has ultraviolet stabilizers to resist the effects of sunlight. Make sure when installing this or any other edging to place it low enough so that the lawn mower can pass over it — this will save you the inconvenience of clipping the grass.

SCYTHES

There are several cutting blades for tall grass and weeds, all of which have a long blade intended to be swung with one or both arms. They are variously referred to as grass cutters, grass hooks, sickles, or scythes.

These can be dangerous tools, of course, and many homeowners have no need for one. However, if you have tall weeds in isolated patches to deal with, one of the lightweight hooks or cutters will handle most jobs. I prefer ones with long handles; not only can they be used for clearing tall grass, but they also come in handy for a quick pruning of dandelions and similar weeds blotching the lawn. (This is not a permanent solution, however, just a temporary face-lift.)

The large, 2-handled scythe is a beautiful cutting instrument meant to skim just above ground level, cutting off tall grasses cleanly without pulling them up and disturbing their roots. Unless you frequently have fields to clear, you'll have little use for this tool.

All of these tools should be kept sharp, clean, and dry and given a wipe with an oily rag after use. With a serrated-edged grass cutter, it's probably easier to buy a new blade than to try to sharpen the old one. Make sure no one is near when swinging one of these blades, and store it securely out of reach of children.

33

Scythe, MODEL 15,
TRUE TEMPER, $4.60–5.00 **(31)**

Curved steel blade, 15½ inches long, with nail hole near tip and wood handle.

This one-handed scythe is good for that occasional job when the grass gets too high for the lawn mower to handle, or for places where heavy, thick weeds have moved in and taken over. It's easily sharpened for clean, comfortable cutting.

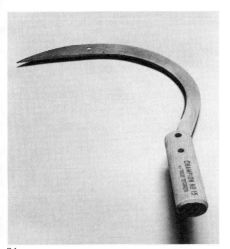

31

Scythe, MODEL 29,
TRUE TEMPER, $5.80–6.30 **(32)**

Deeply serrated, 9½-inch blade with cutting edge on both sides is attached to 36-inch handle of steel and wood for stand-up cutting.

The steel rod handle is slightly limber, which helps give a whip action to this tool, while the serrated blade

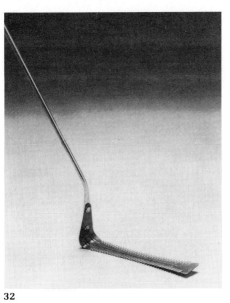

32

holds and cuts grasses and weeds that used to slip, uncut, along smooth blades. This is a nice tool for getting rid of tall grasses in areas difficult to control with other equipment.

Scythe and Snath, SCYTHE
(MODEL 263-20) AND SNATH (JHG-G GRASS SNATH),
DISTRIBUTED BY JOHN H. GRAHAM, Scythe ($17.00–19.00); Snath ($19.00–21.00) **(33)**

Scythe blade 20 inches long and 3 inches wide; curved ash snath (handle) tapering from 2 inches thick at the blade to ¾ inch at the other end, with 2 hand grips; 62 inches long.

If you have plenty of grass, light brush, or weeds to cut, this is the tool you want. It's a beautifully balanced scythe of traditional design. The first view of the twisted handle may confuse you, but after a little practice, you can develop a smooth, swinging rhythm, cutting as you walk. The scythe is especially handy among rocks, tree stumps, and other obstacles where it might be dangerous to use modern power equipment.

GRASS TRIMMERS

Trimming grass borders has always been a tedious business and one that some gardeners find very difficult because of arthritis or other handicaps.

Fortunately, power has come to the trimming business so that we now can choose among fine metal hand shears, power shears that take away most of the work, and one of the newest entries on the front, the nylon cord trimmer. Any of these tools will do the job well. The major differences are in price, durability, and ease of use.

If you consider this work drudgery and own property spotted with stone walls, trees, paved areas, and various other irregularly shaped objects bordered by grass, take a close look at the nylon cord trimmers. Not only are they simple to use (especially the electric ones), but they bring a genuinely new approach to the problem.

The nylon cord trimmer cuts with a tough, flexible nylon filament, whirled about at high speeds, slashing its way through grass and weeds (but not brush or woody vines) with remarkable ease. One of the genuine beauties of this filament over a whirling blade is it can cut close to a fence post or stone wall, building, or other hard surface without significantly damaging either the tool or the obstruction. I say "significantly" because if you strike a hard surface with the filament, it will fray and split much more quickly than if it is slashing only weeds and grass. But this isn't serious. You simply have to pull out a new section of filament from the storage reel, a relatively minor expense and bother which has to be done at intervals anyway.

These tools cut with the tip of the filament, and since they are whirling in one direction, they cut on only one side of the tool. To use it, hold the tool just above ground level (most are light enough for just about anyone to hold) and move in slowly, sideways, to your target. Don't jam the filament housing up against the side of a wall or tree trunk because you'll only damage the filament. The tool can be used on edge or at an angle to trim around objects such as paving stones sunk in the ground.

These tools all vary in the diameter of path they cut, the power of the motor, and the type of power they use — alternating current, rechargeable battery, or gasoline engine. Basically, larger, more powerful units are needed for heavy-duty work, but it doesn't hurt to get a little more powerful motor than you think you need simply because a more powerful unit is less likely to be choked by grass or weeds, straining the motor and shortening its life. The choice among the various power modes is largely one of convenience and cost. Generally, the least expensive ones run off ordinary alternating current. Even if you calculate the price of a heavy-duty, 100-foot, 3-wire extension cord in the cost, electric trimmers may still be a good buy. For portable power, the gasoline model gives you the most flexibility and the small, lightweight engine is likely to be more powerful than a battery model. However, the rechargeable battery offers maintenance-free portability, should last as long as the typical routine trimming task (about 45 minutes would be normal), and can be recharged overnight in a house outlet.

Always remember that these are power tools. That nylon line is probably spinning at more than 6,000 revolutions per minute and at that speed can cut any soft object that gets in its way. It's not as dangerous as a metal blade, for it won't cut through your shoe, but it still must be used with respect. Wear boots or heavy shoes, tight-fitting clothes, long pants, and protection for your eyes. (In the course of about an hour's use it's not unusual to feel the sting of a bit of leaf or stem against the side of your face. No harm in that, but if it hits your eye . . .)

Nylon cord trimmers need occasional replacement of the cords and parts to the electric motor, or routine maintenance on the gasoline engine. Other grass shears should be sharpened periodically, wiped clean after use, wiped down with a light oil for rust protection, and stored in a clean, dry area. Even if you have a nylon cord trimmer, you'll probably find that a pair of hand shears will still come in handy for occasional precision work or some small jobs like trimming around young trees or shrubs whose tender bark may be damaged by the whirling filament.

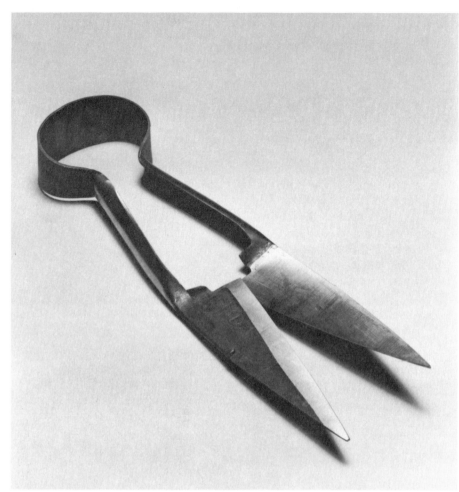

34

Grass Trimmers, MODEL 6S, BURGON & BALL, IMPORTED FROM GREAT BRITAIN BY JOHN H. GRAHAM, $8.00–9.00 **(34)**

Traditional sheep shear design of Sheffield steel, about 12 inches overall with 5½-inch blades.

These shears work with an easy horizontal squeeze action of fingers and thumb, the spring of the steel forcing them open. This old style was once used for nearly all edge trimmers.

Grass Trimmers, MODEL 727, SEYMOUR SMITH, $6.75–7.50 **(35)**

White plastic handles, 5-inch blades, one fixed and horizontal, the other mobile and vertical; spring on pivot bolt permits override of about ½ inch when striking obstacles.

These shears operate with a vertical squeeze of the hand, but the vertical, moving blade is an interesting variation of the more common horizontal blades. There's a slight self-sharpening action as this blade crosses over the fixed one, and it tends to throw cut grass and vegetation away from the tool, which reduces jamming.

Grass Trimmers, MODEL 2, AMES, $7.00–8.00 **(36)**

Red handles with rubber grips close with a vertical squeeze of the hand to

35

move 1 inch cutting edge; blade tension is adjusted with spring under the pivot bolt nut; quick-closing loop unit will keep the blades closed safely when not in use.

This was one of the first shears to use the comfortable squeeze of the whole hand for trimming grass. I've used these shears for many years, and they've stood up through several home sharpenings. The rubber grips absorb vibration and make for a more secure hold.

36

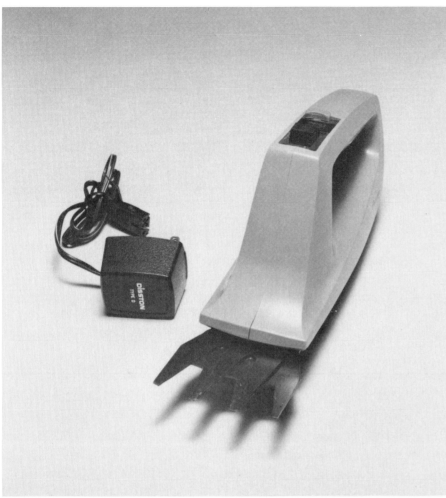

38

Grass Trimmers, MODEL L22, TRUE TEMPER, $16.50–18.00 (38)

Standard squeeze action shears mounted on 2 3-inch plastic wheels with chrome-plated, tubular shaft for an overall length of 37½ inches; squeeze cutting controls are at top of handle; cutting blade has an override when striking stones or sticks.

This is a "floating blade" design in which the upper blade draws back and over the lower blade as you cut. The blades can be sharpened without disassembly by crossing the top blade over the lower blade stop. The blade locks in the closed position when the tool is reversed, so hang this with the handle end down and the blade up when storing on the wall. These are the same firm's Model 22 hand shears, only mounted on a long handle.

38

37

Grass Trimmers, MODEL EGS-1A2, DISSTON, $25.00–27.50 (37)

Battery-operated, rechargeable electric grass shears in plastic case about 10 × 3 × 4 inches with space for solid grip by one hand and thumb control of on/off switch; lock switch to prevent accidental start; 3 thin, black metal blades swing back and forth across 4 holding blades to cut grass.

As with a power lawn mower, these shears require only that the operator push and guide them in the right direction. The real work of cutting is handled by the electric motor. Be careful not to overload the motor by cutting heavy vegetation, but for the typical lawn trimming, there shouldn't be any problem. Recharging is just a matter of plugging the charger into a conventional 110-volt wall outlet. The blades are sharpened at the factory and must be replaced when they become too dull.

Grass Trimmers, MODEL 108,
WEED EATER, $50.00–55.00 **(39)**

*Nylon cord trimmer powered by a re-
chargeable battery; has 7½-inch cutting radius and 25 feet of .051 nylon
line; weight is about 6½ pounds;
length is 34 inches; has handgrip with
trigger at top and second handle that
can be slid up and down metal shaft
by loosening a single wing nut.*

I like this trimmer because of its portability. It takes about 24 hours to
charge the battery fully, then you
have about 45 minutes of trimming,
which is all you need for most work.
It's lightweight and easy to use. Although it is not promoted as an edger,
it did a fine job clearing matted grass
from around paving stones when it
was held so it cut nearly vertically. Its
main disadvantage is its 1 line size; it
is the smallest, lightest line that Weed
Eater uses because the motor simply
isn't as powerful as the ones in the
plug-in or gasoline units. Still, it will
do just about any trimming task
around the yard and you don't have to
wrestle with a cord or fiddle with a
noisy gasoline engine.

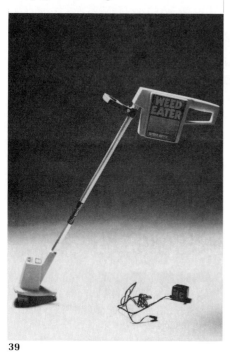

39

Grass Trimmer, MODEL 7802,
ALLEGRETTI, $60.00–66.00 **(40)**

*Nylon cord trimmer gives 16-inch cut
with electric motor that normally delivers .4 horsepower, but power can
be doubled by throwing switch on
handle; includes handgrip that adjusts to different position on handle
by loosening a wing nut; automatic
line feed and cord cutter; uses .08-
inch cutting cord; spool holds 40 feet;
permanent magnet-type motor runs
off 120 VAC, using 5 amps.*

If you are close to an extension cord
and normal house current for most of
your trimming efforts, this unit will
do a fine job. The sliding handle fea-

ture makes it easy to adjust quickly
for the safest, most comfortable holding position. The automatic line feed
is easier and safer than other types
which require you to pull a new
length of cord out by hand. With this
unit, you simply tap it on the ground
and the spool automatically delivers
one more inch of cord which is
trimmed to precise size by the knife
blade fixed on the bottom. Be sure to
read the directions carefully and take
the safety precautions recommended
by the manufacturer. Remember that
any machine that can whip through a
tough weed stem could also do a
nasty job on flesh, and the whirling
motion can send tiny bits of debris
flying outward and upward.

40

Grass Trimmer, MODEL 599,
WEED EATER, $125.00–137.50 **(41)**

Nylon cord trimmer with 12-inch cut powered by 14cc, 2-cycle gasoline engine with recoil starter; handgrip, throttle control, and engine shutoff button on main handle; second handgrip is on bar that runs at right angle to main handle; height of this second handle bar is adjustable.

Once you've started the gasoline engine, you hold this unit with your right arm almost straight down, comfortably at your side. At that point the horizontal bar will be in easy reach of your left hand and guidance of the machine is simple and sure. The motor speed is controlled with a throttle at the right-hand position and the engine can be shut off by pushing a button. The cutting line should be pulled out and manually cut off to the correct length before you start the engine. As with other gasoline-powered devices, this will require periodic maintenance. At the end of the season, the tank should be drained and cleaned with a petroleum solvent, and other seasonal maintenance chores should be carried out as recommended by the manufacturer. The advantage of this machine over household current or battery models is it will go anywhere and will run as long as there is gasoline. The disadvantage is in the maintenance of the motor.

A nylon cord trimmer in action.

41

LAWN MOWERS

A well-grown lawn can be the key feature in your landscape, setting off your flower beds, shrubs, and trees, while providing an area for pleasant outdoor living. Several tools will help you create and care for such a lawn, but none will get more use than a lawn mower. For this reason alone, it's worth spending some extra time selecting a mower that matches the requirements of your property and your abilities to handle it.

Throughout the first half of this century, the most common mower was the reel type, which worked with a revolving blade moving against a single fixed blade in a scissors type action. The reel mower gave a professional close cut on level stands of grass, but ran into trouble on rough terrain. Constant maintenance was necessary because blades easily went out of alignment or became dull. With the invention of the rotary mower, after World War II, manufacturers gradually discontinued the reel mower until now it is available only in a hand unit or a commercial model designed for golf course maintenance.

The rotary mower uses a single blade revolving at high speed to cut the grass. It's excellent for any lawn surface because its whirling blade literally whacks the grass — cutting flat surfaces, slopes and rough terrain with equal ease. The cutting widths of rotary mowers range from 18 to 24 inches, with even larger widths on ride-on types. Obviously there's a convenience to having a wide cut, but you pay for this width with added weight. Since you'll be supplying the muscle, make sure the weight isn't too much for you to control, especially on hilly areas.

Mowers now come with all kinds of options, such as electric starters (which are handy but carry an additional $40-plus price tag). Personally, I prefer a good solid mower without too many fancy extras. I don't find a self-propelled mower necessary. Since you have to walk behind it anyway — and the hardest part of the job is the actual cutting — there's little to be gained by having powered wheels unless you have a large, regularly shaped yard with some long gradual hills.

What type of engine power you choose depends somewhat on your lawn conditions, but is not as critical as other decisions about the mower. Electric mowers are quiet, start with the flip of a switch and require relatively little upkeep. Their main limitation is the cord, which shouldn't exceed 150 feet and thus limits you to a small area. The cord is definitely a bother if you have many trees, flower beds, or other obstacles on your lawn.

Gasoline mowers use either 2-cycle or 4-cycle engines. Two-cycle engines have fewer moving parts and usually last a little longer. However, you must mix oil with the gasoline used. The 4-cycle engine runs on regular gasoline alone (90 octane or higher), but once or twice a season you'll have to check the crankcase, drain the old oil, and add a new batch. I am generally more concerned with the overall quality of the product, the reputation of the local dealer, and the availability of speedy, reliable service than whether an engine is 2- or 4-cycle, as excellent products are available in both types.

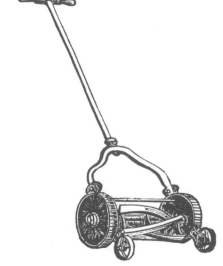

Carelessly used, a rotary mower is highly dangerous, and it's not surprising that the federal government now requires a number of safety features on these machines. Bear in mind that the steel blade revolves at extremely high speeds and can quickly demolish a foot or hand that accidentally slips into its path. A rotary mower passing over loose stones can hurl them with great speed from under the housing, striking the operator's legs with the force of buckshot. So be sensible with this machine. Don't use a mower too powerful or complicated for you to handle comfortably. Don't *ever* let a small child use it. Don't run it over your gravel driveway or any sandy area. (You could end up with bloody legs as well as a dull blade.) And *never* leave a running mower unattended. Add fuel outdoors and never when the engine is hot, for gas falling on a hot engine could start a fire.

Even when the machine's not running, don't reach under the blade housing unless absolutely necessary, and even then it's wise to disconnect and tape out of the way the spark plug wire so there can be no accidental starts.

An interesting new product which will be on the market by the time you read this book is the nylon cord mower. In this unit, the metal blade is replaced by a cord similar to that in the nylon cord trimmers. If these prove efficient lawn mowers, there's little doubt they'll be much safer.

Whatever type of mower you have, keep the blade sharp and clean. Blades are not difficult to sharpen with a file, but if you have doubts about handling this chore, buy 2 blades so one can be on the mower while the other is in the shop. At the very least, have your mower blade sharpened at the start of each season. You'll also want to check the underhousing periodically to make sure it's clean and free of clippings. With aluminum housings, there isn't as much worry about corrosion from damp deposits as with steel, but grass jammed underneath the housing increases the risk of undue strain on the motor. How often you decide to mow your lawn and what the correct grass height should be are factors determined by your particular grass type and local weather conditions. My general rule is: low in cool, damp weather when the lawn is growing fast; high in dry warm weather when growth slows down. Let your lawn grow about 1 inch between mowings. Generally speaking, southern lawns such as Bermuda grass are mown to a height of no less than 1 inch, while northern lawns are cut no lower than 1½ inches. Whenever possible, avoid mowing when wet grass makes surfaces slippery and clippings clump and are difficult to pick up.

Don't throw away those grass clippings, or the fine leaf mulches you get from a mulching attachment in the fall. They can be used directly on the garden or put into a compost pile. The leaf mulch can go in a separate bin for creating leaf mold, an especially rich compost. Don't attempt to make a compost of just grass clippings. They will mat down into a soggy, smelly mess, making you wish you had left the clippings scattered on the lawn where they fell.

Lawn Mower, MODEL 15515, YARD-MAN, $95.00–105.00 **(42)**

6 cutting blades, double-riveted to 4 spider supports, cut a swath 18 inches wide in this push-type reel mower. Adjustable blades; ½- to 2¼-inch cutting height possible by moving a single lever; 2½-inch-diameter plastic roller; tubular steel handle with wood handgrips.

If you have a small, smooth, level area of grass to mow, a gasoline or electric power mower is probably more bother than it's worth. This is a fine, quiet mower that is easier to push than others on the market. There's a grass catcher available, and another model (15510) which cuts a 16-inch width.

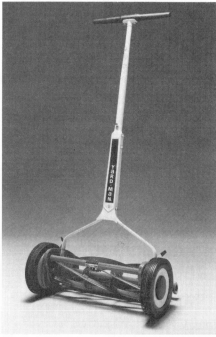

42

43

44

Lawn Mower, "BOB-CAT,"
MODEL M21-4B, WISCONSIN MARINE,
$275.00–300.00 **(43)**

Hand-pushed, rotary-type mower with 21-inch cut and 4-horsepower, 4-cycle engine, weighing a total of 73 pounds. Cutting height adjustable from 1 to 3¼ inches in 13 ¼-inch increments. Magnesium-aluminum alloy frame; heavy-gauge, zinc-plated, tubular steel handle; wheels: 8 × 1¾ inches in the front and 10 × 1¼ inches in the rear.

This is a heavy-duty "commercial" mower of the sort bought for private business or municipal work. There are no frills like throttle and choke. You just pull the recoil starter and go. The virtues of this machine are performance and durability. It's built to take the kind of continuous wear expected in commercial applications, so it should stand up very well in home use. I used mine once on a wet field where the grass was about 1 foot high! These weren't ideal mowing conditions and should generally be

avoided, but the "Bob-Cat" did the job well. An accessory grass catcher attaches to the rear of the mower.

Lawn Mower, "LAWN-BOY,"
MODEL 5026, OUTBOARD MARINE,
$215.00–235.00 **(44)**

2-cycle, 4-horsepower engine with 19-inch cutting blade on rotary mower that weighs just 48 pounds; manual start, solid-state ignition; aluminum-magnesium alloy deck and individual height adjustments at each wheel for cutting heights of 1 to 3 inches in ½-inch increments. No throttle, but switch on engine selects either "light" or "normal" speeds.

If you want a lawn mower that's easy to push and handles well on hills, this one fits the bill. It weighs significantly less than many of the larger mowers at the sacrifice of a few inches of cutting width. Its long handle is a good safety feature, for it keeps the operator far away from the blade. Although it has 2 speeds, you'll want to use the "normal" speed most

of the time, for this is a 2-cycle engine and they run best at high rpm's. The manufacturer won't warranty this product unless its lubricant, which has a synthetic base, is used in the gasoline mix. This lawn mower also has a good vacuuming characteristic. Accessories for this include a grass catcher, a mulching attachment (that attaches with a single wing nut), and a leaf mulching attachment that chops leaves into fine pieces, blowing them through a screen on the way to an extralarge collecting bag. The mulching attachments should be used with the mulching blade, which has about 3 times the cutting edge of a normal blade. This unit will take either a side-mounted or rear-mounted leaf or grass catcher. "Lawn-Boy" also makes standard rear bagging units such as Model 4570.

Lawn Mower, "SNAPPER,"
MODEL V212,
MCDONOUGH POWER EQUIPMENT,
$225.00–250.00 **(45)**

Rotary mower with 21-inch cut is powered by 4-cycle, 3½-horsepower engine; weighs approximately 73 pounds. There's an automatic choke, recoil start, and cast-aluminum deck with cutting height adjusted at each wheel from ⅞ inch to 3⅛ inches in 5 steps. Throttle is on handle and grass catcher hangs from handle behind mower.

This well-balanced mower can be made more versatile with accessory "Mulcherizer" and "Snapperizer" kits. During the spring when the grass frequently tends to be wet, you'll want to use this mower the way it is. As the weather begins to dry out, put on the "Mulcherizer" and you have a mulching mower. This kit includes a special blade and housing, so it isn't the type of thing that you simply snap on and off, but it's certainly no bother to install or remove it a couple of times a season. The "Snapperizer" kit includes an expanded metal shredder plate, a bottom plate, and attaching hardware. This converts the mower into an outdoor vacuum and leaf shredder, especially useful in the fall.

Lawn Mower, MODEL 18060,
TORO, $310.00–340.00 **(46)**

Self-propelled, mulching-type mower with 4-cycle, 10-cubic-inch engine produces 4.5 pound/foot torque at 2,650 rpm; 21-inch cutting width. Adjustable cutting height in ½-inch increments from 1 to 3½ inches by use of a single lever at rear right wheel. Weighs 75 pounds; belt-type drive, handle folds forward for storage, so folded length is 33½ inches and width just under 22 inches; recoil starter; gas tank holds 1⅓ quarts.

Self-propulsion makes this mower primarily useful on large, regularly shaped lawns. The mulching feature means no bagging or raking of grass clippings, since they are cut and recut finely by the whirling blade. However, don't count on the mulching feature to work well in wet or long grass. It's a nice convenience to be able to change the height of cut with a single lever.

45

46

47

Riding Lawn Mower, MODEL 57360, TORO, $1,650.00 1,800.00 **(47)**

32-inch swath cut; 11-horsepower, 4-cycle engine. Electric start, headlamps, 5 forward speeds, plus reverse. Blade adjustment varies cutting height from 1½ to 4 inches. Steel framework; fiberglass body. The turning radius is 32 inches and the overall width is 38½ inches. Overall length is 62 inches and height is 40 inches.

If you can drive a standard-transmission car, you should be able to operate this mower. The large cushioned seat is comfortable and includes a cut-off switch so that the motor is automatically shut off if the operator leaves the seat while the vehicle is in gear. One foot operates a clutch, the other a brake; the throttle is controlled by a hand lever (its top speed is just a little over 5 mph). Another lever reachable from the seat engages and disengages the blade. Clippings are blown into a catcher behind the seat. You can get a blade-type plow for snow or grading as an accessory, but don't expect to do much heavy work with a mower of this sort, because it's primarily a grass-cutting machine. This is an expensive unit, so it will only make sense to buy one if you have a very large area to mow or health or age makes it advisable.

LAWN RAKES

When grass clippings, leaves, sticks, stones, and assorted debris gather on your lawn, you run the risk of having the grass smothered and its beauty destroyed. To cure these problems, you want a sturdy, lightweight lawn rake that will move over and through the grass without damaging it, collecting material into piles so it can be removed.

The most common lawn rake has many tines of spring metal, bamboo, or plastic in a fan shape. These not only move gently over the lawn in a sweeping action, but they also have a large surface for collecting the clippings or leaves and hoisting them into a wheelbarrow or cart to haul off to the compost pile.

You'll find a few special rakes in this section, one of which is designed to travel just above the surface of the soil, hooking out dead grass. The other is a rake made of 28 wooden pegs sometimes called a hay rake. It's used for preparing a smooth seedbed, moving about piles of straw, weeds, and sticks, or, in a pinch, raking leaves.

The type of rake you choose depends on the specific task you have in mind. In most cases, the fan type rake will do the job. The durable plastic ones are finding more favor recently, as they are inexpensive, light, and don't rust.

48

Lawn Rake, MODEL 24, GEORGE W. MCGUIRE, $7.70–8.50 **(48)**

Bamboo lawn rake 24 inches wide with 4-foot hardwood handle; teeth are ½ inch wide, held together with metal band and spiral links to distribute pressure, yet allow rake to move smoothly over uneven ground.

Bamboo lawn rakes have been used for some time because they are springy and flexible, as well as gentle on the lawn. There are 5 models in this line, starting with a 10-inch-wide and going to a 30-inch-wide model. As with all bamboo, the tines will dry when not in use. When a bamboo rake has been stored for several months, soak it in soapy water the night before using it. That way you can bear down harder on the tines without breaking them.

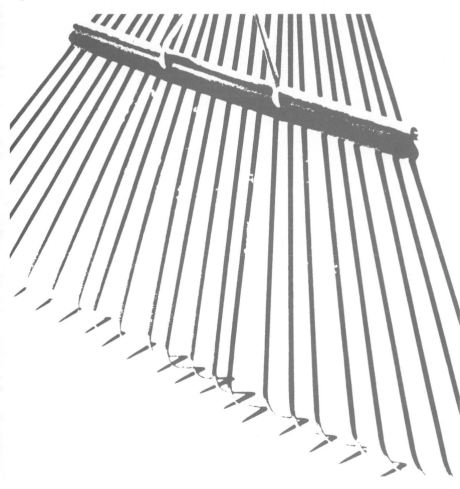

Lawn Rake, MODEL 2-A,
CALIFORNIA FLEXRAKE, $7.50–8.25
(49)

27 flat, green plastic tines supported by a yellow "spreader band" welded across the middle; 4-foot aluminum handle coated in vinyl; rake is 20½ inches wide.

This lightweight lawn rake is easy and efficient to use. The aluminum and tough polycarbonate stand up well in cold or warm weather, making this a durable tool. The spreader band is sonically welded for extra strength.

Lawn Rake, MODEL 19-200,
AMES, $5.50–6.00 **(50)**

Heavy-duty plastic rake head 24 inches wide with 26 tines secured to 4-foot wooden handle with a single screw through the side.

The polypropylene material in this rake stands up well to hot and cold weather. The rake is light, and the large, solid triangle of plastic joining the teeth to the handle is a boon when you're trying to gather and carry piles of leaves or other light material on the rake.

Lawn Rake, MODEL 19-237,
AMES, $8.20–9.00 **(51)**

24 metal tines are joined together in a 23½-inch wide rake with 54-inch wood handle; special reinforcing spring on the back of the rake helps maintain tension on the tines; stress distribution bar prevents tines from twisting and breaking; finished with blue paint.

This is the "deluxe" model in the Ames lawn rake line. It is a comfortable tool to use, but the tine spacing is a bit large for picking up small quantities of grass clippings.

49

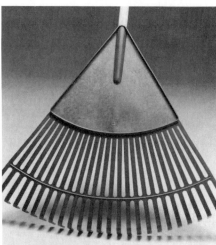

50

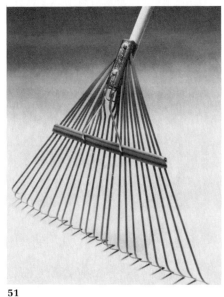

51

Shrub Rake, MODEL D-6B,
DISSTON, $5.00–6.00 **(52)**

6-inch-wide rake with 6 spring steel tines, attached to 48-inch handle.

If getting in close underneath shrubs has been a problem for you, you may want this little rake in your tool shed. It's meant just for those tight spots where the big lawn rakes get all tangled up in low-growing foliage.

52

Lawn Rake, MODEL 19-140,
AMES, $10.80–12.00 **(53)**

*21 curved metal tines form the head
of this 15-inch-wide rake; 2 wing nuts
make the angle of the head and tines
adjustable; rake head is attached with
2 bolts to 54-inch wood handle.*

Matted grass, thatch, and horizontally
growing grasses can frequently
smother your good grass plants. This
rake is designed to work just above
the surface of the soil to pull out that
thatch and give the more desirable
plants some breathing room. The adjustable head can be set at the desired
angle (you want the points on the
tines to ride about ¼ inch above the
soil) no matter how tall or short the
gardener.

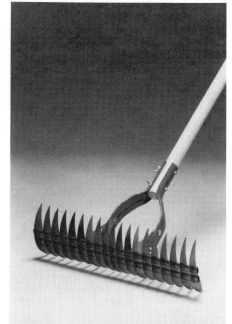

53

Lawn Rake, MODEL 39, RUGG
MANUFACTURING, $9.20–10.00 **(54)**

*Wooden head, 28 inches wide, with
28 4-inch wooden teeth; head is secured through the 6-foot handle with
3 metal bows.*

This is a modified version of the hay
rake used for more than 100 years on
small farms. The head is angled

slightly to give better pickup and raking action. The durable wooden teeth
are replaceable and are quite gentle
on the lawn surface. The bows fastening the head to the handle will add
extra pulling surface action against a
pile of grass clippings or leaves. This
is a traditional light, strong tool
which will last for years.

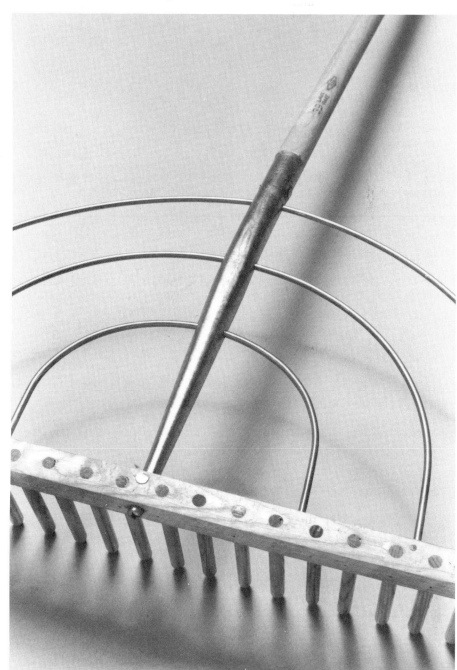

54

BROOM

Broom, MODEL 900-18,
PERFEX, $14.50–16.00 **(55)**

Heavy-duty "garage" broom; 54-inch handle; 18 × 3–inch synthetic fiber brush.

You can use this broom to sweep the clippings from a finely cut lawn, brush off patios, walks, and driveways, or clean the garage, deck, or sunporch. The brush fibers are resistant to chemicals, gasoline, and other petroleum products. When you notice the bristles getting a little worn, switch the handle to the other side for longer brush life. As with all push brooms, this shouldn't be stored resting on the ground. Hang it up to take the pressure off the bristles.

55

LAWN CART

Folding Lawn Cart, MODEL LC-2,
HALL INDUSTRIES, $80.00–88.00 **(56)**

Tubular metal framework with mildew-resistant vinyl-coated fabric; 2 8-inch wheels; cart measures 61 × 38 × 33 inches and holds up to 25 bushels; sides and end fold in for flat storage.

This is a handy cart for loads of grass clippings or leaves. The end opposite the wheels sits flat on the ground so that leaves or grass can simply be swept right in. To unload, the "Big Tote" is dumped over on its top edges.

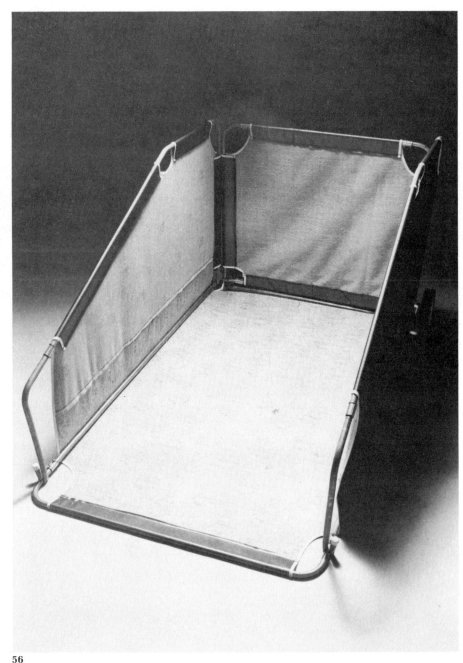

56

HEDGE SHEARS

Hedge shears are pretty straightforward cutting tools. My only caution is not to overuse them. Resist the temptation to trim shrubs that really should have their branches individually pruned. Not everything benefits from a crew cut.

When buying hedge shears, I first look for good steel. They're cutting tools and you want them to take and hold an edge. My second concern is lightness and a rubber bumper to ease the shock of closing. This is important because the shears are usually held in a horizontal position that can tire you out quite quickly; a few ounces can make a big difference. The continuous shock of metal striking metal is also tiring, so the rubber bumper on the better models is well worth the slight difference in price.

I like shears with a serrated or wavy edge because they tend to do a better job of holding the branches to be cut than do those with straight, smooth edges. Electric or gasoline-powered shears certainly make the job easier, but their cost has to be weighed carefully against how often you use them. As with any cutting tool, keep your shears sharp, wipe them dry after each use, and give them a quick once-over with an oily rag to ward off the inevitable onslaught of rust.

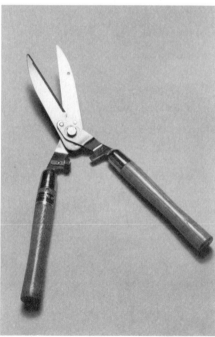

57

Hedge Shears, MODEL 2H, WALLACE MANUFACTURING, $12.00–13.50 **(57)**

8-inch, hollow-ground beveled blade, 21 inches overall, with cushioned ash handles that have hanging hole in end; upper blade is serrated, with a branch notch at the base for cutting larger wood; includes rubber bumper to cushion shock of closing action.

The blades are engineered to minimize sap buildup, which can eventually foul the mechanism. This is a moderately heavy, very strong tool, designed for long hours of continuous work with a minimum of fatigue.

Hedge Shears, MODEL 7, CORONA, $20.00–22.00 **(58)**

Wooden handles bolted to drop forged steel blade; 21 inches overall; oversized bearing bolt and rubber bumper; top blade is serrated.

The rubber bumper absorbs repeated closing shocks making these comfortable to use, and the serrated edge will keep twigs from slipping off the ends of the blades, as they will with some shears. A similar shear, Model 7-L, is 31 inches overall. It has the same 7-inch cutting blades, but the extralong handles make it especially useful for trimming large hedges, particularly those that can be reached from just one side.

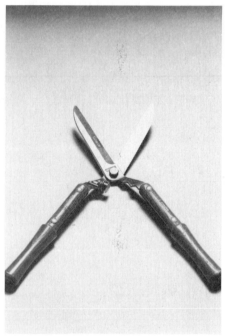

58

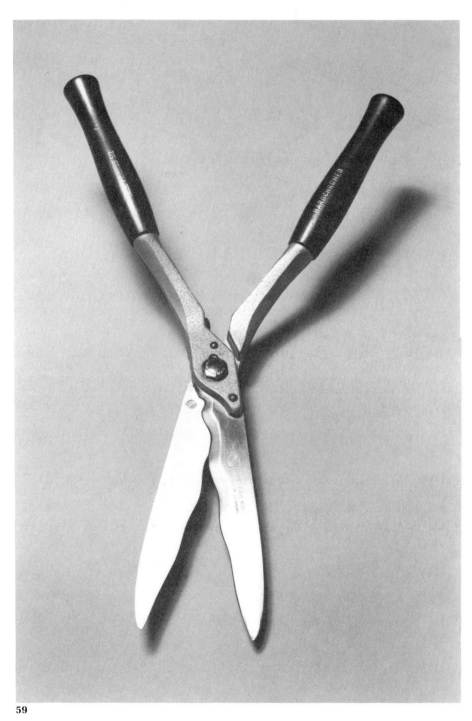

59

Hedge Shears, MODEL 2222,
LITTLE WONDER, $132.00–145.00
(60)

2 sets of dry-lubricant-coated, chrome vanadium tool steel blades provide a 30-inch cutting edge for this electric-powered hedge shear; 110 VAC, double-insulated to provide protection without grounding; plugs into any ordinary home outlet; 30-inch blades.

These professional-quality shears do their job with a minimum of vibration and are guaranteed to cut every known variety of shrub up to ¼ inch in diameter. All moving parts are sealed in a permanently lubricated housing. The extralong cutting blades give a very even cut; however, this unit is also available with 16-inch blades.

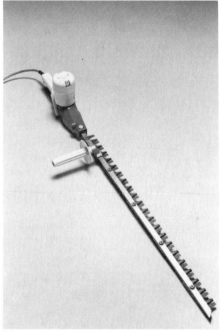

60

Hedge Shears, MODEL 512,
TRUE FRIENDS, $35.00–39.00   **(59)**

Overall length 20 inches; 2 wavy, chromed 9-inch cutting blades, rubber bumper, ¾-inch hex nut; wood handles.

The key to these shears is the wavy edge on the blade, which was designed to maintain an efficient cutting angle at every point along the entire length. This pair of shears doesn't quite work all by itself, but it does make hard work easier.

BRIAR HOOK

Briar Hook, COLEMAN TREE PRUNERS, $4.00–4.50 **(61)**

Pruner, 28 inches long with 5-inch wood handle; chrome nickel steel, bent into a hook shape at one end and the inside of the hook (about 1 inch) is sharpened; weighs less than 12 ounces.

If you're ever faced with a thicket of briars and brambles preventing easy access to the wood you're trying to cut, this tool can solve your problem. Merely reach in, hook the small branch or water sprout, and pull, cutting it off cleanly. Like most precision pruning tools, this needs to be sharpened on one side only.

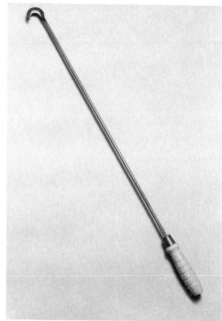

61

SOAPS

Soil I like; dirt I can do without. Unfortunately, working in soil — giving plants a proper start in life, pulling weeds, or even raking leaves — can lead to some heavy dirt that ordinary hand soaps can't get out. Here are a couple of special soaps for extra dirty jobs.

Hand Soap, "MICRO-BRUSH HAND SCRUB," TEXAS NOVACHEM, $2.50–2.75 (for 1 pound) *(no photo)*

Green-colored soap compound that includes tiny plastic granules instead of grit.

This is a fascinating chemical formula designed to remove a variety of different problem dirts such as tar, grease, ink, paint, typewriter ribbon, oil paints, wood stain, varnish, fiberglass resin, and adhesives. The granules give the compound a gritty feeling, but they're gentler on the hands than pumice. Since these granules and the various chemicals in the soap are selected to attract the dirt particles, you'll find little or no residue left in your sink. It all goes down the drain, your hands get clean, and the granules are so small there's no worry about them clogging the drain. Although they are not biodegradeable, they are made of what chemists call a straight chain polymer of hydrogen and carbon. This means they don't break down into something that is harmful or toxic. If you're having trouble finding a soap that does a heavy cleaning job, but doesn't leave your hands raw, try this.

Hand Soap, HOMESTEADER AND ARNOLD, $2.20–2.50 (for 1 pound) *(no photo)*

Soap and pumice compound in plastic container.

You'll get a minimum amount of lather but a maximum amount of cleaning from this old-fashioned soap, which includes many small particles of pumice that act as an abrasive to get out embedded dirt. Pumice is a light, porous, volcanic rock and some people find its abrasive action a little too harsh on the skin.

WATERING YOUR GARDEN

Whether you want a green lawn, juicy fruit, or flavorful, tender vegetables, water is the key ingredient. When nature doesn't supply the proper amount at the right time, the gardener has to step in and become rainmaker. There's a wide range of watering equipment available these days, from the simple to the sophisticated. Whatever you select, however, your basic goal is always the same: to provide enough moisture to the soil so that plant roots can absorb both nutrients and water easily.

If your soil is in condition, water management is off to a good start. Organic matter such as peat moss, manure, or compost will build texture and hold water longer. Hard-to-penetrate clay soils waste water because it runs off before seeping in, while sandy soils drain too fast. If your problem is drought, mulches are an excellent way to cut down on watering needs. Gardeners use everything from hay to old newspapers to the new plastics to keep water in the soil and slow down evaporation. Windbreaks, too, can reduce water loss by evaporation.

Don't be alarmed if the top of your soil looks dry. Most plants forage deep for water. (In fact, watering a little at a time encourages surface root development, which can cause the roots to dry out too quickly. That's one reason why I try to apply a lot of water at each session, putting down about 1 inch at a time, rather than sprinkling the garden every day.) To check if your garden needs water, dig down 6 or 8 inches with a trowel. If the soil is warm and dry, get out the hose. But if it's cool and moist, your plants are fine for the next day or two.

Don't overburden yourself with watering equipment. Although you'll find here several different options to meet specific needs, it would be the rare homeowner who needs one of everything. The same oscillating sprinkler that does the lawn one day can water the flower garden the next. If you're just starting out, I suggest you start with a top-quality watering can, hose, brass nozzle, and sprinkler. You can take care of just about any watering need with those four items, and add specialty tools later on.

SPRINKLING CAN   HOSES

Sprinkling Can, MODEL 710, DOVER, $10.50–12.00 **(1)**

10-quart water carrier of hot-dipped galvanized metal, 8⅞ inches in diameter; replaceable 3½-inch brass rosette, painted red; large carrying handle on top and pouring handle on back; also available in 6-, 8-, and 12-quart models.

This rugged-style sprinkling can, used for more than half a century, is still one of the best. Galvanized metal delays corrosion, and the spout's small ridges add extra strength — it would take a major accident to damage this can. The brass rosette gives fine streams, making it suitable for watering a seed bed of young plants, and it screws on snugly so there is no drip.

Any galvanized metal will eventually give in to corrosion, so if you want your can to last longer, make sure you drain it totally dry after using. This can has a slot at the back of the top cover, making it easy to drain completely.

1

A hose is "nothing but a long, thin bucket," goes a piece of country wisdom; but, as with a bucket, there are proven ways to make hoses more durable. Hoses come in various combinations of vinyl, nylon, and rubber. Rubber is the most flexible material, but it's also the most expensive. Although vinyls have tended to be less flexible in the past, new high-quality vinyl hoses have almost the same virtues as old-fashioned rubber hoses: staying flexible at low temperatures, having a high minimum burst strength, and being able to take quite a bit of abrasion.

When it comes to hoses made out of a combination of materials, the choice is more difficult. There are so many different formulations of plastics and nylon, with varying thicknesses and knits, that the manufacturer's reputation and the price become your main guides. Most major hose manufacturers make hoses that sell under more than one brand name and are dubbed "good," "better," "best." I would suggest you purchase the best quality line in at least a ⅝-inch diameter.

It's no saving to purchase a hose too narrow for the job. A less expensive, ½-inch-diameter hose may sound as if it's just a little smaller than a ⅝-inch-diameter hose, but there's a marked difference in the volume of water the two will carry in a given amount of time. For example, to put down 1 inch of water on a 5,000-square-foot area, a ½-inch hose will take about 6.5 hours; a ⅝-inch hose, 4.3 hours; while a ¾-inch hose can do it in only 2.6 hours. That's why I use a ⅝-inch hose for my garden, and feel there are some advantages to going to ¾-inch hose. However, first check the water piping in your home, and match hose and pipe diameter size. If you decide to join together two hoses of different diameters, put the larger one closest to the faucet. As you get away from the faucet, the pressure automatically drops, so a smaller diameter hose will be more useful on the distant end, helping to maintain pressure by constricting the space through which the water flows. Incidentally, use the shortest amount of hose necessary for a job, as the amount of water you'll get from a hose in a set time period will drop significantly the longer the hose.

When you're purchasing a hose, look at the couplings on each end. On any reasonably well-made hose, they'll be brass. On the top-of-the-line hoses, they'll be a thicker brass, and will have a flattened (octagonal or hexagonal) edge that makes them more crush resistant.

It's tempting to leave hoses stretched out, but it's a good idea to get in the habit of coiling a hose near the faucet and preferably putting it on some sort of holder, such as a hose reel. This keeps the hose from baking in the hot sun, where ultraviolet rays eventually can harm it, and makes it less likely that an accident will happen to the hose, or that someone will trip over it. Be especially careful of the way you treat hose couplings. Dragging the hose is one thing, but when you drag the coupling, you're just asking for it to get banged up and become impossible to tighten for a leak-free connection.

Hose, "HEIRLOOM," MODEL HR-546-25, AMERACE, $10.00–15.00 **(2)**

Rubber hose, 25 feet long, ⅝-inch diameter, with octagonal brass coupling; also available in 50- and 75-foot lengths.

You'll pay a premium price for a rubber hose such as this, but it is more wear resistant, and, given a minimum amount of care, it will last a lifetime — assuming, of course, that you remove it from the lawn before mowing the grass.

Hose, MODEL 2600 SL, COLORITE PLASTICS, $20.00–22.00 **(3)**

50-foot, ⅝-inch-diameter, reinforced vinyl hose with octagonal brass coupling; also available in 25- and 75-foot lengths.

This hose is very flexible and has a burst pressure of more than 500 pounds. It is of "4-ply" construction, which means there's an inner core of vinyl, a second coat of vinyl, a knitted nylon coat, and then another coat of vinyl. This type of hose is not for hot water use, but it should stay flexible enough to coil easily, even under near-freezing conditions. The area near the faucet joint is reinforced, since that's where there's usually a sharp bend, putting extra pressure on a hose.

2

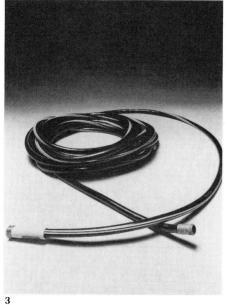

3

NOZZLES

A hose with water gushing unchanneled from it is of little use to gardeners because it usually supplies too much water, too rapidly, in too limited an area. The simple solution is to cover the hose end partially with your thumb, but since nozzles are inexpensive and do a better job, this seems unnecessary.

Choosing a nozzle doesn't have to be a complex business. Most gardeners get along just fine with a single brass adjustable nozzle that they can twist to get anything from a spray gentle enough to water a seedbed, to a stream forceful enough to wash dirt from the patio or insect pests from trees and shrubs.

Other adjustable nozzles work with either a pistol grip that you squeeze, or a thumb slide to change the water pattern. I find these handier for specific short-term tasks or for washing the car than for steady watering. The gardener usually wants to apply a lot of water at infrequent intervals. To do this, he doesn't want to have to keep a constant pressure on a pistol grip or thumb slide. You'll find a "rose" or "flaring" nozzle with many tiny holes does an excellent job of watering seedlings without washing them away and can also be good for pot plants whether outside on a deck or in a greenhouse. The fogging nozzle produces a superfine mist that can't be beat for adding humidity to a greenhouse or providing the extra delicate touch to cuttings or a seedbed. If you're in the habit of washing down your driveway, deck, or picnic table, you'll find the special "sweeper" nozzle does a good job.

If you decide to buy individual nozzles, start thinking right away about how you're going to store them. The main problem with having several nozzles is that it's so easy to misplace them. Perhaps a small rack next to the hose holder is best. Treat them with reasonable care and don't drag them over a driveway or across a stone wall. A solid brass nozzle of good construction should last a lifetime. Poorly constructed nozzles may eventually corrode and are likely to leak from the outset, an irritation and a waste of water.

4

Nozzle, "RAINBOY," MODEL N-21, L. R. NELSON, $3.80–4.20 **(4)**

2-piece, solid brass construction, 4⅞ inches long.

This style of adjustable nozzle has been used by many thousands of gardeners over the years. At 7½ ounces, it's heavier and more solidly built than many less-expensive versions. The 3 knurled rings make it easy to twist and adjust from a fine spray to a powerful, thin stream. On some twist nozzles there is a stop to prevent the barrel threading from turning right off the spindle, but there isn't on this one, so don't twist too far or you'll end up getting some of the water meant for your plants.

Nozzle, "REMINDER PISTOL," MODEL 2230, L. R. NELSON, $5.40–5.95 **(5)**

Solid brass nozzle parts, brass-plated zinc body, pistol-grip flow control with spray adjustment.

As with other pistol-grip nozzles, you squeeze the handle to turn it on. What's different about this one is that you can adjust the spray from fine to coarse by twisting the nozzle. The volume of flow is adjusted by setting the brass selector knob at the rear. You can therefore preadjust this to a

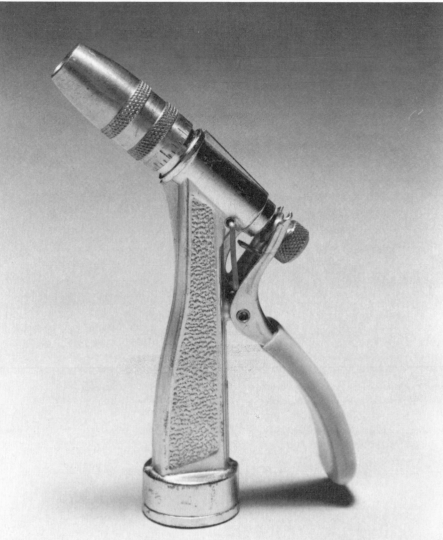

5

6

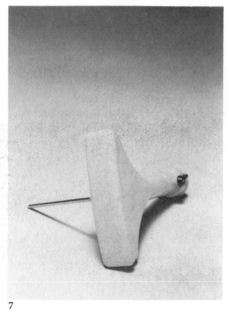

7

desired volume and spray pattern and it will return to that pattern every time the grip is squeezed, instead of having the pattern and volume vary with the pressure put on the grip. A clip is used to lock the nozzle open.

Nozzle, MODEL 2661, L. R. NELSON, $5.70–6.30 **(6)**

Brass "rose," 2⅜ inches in diameter with many small holes; 1¼ inches long.

This looks more like the conventional "rose" on a sprinkling can than a hose nozzle. It accomplishes the same purpose as the flaring, or fan style, but doesn't give such a wide pattern.

It is fine for low-pressure, gentle watering of seeds and young plants and will find a place in the greenhouse as well as outdoors. The front is easily unscrewed and the plate removed for cleaning.

Nozzle, MODEL 2635, L. R. NELSON, $2.00–2.20 **(7)**

1-piece yellow polystyrene nozzle with about 80 small holes in a rectangular pattern 4 inches wide; built-in shutoff valve and short spike to position in ground.

This is a good nozzle for a gentle spray watering of a seedbed or young plants. The pattern will vary with

pressure, of course, but typically, it will strike about 8 feet away, covering an area about 3 feet by 6 inches. The metal spike folds safely against the bottom of the nozzle. Since you can put a lot of water in a small space quickly, you won't use this spike often, but it does allow you to set the nozzle down and leave it running while attending to some other nearby chore for a few moments. The shutoff valve is handy and a water-saver as well.

8

9

10

Nozzle, MODEL B-50-C,
RAIN BIRD SPRINKLER, $3.00–3.30 **(8)**

*Brass fogging nozzle, 1⅛ inches long
with washer and inlet screen.*

At a typical pressure of 50 pounds per
square inch, a ⅝-inch hose will deliver 17 gallons of water a minute.
This nozzle discharges less than half a
gallon per minute in a cloud of fine
mist a few feet in front of the operator. Such a superfine spray is useful
for misting ferns, adding humidity in
a greenhouse, watering fine seeds, and
misting cuttings while roots are forming. The inlet screen helps prevent
particles from clogging the mechanism.

Nozzle, "NOZZ-ALL," MODEL 2640,
L. R. NELSON, $3.40–3.75 **(9)**

*Bright yellow plastic, about 2¼ inches
at widest point and 3 inches long;
brass connector.*

This can be used as a conventional
twist nozzle to give various patterns
of water, or as a gentle soaker. Twist
it one full turn past the shutoff point
and you get a large but gentle stream
of water mixed with air that is especially useful for the roots of trees and
large plants.

Nozzle, MODEL 4120S,
MELNOR INDUSTRIES, $.45–.55 **(10)**

*1 piece, molded orange plastic, 2
inches long with 3/16-inch opening.*

A "sweeper" nozzle such as this can
put plenty of water in a small area
fast and with a force that is meant to
knock things down, or wash them
away. This is not intended for water-

ing flowers and vegetables — it will
dig up the soil and harm the plants.
But it is good for knocking down
webworm nests, for example, and its
main use will be cleaning the patio,
picnic table, driveway, or birdbath. If
this is a tool you think you'll use
often, perhaps you'll want a brass
nozzle, such as the Nelson Model
N-26.

ROOT WATERERS

A device that puts water underground in the root zone of trees and shrubs is the most efficient way I know to get water to these large plants. Such "root waterers" are essentially long, metal tubes with holes near the bottom and a hose connector at the top. You connect the hose, insert the tube in the ground, and turn on the water. The result is that your trees and shrubs get water where they need it most, and precious water is not spilled on the surface to evaporate, an important consideration in many dry regions.

To use a root waterer, simply mark off an imaginary circle at the "drip line," the farthest extension of the branches from the tree, and water at intervals of up to 6 feet around this circle. Don't apply too much pressure; you're just trying to get the soil wet. (To check pressure, turn the hose on with the root waterer above the ground, noting the position of the faucet handle when the pressure is about right. When the models listed here put out about a 1-foot-long stream, that indicates sufficient pressure.)

Some root waterers can also be used to apply fertilizer in a soluble form.

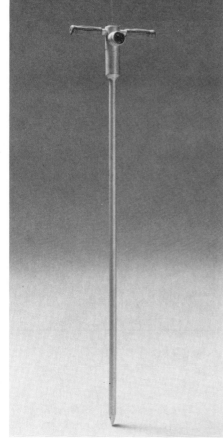

12

Root Waterer, MODEL 160, ROSS DANIELS, $14.00–15.50 **(11)**

Steel tube, 28 inches long, with 4 irrigating holes near the bottom point, 2 handles at the top, and a clear plastic chamber for holding fertilizer cartridge.

The handles make it easy to push this tool into the ground for watering or feeding trees. To feed, you simply insert an appropriate fertilizer cartridge and turn on the hose. Too much pressure causes the chamber to leak, however, so be careful. There's a control valve on this unit so you can turn the water on and off without going back to the faucet — a handy feature. Special cartridges are available for feeding evergreens, fruit trees, roses, and other trees and shrubs.

11

Root Waterer, MODEL 130T, YOUNG INDUSTRIES, $8.00–9.00 **(12)**

½-inch-diameter pipe, 34 inches long, with brass swivel hose connection at the top; "T" handle with two red plastic hand grips.

This tool applies water easily and efficiently to the root zones of large plants, trees, and shrubs. With the hose connected and water coming through, it's possible to insert the tool up to 30 inches deep in average soils. The water volume is controlled at the faucet where the hose is connected. The water is applied gently, mixed with air, at a rate of about 1 to 2 gallons a minute.

HOSE ACCESSORIES

Ever wish you could hook two hoses to the same faucet? Or stop the flow of water and switch nozzles without having to walk back to the faucet? Or be able to salvage that hose with a broken coupling? Here are some accessories that will solve these and other watering problems. Included are hose reels, one item that if used diligently will probably save you from needing some of the patch-up items. In several instances, similar units are available in plastic, chrome-plated zinc, and brass. When choosing among these, simply match the quality of the hose it will go on. That way your hose will be like the parson's "wonderful one-horse shay," with no weak links. When it gives out, everything will go at once!

13

Hose Coupling, "POSI-CLAMP" FEMALE COUPLING, MODEL 01F-C, GILMOUR MANUFACTURING, $1.00–1.10. **(13)**

Black nylon, plastic-threaded coupling with two nylon half clamps, fits ⅝- or ¾-inch hoses; also available for ⁷/₁₆-, ½-, and ⁹/₁₆-inch hoses (Model 05F-C).

Two sizes of these couplings will fit all standard rubber or vinyl hoses to replace broken couplings, and are available in male or female units. The half clamps are tightened over the shank with two screws.

14

Hose Mender, "POSI-CLAMP," MODEL 01HM-C, GILMOUR MANUFACTURING, $1.50–1.75 **(14)**

Two black nylon couplings; mender section 2 inches long, clamp 1½ inches in diameter; fits ⅝- and ¾-inch hoses.

When you damage your hose, this reusable hose mender will make it almost as good as new. Cut off the damaged section of hose, insert the tapered portion into the hose opening, place both sets of clamps around the hose, and tighten the screws. It's as easy as that. This model will work on all standard garden hoses, and Gilmour's Model 05-HM-C will fit smaller-sized hoses.

Hose Patch Tape, MODEL RT-07, ARNO ADHESIVE TAPES, $1.10–1.20 (no photo)

Green plastic tape, ¾ inch wide, 250 inches long, with adhesive on one side.

This tape isn't a substitute for a permanent hose mender, but if applied tightly in warm weather (above 50° Fahrenheit), it should stop a garden hose from leaking for a while. Make sure the surface of the hose is clean and dry, then apply this over the hole and about 1 inch to either side. You'll also find this tape useful for patching boots, rainwear, and similar items.

Hose Coupling, MODEL N-1558F, L. R. NELSON, $1.75–1.95 **(15)**

Heavy-duty brass female coupling for ⅝-inch hose.

If you want a durable coupling, this is the choice. It's of the same heavy brass found on top-quality hoses. To use it, simply insert it in the hose and tighten a standard galvanized steel hose clamp over it. Both female and male couplings are available with standard threads. Other models fit ½-, ¾- and 1-inch hoses.

15

Shutoff Coupling, MODEL N-111C, L. R. NELSON, $3.20–3.50 **(16)**

Die-cast zinc shutoff connector 2⅛ inches long with female fitting on one end, male on the other, and ball valve in between controlled by plastic lever.

If you want positive shutoff of the water in a hose, try this coupling. You might want to use it behind a nozzle that contains no shutoff provision of its own, or simply as a step-saver for changing nozzles without having to shut off the water at the faucet.

16

17

Dual Shutoff Coupling, MODEL N-78C, L. R. NELSON, $4.30–4.75 **(17)**

"Y"-shaped zinc coupling attached to faucet at one end, with two connections for hoses; plastic levers control water flow to hoses.

If you're short on outdoor faucets and long on watering needs, this is a convenient accessory. Two hoses can be connected at once and with the lever-controlled ball valve, either can be shut off independently, or the volume of water regulated. Of course you can only get so much water out of a faucet at a time, so expect a drop in pressure if you're using both hoses simultaneously.

Gooseneck Coupling, MODEL N-95C, L. R. NELSON, $2.30–2.50 **(18)**

Chrome-plated zinc alloy fixture bent at 60-degree angle; 3 inches long; standard coupling for faucet on one end, female hose coupling on other end.

This small coupling may save you some scraped knuckles, especially if your faucet comes close to the side of the house. It makes it a little easier to attach a hose and helps eliminate hose kinks at the faucet end.

18

Nozzle Holder, "RACKY'S NOZZLE RACK," RACKY'S ENTERPRISES, $3.75–4.50 **(19)**

Sharp, 16-inch metal spike with adjustable nozzle holder at top and large, plastic wing nut for tightening.

A California woman who got tired of holding a hose nozzle while watering her seedbed invented this simple device. It's just a clip on a stick, but it allows you to adjust the nozzle to the desired spray, aim it at the angle that will do the most good, then clip it in place and go about your other garden chores.

19

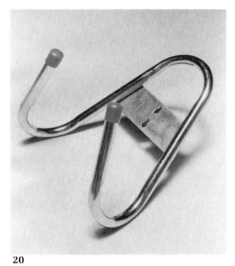

20

21

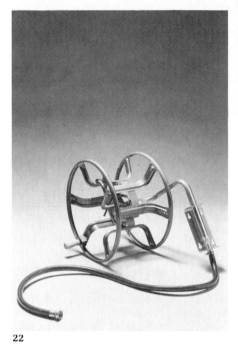

22

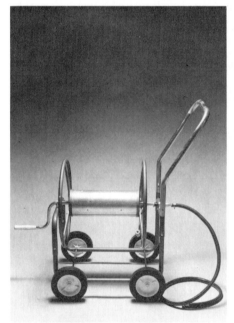

23

Utility Hanger, MODEL HH2,
TRUE TEMPER, $4.20–4.60 **(20)**

*Chrome-plated tubular steel, ends
capped with plastic, 10¼ × 8¾ × 6½
inches.*

This strong steel hanger will support
a garden hose or heavy equipment
such as a mower or a spreader.

Hose Reel, "SPOOLTOOL,"
SPOOL TOOL, $12.00–13.00 **(21)**

*Heavy orange plastic reel, 15 inches
in diameter; width adjustable from
1¾ to 3 inches. Holds up to 50 feet of
⅝-inch hose.*

This simple and attractive tool could
qualify as a toy for all ages. You can
wind and store a garden hose or a variety of other things, such as electric
extension cords, microphone or coax-
ial cable, chains, clothesline, and utility ropes. Eight holes on each side of
the reel can be used to hold the outer
end of the item being stored, or for
hanging on nails, hooks, dowels, or
cord.

One or two of the spacers included
may be removed for a more limited,
narrow storage capacity.When electric
cords or hoses are rolled, the male
cord fitting or the female hose fitting
may be brought through the center
hole for attachment, and only a small

part of the other end need be unrolled
for use.

The tool cleans easily; it is strong,
and will float if it falls into water.

Hose Reel, "SWINGER," MODEL 23 815,
AMES, $20.50–22.50 **(22)**

*17-inch reel holds 150 feet of ⅝-inch
hose; wood handle for winding; metal
mounting bracket locks into different
positions; 4½-foot leader hose.*

I like the way this reel is mounted.
The swing-out feature allows it to sit
flush against the house, or be brought
out at a right angle. You can also lift
it out of its mounting plate for use in
another location, or for storage.

Hose Wagon, MODEL 23-804,
AMES, $58.00–63.00 **(23)**

*Four 8-inch diameter wheels; 20-inch
reel holds up to 400 feet of ⅝-inch
hose; 6-foot rubber leader hose; large
metal crank handle; zinc-coated handle with zinc and enamel coating on
reel.*

Those large wheels make it easy to
move plenty of hose from one area of
the yard to another, or back to the
shed for storage. This is the most
elaborate of four cart-type reels Ames
makes. Two of the smaller ones,
Models C 23-805 and B 23-808, will
double as small carts for carrying
trash cans or a bale of peat moss
when the hose reel is detached.

SPRINKLERS

It's hard not to be captivated by the fascinating array of lawn and garden sprinklers now available. The most elaborate will do everything except pay the water bill, while even the simplest can be quite effective for many applications.

No matter how elaborate, however, sprinkler choices break down to four basic approaches. The simplest is just to have a spray head with no adjustment and no movable parts, such as a "rose"-style nozzle for a hose. Whirling-type sprinklers use two or more arms and the force of water pressure to spin them as they throw water in a circle. Impulse, or impact, sprinklers give a long stream of water that is broken into droplets in the air. The water is directed in a slow, circular pattern by the impact of a small hammer, deflected by the water stream. Oscillating sprinklers provide a rectangular pattern through a horizontal tube with several nozzles on it. The tube turns slowly from side to side.

Sprinklers can be mounted on a simple fixed base that can be slid across the lawn, or on a wheeled base, a fixed spike, or in a traveling arrangement that follows the hose in the pattern laid down by the gardener. Such traveling sprinklers are the most complex and expensive, involving a water motor and different gears to vary the speed.

In deciding which sprinkler best suits your needs, consider first what you most want it for, then look at the operating characteristics of the different types in this section.

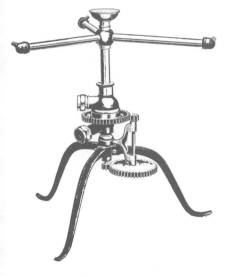

For example, an impulse sprinkler puts out a low, coarse stream of water. It may be a bit rough on a newly planted flower or vegetable bed, but its low angle and long throw make it a good choice for a lawn or an area where there are many trees to water. For large open areas, as well as some garden watering, I like the oscillating sprinkler. Its rectangular pattern makes it easier to match sections for total coverage than is the case with circular patterns, and its spray is fine enough not to upset the soil. During a significant part of its cycle, however, it is shooting water high up, which makes watering under trees difficult. Moreover, many of the less expensive models do tend to "hang-up" at the ends of each cycle, putting more water at the extremes of the pattern and causing some puddling. I've included some models where this problem is minimized.

Many of the whirling models are adjustable for height, allowing you to water a fairly narrow area near the ground, or a larger area by shooting the water at a higher angle. This high angle can get over some nearby obstructions, but if you're really looking for a way to get some extra height, consider a sprinkler on a pole stuck into the ground. (Choose firm ground for any spike-type mounting, as softer ground is likely to get muddy and the sprinkler will soon tip over.)

Generally speaking, you'll find the more expensive sprinklers tend to use more brass and stainless steel in their working parts. An inexpensive oscillating sprinkler, for example, will simply have holes punched in the bar. When cleaning these, it's easy to damage the sprinkler by enlarging the holes. I prefer to spend a few extra dollars for the type that has individual brass nozzles that screw into the bar. These are easier to clean and can be replaced if damaged.

Traveling sprinklers either drag the hose behind them, or coil it up on a reel as they go. The latter is convenient when using the sprinkler, but not so convenient if you then want to use the same hose for another job. Most traveling sprinklers move fast enough to set down just ½ inch of water at a time, and then they have to be reset, which is a disadvantage if you want to give your lawn a good 1-inch drenching of water a week. They're still handy, however, for the gardener who will be away from home during the day and will not be able to pull an oscillating or other type of sprinkler to a new position once enough water has been applied.

Always make sure your sprinkler is drained before freezing weather arrives. With many oscillating sprinklers, it's nearly impossible to drain them completely, so they should be stored in a warm garage or basement, out of freezing temperatures.

If it isn't clear to you exactly what the different sprinklers do, visit a garden supply place that can demonstrate the different patterns of their sprinklers, or at least take a tour of the neighborhood and see if you can spot different types in use. Don't take the manufacturer's stated patterns and sizes of covered areas too literally. These will vary with water pressure, hose diameter, hose length, and wind conditions. They're given here as rough guides for comparative purposes.

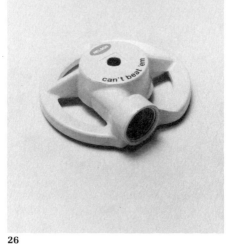

26

Sprinkler, "CAN'T BEAT 'EM," MODEL N-48SC, L. R. NELSON, $3.20–3.50 **(26)**

Cast-metal sprinkler, no moving parts; produces square pattern covering 25 feet on a side.

This is a simple, fixed-pattern sprinkler with a water nozzle large enough so dirt and debris will not clog it. Model N-48FC is essentially the same sprinkler, but it produces a circular pattern about 30 feet in diameter.

Hose-End Sprinkler, "CIRCULAR SHOWER," MODEL 100 C, THOMPSON, $2.90–3.50 **(24)**

3½ × 4¼-inch metal hose-end small-area sprinkler with approximately 50 holes; covers a 25- to 30-foot area.

This small but heavy sprinkler can be used for small-area watering when you need a gentle rainlike shower. There are no moving parts to break and it comes with a lifetime unconditional guarantee from Thompson.

Hose-End Sprinkler, "TWIN CIRCLE," MODEL 70, THOMPSON, $2.90–3.50 **(25)**

3 × 4-inch metal hose-end attachment; sprays overlapping 25-foot circles.

Useful for small-area coverage, this sprinkler has no moving parts and because it's heavy for its size, it doesn't flop around on the end of your hose. Thompson gives it an unconditional lifetime guarantee.

24

25

27

Sprinkler, "DAISY," MODEL N-65,
L. R. NELSON, $12.00–13.00 **(27)**

Yellow, cast-metal housing sits on 2 small plastic wheels and holds 2 sprinkling arms, each with an adjustable brass nozzle.

This is a most versatile small sprinkler, suitable for lawn or garden. Under normal operation, the arms spin from the water pressure and thus water a circle up to 50 feet in diameter. However, the arms may be locked in position to water a narrow strip. Each nozzle is on swivels and, as with a twist hose nozzle, is adjustable from a fine spray to a heavy stream. Since the nozzles can be turned off independently and aimed below the horizontal, you can lock the arms in place, aim a nozzle to cover a freshly seeded row of vegetables, and apply a light sprinkling to that area. Water can either be applied close to the ground without wetting foliage or aimed to shoot over some low flowers or vegetables to water a section beyond.

28

Sprinkler, "WARBLER," MODEL 225,
RAIN BIRD SPRINKLER, $21.00–23.00
(28)

Aluminum, impulse-type sprinkler head on green metal base with adjustable dial to cover up to 80-foot-diameter circle or any segment of a circle.

The two tabs near the base of this sprinkler are really stops that cause the sprinkler to retrace its course. The portion of a circle covered depends on where you set these tabs. The distance adjusts for a throw of up to 40 feet at a relatively low angle. The WB-425 is similar, but it has a 2-wheeled base for easier dragging along the lawn to different positions and has hose couplings at both ends so several sprinklers can be hooked in a series.

29

Sprinkler, MODEL PS-125,
RAIN BIRD SPRINKLER, $16.00–17.50
(29)

Impulse-type sprinkler with brass and stainless-steel head on heavy plastic base with 2 hose couplings; diffuser pin adjusts spray; covers up to 80-foot diameter.

This sprinkler can be set to cover a full circle or any part of it with a low-angle stream. The diffuser pin adjustment is a screw type that holds the preset adjustment well and makes this useful on garden or lawn, since it can apply a fine spray that won't disturb the soil. Thompson also makes a sturdy impulse sprinkler, "Ranger," Model 505 SSP.

30

Lawn Sprinkler, "SQUARESPRAY,"
MODEL 433,
PROEN PRODUCTS, $5.25–5.75 **(30)**

*Square red base, sled pattern about
5½ inches; rigid hose connections and
2-inch-square aluminum head; water
coming through these holes hits rotating aluminum sprinkler deflector.*

The pattern of this spray in varying
water pressures is generally square,
with a normal maximum size of about
35 feet. Where a circular-type sprinkler can over- or underwater a square
or rectangular area, square-patterned
sprinklers can solve the problem.

Sprinkler, MODEL GS-25-2,
RAIN BIRD SPRINKLER, $30.00–32.00
(31)

*Impulse-type brass and stainless-steel
sprinkler head mounts on top of 3-
pronged steel spike at ground level, or
2 or 4 feet above the ground; coverage
from 30 to 80 feet in diameter in a
full or part circle; 2 hose couplings
for series operation of sprinklers.*

The advantage of this sprinkler is its
ability to get over flower beds, bushes,
or other obstructions and apply water
to otherwise hard-to-sprinkle areas.
The 3-pronged base holds well, even
in moist ground. The base can be
used alone, or with either of 2 pipe

31

extensions to get desired height. The
soft green color blends well with the
landscape.

Sprinkler, MODEL 1049,
L. R. NELSON, $17.00–19.00 **(32)**

*Oscillating-type sprinkler with adjust-
able pattern and throw; yellow plastic
base, gold anodized metal tubes; 19
brass jet nozzles threaded into tube;
red plastic hose coupling; coverage up
to 2,800 square feet in rectangular
pattern.*

A dial selects 4 basic watering positions (left, right, center, and full), and
you can select from 16 "fine tune" positions to adjust the throw, which
should make it easy to water any portion of garden or lawn.

Sprinkler, MODEL 371,
BURGESS VIBROCRAFTERS, $16.00–
18.00 **(33)**

*Oscillating sprinkler with yellow plas-
tic housing on aluminum runners
bent to form a carrying handle; 16
plastic nozzles; adjustable coverage
up to 2,800 square feet in rectangular
pattern.*

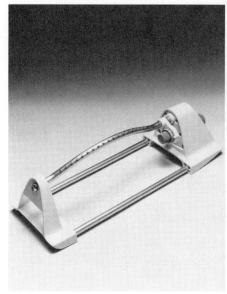

32

There are just two moving parts in
this new-design oscillating sprinkler.
It operates on less than 10 pounds of
water pressure and automatically
speeds up near the end of each cycle
so there is even distribution of water
and no puddling. It can be adjusted to
water narrow strips, or to keep the
stream low under bushes or trees. The
sprinkler head holds a plastic clean-
out plug with a small tip for clearing
a nozzle that might be clogged with
dirt.

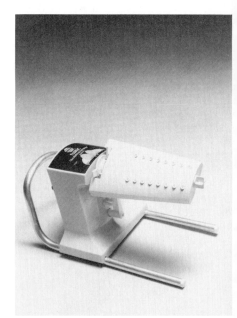

33

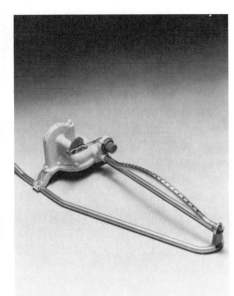

34

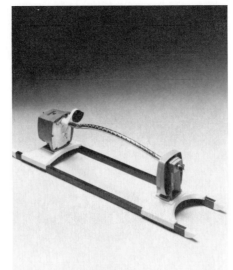

35

36

Sprinkler, "DIAL-A-RAIN," MODEL N-055A,

L. R. NELSON, $29.00–32.00 **(34)**

Oscillating sprinkler with yellow metal motor housing mounted on 23-inch gold anodized runner; water tube holds 19 threaded brass nozzles; dial adjusts for four patterns (right, left, center, and full) and 16 settings of throw; effectively covers rectangular area of about 2,700 square feet.

This top-of-the-line oscillating sprinkler has an unusual, heart-shaped "cam" that changes the rotational motion of the water motor into the back-and-forth motion of the sprinkler. This model starts the return stroke quickly so there's no puddling at the ends of the pattern. The high-torque water motor is designed to operate even under very low pressure.

Sprinkler, "TIME-A-MATIC," MODEL 890,

MELNOR INDUSTRIES, $29.00–32.00 **(35)**

Oscillating sprinkler with timer that shuts off automatically after preset volume of water is reached; black and white plastic base; metal tube with 20 brass nozzles; plastic drain plug and nozzle cleaner; size of rectangular pattern selected by dial; waters rectangular areas up to 3,500 square feet.

The main feature of this sprinkler is the "timer" which allows you to choose one of 12 settings in 100-gallon increments to a maximum of 1,200 gallons. It will take about 1,100 gallons to put down ½ inch of water over 3,500 square feet, which is roughly half the amount a lawn or garden needs in a week. For the most precise use, check the dial settings against a rain gauge or other water-measuring device the first few times. As with many oscillating sprinklers, this one tends to leave more water at the ends of the pattern where the sprinkler reverses itself. A disadvantage of having a timer on the sprinkler is that you may be tempted to leave water under pressure in the hose as it

bakes in the sun after the sprinkler has shut off. While this shouldn't burst a good-quality hose, it isn't a wise practice, as it can eventually weaken a hose.

Portable Sprinkler System, MODEL 113 H,

THOMPSON, $20.00–22.00 **(36)**

Two 12-foot hose lengths; 3 metal sprinkler units, 8 × 2 inches, with all-brass adjustable nozzles; covers 3 20-foot circles.

This unit, patterned on underground sprinkler systems, allows you to water specific areas that are far from your water source. Attach the first sprinkler to the end of your garden hose, and then alternate hose ends and sprinklers. Its main benefit is control, because you can place the heads wherever you want them. Thompson also sells the sprinklers alone (in 3-sprinkler units) for owners who have left-over sections of hose lying around ($9.00–10.00).

37

Traveling Sprinkler, "RAIN TRAIN," MODEL 1820,

L. R. NELSON, $57.00–63.00 (37)

Die-cast metal body and wheels; 2-armed aluminum whirling sprinkler with height of nozzles adjustable; 2 speeds; weighs more than 17 pounds; maximum coverage of 16,000 square feet.

This looks for all the world like a child's little yellow tractor, but it does a practical job of sprinkling in a path about 50 feet wide along a pattern set by the way the hose has been laid out. It will propel itself up a grade and around corners and an automatic shutoff device can be applied to the hose to bring it to a halt.

You'll get a little less total coverage, but put down more water, if you use this sprinkler with a ⅝-inch hose. It can drag up to 275 feet of ½-inch hose, up to 200 feet of ⅝-inch hose, or up to 150 feet of ¾-inch hose. With ⅝-inch hose, the speed adjustment allows you to put down about ¼ inch of water at high speed, or twice that at low speed. The effective coverage (where water distribution is even) is about 11,900 square feet. The maximum coverage is arrived at by using ½-inch hose and including the uneven sprinkling at the edge of the

38

sprinkler's reach. The spray arms can be rotated to point downward to cover a path as narrow as 15 feet wide. Since this sprinkler is all cast metal, be careful not to drop it.

Traveling Sprinkler, "RAINGER," MODEL 2000,

H. B. SHERMAN, $77.50–85.25 (38)

Metal motor housing; large, die-cast wheels; aluminum spray bar with nozzles for fine mist or full-stream spray; nozzles also adjust for height; 2-speed motor.

By reversing the wheels, you can select one of two speeds. At the slower speed, you can put down about ¾ inch of water over an area 80 feet long and 50 feet wide in about 2 hours. (Of course, this will vary with size of hose and water pressure.) Most traveling sprinklers move faster, so more than one application is necessary. Too many lawn sprinklers show up in the spring with ruptured housings because they were not drained properly in the fall and the water in them froze. There's a plainly visible brass drain plug on the bottom of this tool that should remind the user of the need to empty all the water from it before storing. An automatic shutoff that can be placed anywhere along the hose is available.

Traveling Sprinkler, "TRAVEL-MATIC," MODEL 3503,

MELNOR INDUSTRIES, $91.00–100.00 (39)

Reel-type traveling sprinkler; twin nozzles adjust for angle of stream; two speeds; waters up to 16,000 square feet.

This sprinkler coils up the hose as it goes along, which means that the hose is all rolled up when the job is finished. At the slower speed, the sprinkler will spread about ½ inch of water. The reel can hold up to 240 feet of ½-inch hose, but I'd recommend using ⅝-inch hose. Not much water will come out of 240 feet of hose of any diameter. Of course, the larger hose will take up more room, so consider the effective travel of this sprinkler at somewhat less than 200 feet. The front guide wheel will shut off the sprinkler at a special shutoff device located at any joint between lengths of hose. The motor of plastic gears is strong enough to move the sprinkler over level ground and moderate upgrades. This is a costly unit, so make sure your acreage size justifies the expense.

39

WATER CONTROLLERS

If you'd like to water your lawn today, but you have to go out, perhaps you should consider a water controller, a device that shuts off the water after a preset amount has flowed through it.

Earlier water controllers used a clockwork mechanism and were, in the strictest sense, timers, with the disadvantage that because there are so many variables controlling the amount of water coming from a sprinkler, merely setting it for a given time didn't assure that the same amount of water was set down during each session.

Water meters, however, measure the flow of water coming through them and shut off after a certain amount is reached. The system still isn't faultless, so check it occasionally. Put out some straight-edged cans or a rain gauge under your sprinkler and see just how much water is actually delivered at a specific setting. Instructions with the timers will be helpful as a rough guide, but trust your own measuring and adjust accordingly. You'll find these devices will really save you frustration while watering a garden or lawn.

41

Water Timer, MODEL 100,
MELNOR INDUSTRIES, $12.00–13.50
(40)

Round, sealed black plastic case about 3 inches across, 2 inches high; raised dial can be set at any of 48 click-stops to deliver up to about 625 gallons of water; hose coupling attaches easily to faucet.

The package has a chart that recommends the dial setting for 4 different types of sprinklers from different manufacturers, and an approximate time period required to apply ¼ inch of water from each sprinkler at 2 different water pressures. This unit does restrict water flow to a smaller amount, but it is valuable for shutting off the water when it has given the plants what the gardener believes they should have. Each of the 5 major settings indicated on the dial will deliver about 125 gallons of water.

40

Water Timer, MODEL 500P,
H. B. SHERMAN, $17.60–19.40 **(41)**

Beige plastic case, 3 × 4 × 6 inches, with metal faucet coupling; 14 dial settings deliver from 100 to 1,400 gallons of water in equal increments; filter washer included.

This water controller can be awkward to attach to the faucet, but it is well made and durable. It can be set for light, medium, or heavy soaking and shuts off automatically. There's an antihammer valve included to prevent back pressure "bang" during shutoff, which helps to avoid possible pipe damage.

DRIP IRRIGATION

Drip irrigation, a technique where water is applied drop by drop to the root zones of plants, is used by many commercial gardeners all over the world. Its proponents say that drip irrigation means less work, less water use, and better crops. While I can't deny that the first two points are important and interest me, what's most exciting is the last — better crops. Why should drip irrigation give you better crops? Those who have been using it give three reasons:

1. You can have excellent control in getting a precise amount of water to the root zones of crops and thus keep the soil moisture level at a healthy point so that plants don't go through the stress periods of drying out.

2. Water-soluble fertilizers can be applied through the system, again going directly to the root zones.

3. Since the water is being applied around the root zones of the selected plants, water is not wasted on spaces between rows, spilled on foliage, or blown off target by the wind. This means fewer weeds and less chance of wet foliage leading to fungi diseases.

The basic principle of drip irrigation has been applied by many gardeners in different ways. For example, some persons like to sink tin cans with several small holes punched in them into the soil around their tomatoes. They fill the cans with water and let it slowly leach out. For a long time, indoor gardeners have used a variation of this system for rooting cuttings. They put a small clay flowerpot inside a much larger one. The drainage hole of the small pot is blocked with a cork and the pot filled with water which slowly seeps out through its sides into the surrounding soil. Yet most gardeners have been slow to try drip irrigation, partially because some early systems sold for home use were simply small, light hoses with holes punched in them that tended to clog with grit and algae. There are better, slightly more complex systems available today, and prices are not out of line with other watering techniques using high-quality sprinklers. A starter kit will cost in the neighborhood of $25.00 and will give you enough equipment to drip irrigate about 45 feet of garden rows. Such a system could also be used to water and fertilize fruit trees, shrubs, or berry bushes.

Drip irrigation is a little more sophisticated than punching a few holes in your garden hose. You need a system that will apply water slowly and evenly at several different locations. You don't want it to clog and you can't afford to have fertilizers pushed back into your home water supply. The technology is now reasonably well developed, however, and while more complex than a hose with holes in it, is not as intricate as many common sprinkler systems.

Acquaint yourself with the accessories available with a system. If you're going to fertilize, you need a back-flow preventer that will not let a change in water pressure draw the fertilizer back into your home system. If you're drawing water from a pond or other open container where algae might form, you'll have to filter it first through a sand filter such as those used for swimming pools. Algae can spell death to a drip system. That's why black plastic hose is used. Some ordinary gar-

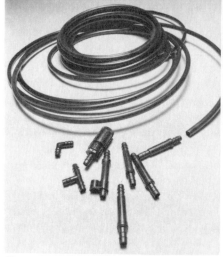

42

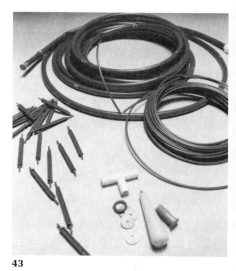

43

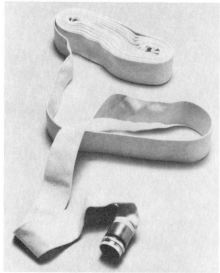

44

den hoses may let through enough ultraviolet rays to cause algae formation in the slow-moving water. If using well water, you'll also want a finer-mesh screen filter than normal to keep particles out of the small irrigators.

I like the idea of using drip irrigation with crops that are especially water sensitive, such as tomatoes, lettuce, and celery. How much water you apply, however, will vary with weather, soil type, and the size and stage of development of your plants. In short, drip irrigation won't replace good gardening know-how, but it can make your job easier and the results more satisfying.

Drip Irrigation, MODEL R-500D, RAINDRIP, $23.00–25.00 **(42)**

Starter kit includes 60 feet of ½-inch, semi-rigid plastic tubing, 28 drippers (each delivers 1 gallon per hour), 3 "T" connectors, 2 elbow connectors, 4 hose ends, 1 hose swivel adaptor, 1 screen filter, ½-gallon-per-minute flow control, and instructions; irrigates a garden approximately 12 × 16 feet; can also be used for shrubs, fruit trees, and other plants.

The parts to this system look simple and in most cases they are, but those "drippers" are less straightforward than they appear. Whether you're looking at the outside, or through one, it seems to be just a rigid, plastic tube. But cut through one and you'll see there is really a tube within a tube. The inner tube has a spiral outer layer that fits tightly against the inside of the outer tube. The result is a dual water chamber, a large inner one to let most of the water through, and a small, spiraling outer chamber that effectively slows the flow of some of the water, making it possible to have a fairly large hole from which the water emerges. Such a large hole doesn't clog as easily as the tiny ones used in many other systems.

The "T" connectors, elbows, and hose ends are just devices that allow you to put your kit down in such a way as to cover several short rows. Although a small system like this could be moved about to different locations, I recommend setting it up to cover one area, at least for several months of a specific growing season,

and leaving it alone. Use it on plants that will most benefit from maintaining a constant moisture content in the soil. This kit can be installed easily in a single Saturday morning. Cut the tubing to length with a knife or shears. The drippers and other parts are easier to insert if the end of the tubing is first dipped in hot water for about 30 seconds to soften it. You use a dripper about every 21 inches along a row of plants.

The manufacturer recommends watering a vegetable garden twice a week for a period of 2 to 8 hours with this system. That's an approximation, of course, and the best results will be obtained by being aware of the needs of your plants, your soil conditions, and weather patterns. There's no magic formula, just common sense. You water far more in dry weather than in wet.

This system can be expanded to cover a far larger area and there are accessories available for introducing fertilizer, regulating the line pressure, and filtering.

Drip Irrigation, "ROBERTS TRICKLE IRRIGATION HOME KIT," MODEL 13-0001, ROBERTS IRRIGATION PRODUCTS, $13.00–14.50 **(43)**

Home starter kit with 50 feet of ½-inch, rigid green plastic tubing, 60 feet of ⅛-inch tubing, 20 "spot spitters," each 4½ inches long and emitting between 4 and 15 gallons per hour depending on water pressure; hose coupling, hose punch, and 4 pressure reducing discs.

This is sort of a hybrid between a sprinkler and a drip system in that the water is emitted continuously in a fine spray a few inches above ground. The ½-inch tubing carries the bulk of the water. The "spot spitters," which are really simple sprinklers, are set in the ground and aimed toward a plant. The water comes out of them in a spray covering about 90 degrees and reaching between 18 and 24 inches. Each of the sprayers is connected to the main tube by a short length of ⅛-inch tubing. This is attached by punching a hole in the main tube and sliding it in place. The hole closes around the smaller tube, making a tight seal.

Roberts also makes conventional sprinkler systems, a home drip irrigation system using just tubing with holes punched in it, several sizes of "spot spitters" for different applications (including one that can be fed from an underground hose to be unobtrusive) and similar units built into the sides of flowerpots.

Drip Irrigation, "ROSE AND GARDEN SOAKER," MODEL S-30, SPECIALTY MANUFACTURING, $7.70–8.40 **(44)**

Seamless white, lightweight canvas soaker hose about 1 inch in diameter and 30 feet long; hose coupling at one end; other end sewn closed.

This is a soaker hose, not strictly a drip irrigation system, but the basic idea is the same. The loose texture of the hose allows water to ooze out its entire length, thus allowing you to apply water to the root zones slowly without wetting leaves of plants. A simple filter added to the coupling reduces chances of the spaces in the hose clogging. Run it across the top of a slope, never up and down the slope, or there won't be even distribution of water. Dry, brush clean, and store in large, loose loops after each use. Also available in 15- and 45-foot lengths.

PROTECTING THE GARDEN
AND LANDSCAPE

When I hear fellow gardeners tell how rabbits destroyed a crop of lettuce in a single evening, or how cutworms massacred the young broccoli plants, or how raising apples is hopeless because of all the insect pests, I sympathize. Just about every gardener has suffered these setbacks. Certainly I have. But the key to keeping them in check is to have what tennis players call a good "follow-through." You can't just plant, you have to protect your crops.

Protection takes two forms — physical barriers and chemical ones. Physical barriers involve few tools or accessories; they're pretty straightforward and are used mainly for keeping birds and a variety of small animals out of your garden. You'll find fences and nets the main weapons in this battle. Traditional garden fencing material is simply galvanized or vinyl-covered wire, 3 or 4 feet wide with a 1-inch mesh, which should be rust resistant. When you build such a fence, bury the first foot of it, and place the barrier at least 2 feet high. And make sure there are no gaps — it's amazing how small a rabbit can get when he's on one side of a barrier and food is on the other. Some gardeners are forced to electrify their fences to keep pests at bay. These fences are far simpler to construct than the uninitiated may fear, as I'll explain later in the chapter.

There are several other ways to protect your crop short of using chemical sprays and powders. But for many diseases and insects, the only solution is spraying.

If I can possibly do without pesticides, I don't use them. A few bugs won't destroy a crop. But when nature gets out of balance, when the bugs look like they're going to take over and it's a choice between them or the garden, my choice is the garden. I look for pesticide devices that give thorough coverage while using the least amount of chemicals. I want as much control over dosage and direction as possible.

Government regulations for pesticide control are constantly changing. Current regulations forbid many pesticides to the home gardener, although the brands on the market now are safer than those of former years. Before you use any pesticide, examine the label carefully; its use and disposal should be explicitly detailed. Don't open a single container until you understand the directions thoroughly.

When I aim dust or a stream of liquid at a plant, it's essential that the pesticide land only on that plant, not on other plants in the general vicinity. Common sense dictates spraying only when the wind is calm or light and making sure everyone in the vicinity is upwind from the spray. Leave big spraying jobs, such as trees over 25 feet high, to professionals.

Keeping a sprayer clean is critical, for if nozzles and filters are clogged with dirt and chemical residues, they become useless. Cleaning also prevents one chemical from mixing with another. One way to be absolutely positive you're not inadvertently mixing chemicals is to have one sprayer for each type of chemical. (You should still clean them after each use.) This is particularly important with herbicides, where the residues left from one spraying operation might actually harm the next plant you try to save. If you have more than one sprayer, be sure to label each one clearly.

When I look for a sprayer, I want one that is easy to fill, adjust, empty, and clean. Before I use it for the first time, or after it has been in storage for a long while, I try a "wet run," using just water. This gives me a chance to see how far the sprayer will reach and the pattern created by different nozzles or nozzle settings.

Sprays come in two forms: in solution (completely dissolved in the water) or in wettable powders (which do not dissolve). Such powders remain suspended in the water, but if a tank containing them sits idle for any length of time, they'll soon settle to the bottom. So, when you use a wettable powder, agitate the tank frequently and keep an eye on the spray stream. When particles are beginning to settle, the stream usually turns from a milky color to clear. After using wettable powders, clean the sprayer especially carefully, as powder particles can plug filters and nozzles quite quickly.

By all means, take extra precautions with all pesticides. Keep them locked up, out of the reach of children and out of sight of people who may not understand their potential toxicity. Likewise, clean and lock up any measuring devices or other tools used in the spray preparation. Finally, know what you are doing. Identify the insects you are after, time your assault to hit at the right point in the insect life cycle, spray effectively (being sure to get the underside of leaves where many insects lurk), and don't make the common mistake of assuming that "more is better." There's an optimum amount for each pesticide stated clearly in the product's directions. Follow them.

INSECT TRAPS

There are several mechanical ways of disposing of garden pests and where feasible I prefer these to using chemical sprays and powders. Their only shortcoming is that they are usually targeted for a limited population and there are still many insects that can't be handled in this fashion.

Insect Trap, MODEL I.D.T.-2, HALL INDUSTRIES, $60.00–65.00 **(1)**

Lantern-style trap, avocado green, 12½ inches high and 9 inches in diameter at widest point, uses 60-watt blue light bulb to attract insects, and brass grills to catch and kill them with an electric current; hook on top for hanging and 6-foot, 3-prong outdoor cord for hooking to 110v standard house current; UL listed.

This is a simple, safe, ecologically sound way of eliminating flying insect pests in outdoor living areas. Bait, such as spoiled meat for flies, or honey for bees and wasps, can be put in it, or you can depend on the special light to lure the night flyers. This one lantern will attract insects from an area about 60 to 70 feet in diameter. Hall also makes larger units of similar design. The upkeep is minimal since it runs off standard house current and the only thing you have to do is remove the dead insects from the base. Replacement bulbs are also available from Hall.

Japanese Beetle Trap, Cage, and Bait, ELLISCO, $11.00–12.00 **(2)**

Green and yellow enamel metal trap about 15 inches tall; lower 6 inches of the trap is a perforated cage from which the beetles are unable to escape; the yellow upper portion contains the bait and 4 fins that serve to deflect the flying beetles down the funnel into the green cage; wire hanger for suspending from tree branches; price includes trap, cage and bait.

When using this trap, remember that the most effective area for beetle control will be downwind from the trap. Beetles from far away will be attracted by the odor that blows toward them. Position the trap in bright sun, but be sure to keep it away from roses, grapes, zinnias or other favorite foods of the Japanese beetle so they don't eat their fill before discovering the trap. When the cage becomes loaded with beetles, lower it into water containing a small amount of soap or kerosene to kill the beetles. A hanger that stands in the ground is available as an accessory.

3

Slug Trap, IMPORTED BY GOOD-PROD SALES, $2.70–3.00 **(3)**

Green plastic cup, 3½ inches by 4 inches deep, with detachable brown roof, 5 inches across.

This nonpoisonous solution to the slug problem combines the stale-beer-in-a-jar-lid method with the shady refuge of the cabbage leaf or shingle. Bury the cup in the soil and fill with beer. The roof keeps the beer undiluted, drawing the slugs by the smell to their death by drowning.

1

2

POCKET MAGNIFIER

Pocket Magnifier, MODEL N8183,
BAUSCH & LOMB, $7.75–8.50 **(4)**

*Black plastic oval case, 2 × 1¾
inches, holds two plastic lenses, one
magnifying 3× and the other 4×;
used together, they give 7×.*

Friend or foe? That's what you want
to know when the insects arrive and
start eating your plants. This pocket
magnifying glass will help you identify some of the tinier species, such as
spider mites; identification is the first
step toward intelligent control.

4

ANIMAL TRAP

Animal Trap, "HAVAHART,"
MODEL 3A,
WOODSTREAM, $48.00–53.00 **(5)**

*Cage made of rust-resistant galvan-
ized metal and wire mesh, 42 × 11 ×
13 inches; weighs approximately 22
pounds.*

This is the humane way to trap small
animals who are making pests of
themselves. The trap is simple to set
and unlike the strong, spring-type
trap, you don't have to worry about
hurting either yourself when setting
it, or the animal. Once you have
caught the animal, give him a one-
way ticket to a distant forest or
meadow where he can set up house-
keeping without harming your garden
or someone else's. These traps are
available in several sizes for mice,
birds, and foxes. The size pictured
here is designed for woodchucks and
raccoons. Woodstream also makes
mole and gopher traps.

5

BARK SPUD

Bark Spud, "OUR BEST BARK SPUD,"
SNOW & NEALLEY, $19.00–22.00   **(6)**

*Blade and socket are 1 piece, 11
inches long, 2¼ inches wide; handle
above socket is 6¼ inches long; end
and both sides of spoon-shaped blade
are sharpened.*

This tool can be used to trim the bark
off trees felled for fence posts, or to
trim old, loose bark from aged fruit
trees to remove insect hiding places.
It's also convenient to remove small
branches from trees that have just
been chopped down. It's a heavy,
well-balanced specialty tool.

6

ANTI-BIRD DEVICES

I'm not sure where the derogatory term "bird brain" came from, but I
doubt that it was originated by a gardener who tried to outwit birds in
defense of a crop. The truth is, short of putting a physical barrier between crop and birds, there are few sure-fire solutions. Besides, most
of the time birds are a gardener's friend.

Starlings, for example, are much maligned, but during the spring
they gather on our lawns and make a meal of the grubs of beetles
which would give us endless problems later in the summer if they sur-
vived. In the summer they eat the chinch bugs and sod webworms,
and in the fall they do a nice job on crabgrass seed and perhaps other
weed seeds. This is not to mention the obvious — that their songs,
colors, and motions are as much food for the soul as the flowers we
plant.

Still, I get irritated with birds on two scores. First, at seeding time,
crows dabble about pulling up the young shoots of corn, eating the fat-
tened kernel at the end. Pheasants are even more efficient. They'll
stroll down a field row pulling every single seedling, execute an
about-face, and return on the adjoining row. If such damage is common, you might try dipping the seeds in a repellant to make them
taste bad. Incidentally, don't be too alarmed about birds feeding on
your grass seed. The seeds they like are the large ones, such as the rye
grasses. Most of the better perennial grass seeds, such as bluegrasses,
are so small they aren't worth the bird's energy to lean over and pick
them up.

When it comes to harvest time, I've heard many a gardener say he
would be happy to share with the birds if only they had better eating
habits. Why must they take a small bite out of several pieces of fruit?
Can't they eat one entirely instead? I wish I had an answer to that.
I've found the only sure protection is to cover the fruit with a net. Nets
should be applied with care so as to damage neither the net nor the
fruit, and must be secured entirely around the edges, or a bird will
sneak through.

Scarecrows are traditional with gardens. What would a picture of a
country cornfield be if it didn't include a scarecrow with a few crows
perched on his shoulder? The basic conclusion I've reached about all
kinds of bird devices is that no one thing seems to work for long.
Those "bird brains" have a way of figuring things out pretty quickly.
So if you're going to try the scarecrow method, use several different
ones and alternate them every few days, moving them to different locations. This may just keep the birds puzzled long enough for your
crop to develop to the harvest point relatively unmolested.

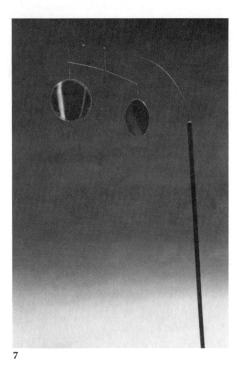

7

8

9

Scarecrow, MODEL "SUNDANCE SCARECROW,"
NATURE WORKS, $8.00–9.00 **(7)**

2 5½-inch-diameter, chrome-plated styrene discs dangle from wires attached to a spring-hardened, stainless steel whip that curves to fit into the top of a 33-inch wooden dowel painted green.

Place the dowel in the ground, hook on the shiny, dangling plates, and away go the birds, frightened by the dazzling reflections and movements . . . or so goes the theory. I'd never want to guarantee that this or any other scarecrow works for all birds all the time. What I can say is that it does seem to do some good in keeping birds out of the garden and even when it isn't doing that job as thoroughly as we might like, it harmonizes with the environment, providing an attractive and interesting garden ornament.

Bird Repeller, "BIRDS-AWAY REPELLER,"
DALEN PRODUCTS, $4.00–4.50 **(8)**

6-foot-long inflatable plastic snake, brown and black on the top, mostly white underneath; 2 eyelets for hanging.

Hang or drape this plastic crawler in your fruit trees and squirrels and birds will be frightened away, for it looks like one of their natural enemies. However, don't count on the birds' being fooled forever. At some point, they will decide that they have no trouble at all coexisting with *plastic* snakes. That's when it's time to move the "snake" to another location in the hope that the birds will think it got there on its own or, at any rate, will find the situation worthy of more contemplation. I look on this as one more item in the gardener's friendly bag of tricks to try to keep from sharing too much of the harvest with the birds. It's not foolproof. It won't work forever, but it should be of some help and children love it.

Anti-Bird Net, "DUREX,"
ANIMAL REPELLENTS, $13.00–14.00 **(9)**

Hexagonal mesh of about ¾ inch, made of lightweight Olefin fabric and measuring 20 × 20 feet. Also available in the following sizes: 9 × 45 feet, 4½ × 75 feet, 9 × 21 feet, and 4½ × 36 feet.

Simply stretch or drape this net completely over the crop to be protected. When using on a thorny crop, you'll want to support it above the crop with a wood or wire frame. And be sure to secure it to the soil on all sides. Birds not only fly, they crawl, and they'll get under a loose net like kids sneaking into a circus tent. Handle this screening carefully, folding and storing it when not in use. With such care, you'll get many seasons of protection from it.

Garden Utility Net,
MODEL 834V144PHBK,
DUPONT, $12.00–14.00 (for 12 × 50
foot roll) **(10)**

*Vexar plastic mesh in about ½-inch
squares.*

Although netting such as this is most
frequently used for covering ripening
fruits and berries to protect against
bird damage, it has several other possible uses. It could also protect young
germinating seedlings from birds or
small animals, or be tied into bags
that will be strong and tight for carrying leaves and small prunings. During
the winter, this material can be tied
around evergreens or shrubs to support them against breakage from
heavy snow loads. Swimming pool
owners can use it as a cover to prevent medium to large leaves from getting into the water. With reasonable
care, this durable net should last for
many years. It can be cut to any desired size with ordinary kitchen
shears.

10

ELECTRIC FENCES

When harvest time comes and you find yourself sharing a dispropor-
tionate amount of the fruits of your labor with a variety of four-legged
freeloaders, you might want to build an electric fence.

Farmers have been using these for years, primarily to keep live-
stock in, but what will keep a horse or pig on the inside of a fence can
also keep some other creature out. Animals are usually smart enough
to remember unpleasant experiences, and once a rabbit has had his
nerve ends jangled by an electric fence, he's likely to give it a wide
berth.

As garden fencing goes, electric fences are neither expensive nor
difficult to install. In fact, they're about the easiest type of fence to
build. A properly constructed and installed fence is not dangerous to
people or pets, although you should take two precautions. First, as
with any electric device, look for evidence that the one you are purchasing has been approved by the Underwriters Laboratory (UL). Second, get or make signs that warn people that this is an electric fence.
(In some states, this is required, but it's a good idea anywhere. The
shock you get from touching an electric fence is not lethal, but it is
unpleasant, especially when it comes as a surprise. Signs are available
from Dare Products and other manufacturers.) Wearers of heart devices such as pacemakers should remember that this sort of fence
poses a potential hazard.

The first item you need to buy is an electric fence charger — the
heart of the system, which can turn either house or battery current
into a high voltage, pulsating surge. There are three basic versions of
such chargers. One uses solid-state electronics to convert house current to the pulsating current used in the fence. It delivers a shock that
lasts about 1/400 second. The extremely short duration of the shock is
the main reason why electric fences will not harm an animal or person. You'll find this type a little more expensive to start with, but
since it will use less than a quarter's worth of electricity a month, its
operating economy is difficult to beat. It must, however, be located in
a weatherproof building or box.

If it's difficult to get your fence charger near a regular source of
house current, the battery- or solar-powered units are the best bet. Batteries can be any 6- or 12-volt type (voltage varies with the fence
charger) that is rechargeable, or a throwaway variety. If you use an
automobile storage battery, it should be routinely recharged every 3
months, even if it doesn't appear low. A new unit on the market, made
by Parker McCrory Manufacturing Company, uses a rechargeable battery powered by solar cells. The initial cost is high, but the maintenance is almost nil. The rechargeable battery should last a minimum
of 5 years and the solar cells for many more. The cells recharge the
battery, so once this is installed, you can forget about it. Don't use any
sort of voltage conversion unit or standard house current with a
charger designed for battery operation.

The one type of fence charger I'd stay away from is the so-called
weed burner. Though the initial cost is low, the operating cost is high,

continued

and because they're potentially dangerous, they don't have UL approval. A weed burner gives a 1-second shock which is long enough to burn weeds and gives more warning than any animal needs.

The other materials for an electric fence are posts, insulators and wire (a No. 18 galvanized wire will do the job). Your choice of posts is a matter of personal preference, but whatever type you choose, you won't need many. Since the posts are required to carry only the weight of just a few strands of wire, they can be spaced 20 to 25 feet apart.

The wire runs from your fence charger to the posts in a continuous strand. Don't let it touch anything — other buildings, the posts, other fences, weeds, trees — or it will cause a short circuit, making the fence ineffective. To attach the wire, while keeping it out of contact with posts, you'll need insulators.

You're probably familiar with the glass or ceramic insulators on telephone and power line poles. Insulators for electric fences accomplish the same task, but they're much smaller. Different models can attach the wire to a round, metal rod, a wooden post, or the so-called T posts. They're also made in various sizes for holding the wire relatively close to the posts, or several inches away from it. At these points, the wire is simply slipped securely into one insulator and run on to the next one. The special insulated connectors for gates are also simple to install.

Any electric installation needs a complete circuit, for current must flow in a closed loop. The current starts flowing at the charger and keeps going through a continuous wire in the electric fence. The device that completes the circuit is the earth itself. To feel a shock from an electric fence, an animal must be in contact with the ground, allowing the electric current to travel from the wire to the animal to the ground and back to the fence charger.

The final link in an electric fence, then, is the connection between the charger and the ground. For this, a metal post should be driven a minimum of 6 feet into the ground beneath the charger. Make sure this post is in contact with moist soil, since that's the best conductor of electricity, then run a wire from this ground post to the charger. The wire should be clamped, not simply twisted, to the ground post. Don't use a water pipe or fire hydrant for a ground because water leakage can create a shock hazard.

How high you put the wires depends on what kind of animal you're fencing in or out. The rule of thumb is that wires should be about two-thirds the height of the animal. For rabbits, woodchucks, and similar small animals, you'll need 2 or 3 wires, about 3 inches apart, with the lowest wire about 2 inches above the ground. (When multiple wires are used, they can all be charged by simply connecting short jumper wire between them at one point.) Or if you prefer, construct a conventional wire fence and string just one electric wire along the top. This is useful for discouraging larger and more clever animals such as raccoons.

Try to keep the area around the fence as free of weeds and any other obstructions as possible. When fence charger manufacturers talk about weeds shorting out a fence, they are frequently thinking of the

11

Fence Charger, "PARMAK," MODEL A-SF, PARKER MCCRORY, $37.00–40.00 **(11)**

Green steel, weatherproof case, 8½ × 12 × 5 inches, contains circuitry for converting power from a standard 6-volt battery to that needed for an electric fence; includes wing-nut type connecting points for fence wire and ground, as well as lightning arresters and built-in test unit; front panel switch selects off, on, and test functions; bracket on rear provides for mounting to posts with 2 screws; UL approved.

This unit is designed for battery operation so you don't have to worry about being near house current. Since the box is weatherproof, it won't need to be mounted inside a building. It can handle up to 15 miles of fence putting out a 1/50-second pulse of current about 45 times a minute. You can expect a typical battery to last about 2 or 3 months, so a rechargeable battery might be worth the investment, especially if the fence charger is used all year. If used for just a few months a year, the large throwaway dry cells are probably just as economical. Installation is simply a matter of hanging it on the post, connecting 2 wires to a battery placed inside the case, and connecting the fence and ground wires. This same company also makes a unit with a rechargeable solar-powered battery, as well as units designed to be mounted indoors and run off 110-volt house current.

rancher with miles of fence and many weeds. For a small home garden, this shouldn't be such a problem, but it is still a good idea to be tidy.

How do you know if your electric fence is working? If the unit you purchased doesn't have a built-in tester, you can purchase a simple testing device from the manufacturers mentioned here. Many a farmer or rancher scoffs at this question. When he wants to test his fence, he touches it. The shock is similar to what you would feel if you accidentally touched a spark plug wire in your car.

Fence Post, MODEL 0-48/25, DARE PRODUCTS, $.70–.80 **(12)**

23/64-inch steel rod with 3¼-inch-wide anchor plate crimped in place 10 inches from one end.

This is an easy-to-install post for a small electric fence, such as one might use around a vegetable garden. Model 414-2W is virtually the same post, just slightly larger (⅜-inch diameter) and includes 2 of the RP/25 insulators. The anchor plate holds the post in the ground and prevents it from turning.

13

Insulator, MODEL RP-25, DARE PRODUCTS, $3.00–3.25 (for package of 25) **(13)**

Hard polyethylene, bolt-and-nut-style insulator, 1⅞ inches long and 1¾ inches in diameter, bright yellow color, fits on round metal posts from 5/16 to 9/16 inch in diameter.

This insulator just slips on a metal fence post and can easily slide up and down to adjust the wire to the desired height; wing nuts make it simple to tighten it by hand. The wire fits between the two small clips on the end, one clip facing upward and the other downward. You can even make a height adjustment while the fence is turned on without touching the wire. This is one of several plastic insulators made by Dare for attachment to either wood or metal posts. Many of the others use the same type of clip for holding the wire.

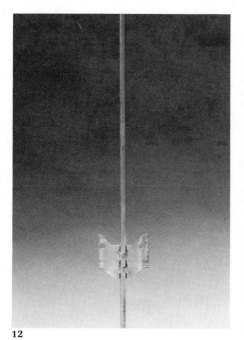

12

Insulated Gate Handle, MODEL 1247, DARE PRODUCTS, $.90–1.00 **(14)**

Double-insulated, black rubber and vinyl gate handle, 6¼ inches long, with ¾-inch piece of metal with hole on one end and 1¼-inch metal hook on the other.

This handle allows for a continuous electric fence with a gate that can be opened without having to turn off the power. The double tubing protects you from the current, and the flanges at either end, plus spiral grip, protect against your hand accidentally slipping and touching wire. For a gate, you'll need one of these for each wire of the fence.

14

POSTHOLE DIGGERS

A posthole digger is the sort of tool you hope someone in the neighborhood has so you can borrow it for that occasional moment when it is really needed.

This is not to say a posthole digger isn't useful. It is. It makes a narrow hole that will do a far better job of holding a pole for a fence post, arbor, birdhouse, clothesline, or whatever, than will a hole made with a shovel. When you dig a hole with a shovel, it is wide and this means a lot of loose dirt around the post.

Even if your use is only occasional, it's good to know what posthole diggers do. The posthole diggers I've seen fall into three basic styles: scissors, the most common; a lever arrangement, which I think offers a real advantage; and an auger type, which looks impressive, but runs into problems when faced with stones the size of the space between the screw blades.

The scissor-type digger still does a good job, but if you read the product descriptions on the units included here, I think you'll see some real advantages to the type that uses a lever part way up a single handle to operate a second blade. However, either style will do an adequate job. Keep the point oiled and, as with any digging tool, keep the blades clean and sharp.

Posthole Digger, "HOMEOWNERS DIG-EZY," MODEL 17-086, AMES, $15.70–17.30 **(15)**

2 9-inch steel blades, 5½ inches wide, bolted to a pair of 44-inch-long handles in a scissor design, pivoting on a bolt through the top of the blades.

This digger was designed specifically for the homeowner so it's lighter in weight and the handles are 4 inches shorter than the traditional model. It will do a fine job of cutting and removing the soil for postholes and there's a convenient 2-foot measuring mark on one handle to check your progress. The ends of the blade remain open somewhat, so it is difficult to remove those last fine soil particles with each scoop, but that is common with this type of digger. In fact, the blades are a little more pointed than usual, which tends to make it somewhat easier to pick up loose soil.

Posthole Digger, MODEL "UNIVERSAL DIGGER," ERIE IRON WORKS, $30.00–32.00 **(16)**

5-foot wood handle holds single, fixed blade about 8 inches wide and 7 inches deep; second blade is movable and controlled by a double lever of black pipe and strap steel attached to the wood handle.

This unusual digger is made in Canada and the design has some real advantages over the traditional scissors-type posthole digger. On this model, you have one blade going straight down while the movable digger blade is operated with a lever well above the soil level. This means you can dig a deep hole without having to make the top wide to accommodate the handle, as with the scissors-type diggers. This arrangement works very well; the movable blade closes tightly against the fixed one and is easy to use in any type of soil. And another plus is that no soil falls out as you haul the blades to the surface.

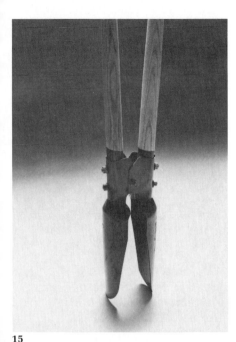
15

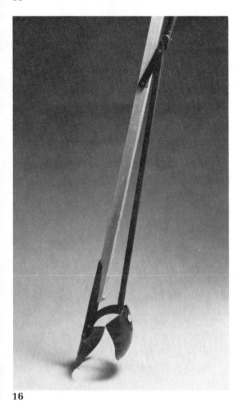
16

PRY BAR

Pry Bar, MODEL W36, TRUE TEMPER, $5.60–6.10 **(17)**

Forged 1-piece carbon steel bar 36 inches long, ¾-inch diameter with one end flattened to a chisel point and the other curved in a hook.

You probably won't buy this tool for use in the garden, as its primary function will be in tearing down old wood construction. However, it has several garden uses, including prying loose stones, making small, deep holes for inserting stakes for plant supports, or light fence and netting poles, or for helping to pull heavy, wire fencing taut against a post prior to attaching. This last is done by wedging the bar in the wire mesh and prying against the fence post.

17

ALTERNATIVES TO CHEMICALS

Rather than automatically reaching for a chemical to get rid of garden pests, consider your alternatives. You may be surprised how much control and protection can be exercised just by using good gardening practices. Here are some time-tested tips:

A brussels sprout plant with a root maggot mat.

A pepper plant with a cutworm collar.

• *Keep your garden clean and weed free. Leaf miners, for example, thrive in weeds, but they're not fussy. They'll gladly step over to your spinach or Swiss chard if it's handy. Burn foliage of plants infested with leaf miners.*

• *Grow melons and cucumbers on a fence. This keeps them out of the reach of slugs and mice.*

• *Try spraying plant foliage with soapy water. This old-time cure often works because the soap film coats the breathing pores of insects, smothering them. In the house, plants do well with a bath in a mild dishwasher detergent every couple of weeks. Rinse them carefully when through. (The rinsing, too, tends to wash insects down the drain.)*

• *Be careful about your watering habits. Give the plants time to dry off before nightfall to avoid fungus diseases.*

• *Pay attention to proper spacing. Plants growing close together means poor air circulation and good breeding grounds for insects.*

• *The cabbage maggot life cycle starts with eggs laid in the soil beneath your plants. Broccoli, cauliflower, and cabbage can be protected from these maggots by using a "maggot mat" of tar paper or carpet, cut in a 12-inch square. Put a hole in the middle for the plant stem. Slit the mat from the hole out to the end and slip around the young plant, then tape the slit with a waterproof tape.*

• *Protect young plants from cutworms with a cardboard collar 2 inches wide and 14 inches long. Form in a loop around the plant and staple, pushing it gently into the soil a bit. On his nocturnal visit, the cutworm will halt at this barrier; even though he could crawl over it, he won't. He'll look for easier pickings elsewhere.*

• *If you forget to put up such a barrier, and you see a young plant that's been lopped off near the base, that's the cutworm's doing. Fortunately, after such a hearty meal, he digs in near the base of the plant for a snooze. Dig in after him and destroy him — messy, but effective.*

• *Oil your ears of corn. After the ears have been formed, put a few drops of mineral oil on the silk near where it enters the ear. The oil smothers ear worm eggs.*

• *If birds and squirrels are enjoying your corn, bag it. Put a paper bag around each ear while it's still on the plant and let it ripen that way. Similar barriers can be used to protect sunflower heads while their seeds ripen.*

• *The weed patch is also a breeding ground for stalkborers, but if they get into your garden, go after them with a knife. Look for a small hole in the stalk of a plant. When you find it, slit upward with a pocket knife. You should come to the borer within a few inches. Pry the stalk apart, dispose of the borer, and chances are the plant will recover.*

• *Consider putting a half grapefruit, cabbage leaf, or sheet of plastic on the ground to deter slugs. They're nighttime prowlers. When dawn comes, they head for cover. If you provide the convenient cover, you'll have them packed into one small area where they're easy to destroy. Or use a slug trap or a can filled with beer.*

• *Where feasible, mix up your plantings. Large insect infestations get started where there's a concentration of the favorite food of a particular insect. Combining several different plant types in a row can confuse the insects.*

• *Use your hose for more than just watering. Aphids and red spider mites, for example, can be knocked from plants with a good stream of water. An aphid knocked from his perch on a zinnia, for example, will find the return trip long and arduous. He may never make it.*

• *A can containing water covered with a thin film of soap or kerosene will drown beetles. Pick them off by hand and drop them in it.*

• *Wrap trunks of young fruit trees loosely in a protective shield of ½-inch-mesh hardware cloth from soil level to the first branches. That way mice and rabbits won't make a winter meal of the tender bark. Keep mulches a few inches away from the base of the trunks, to avoid providing a nesting ground for mice.*

• *There are other ways to control pests which have varying degrees of success. Some gardeners swear by "lady bug" beetles and praying mantis egg cases. Both of these are beneficial insects and I encourage their presence in garden or greenhouse. Putting up homes for tree swallows is also a good idea, as they do a pretty thorough job of keeping the flying pest population, including mosquitoes, to a minimum.*

A mixture of plant varieties helps to avoid insect pests.

SAFETY PRODUCTS

Most of the sprayer safety precautions are just common sense. A few I've mentioned before are worth repeating. Keep everything locked up when not in use; wash thoroughly all equipment used in any phase of a spraying operation; spray or dust in calm weather; don't use sprays in a house or greenhouse where ventilation is poor unless the chemicals are approved for this kind of use; and make sure all people present are upwind from the spraying operation.

There are some other precautions you can take, particularly if you have sensitive skin or allergies. Some people wear old foul-weather gear or an old coat when spraying, just in case a chance puff of wind blows the spray back at them. Rubber gloves, or the disposable ones described here, help keep dusts and chemicals off your hands. They're inexpensive and allow you reasonable dexterity.

Masks and respirators afford additional protection, but be sure you don't overestimate the nature of the protection they offer. A mask isn't going to protect you from a toxic chemical; it will just keep some irritating dusts and fumes to a minimum. A respirator doesn't supply oxygen; it simply puts a filter between you and the chemicals. I can't stress enough that you should know what you're doing when using a mask or respirator. A wrong filter or improperly cared-for respirator can give you a false sense of security ultimately more dangerous than helpful.

Sprays call for intelligent use, respect, and restraint. I think the most common mistake made by the home gardener when using sprays of any sort is to simply assume that more is better. It isn't. There's a right amount to do the job well. When you buy a product, read the directions and follow them precisely.

Dust Mask, MODEL SL-4800, FIBRE-METAL PRODUCTS, $2.25–2.50 (for 5 masks) **(19)**

Green foam plastic, about 12 inches long and about 5 inches wide, can be stretched in both directions to cover the mouth and nose while 2 holes at the ends will fit over the ears for comfortable wearing.

This safety device for the gardener and home worker is an excellent filter for nontoxic dust, sawdust, pollen, and other irritants present when working with the soil or around the home. These masks may be washed or sterilized. The mask is lint-free, non-allergenic, nontoxic, and does not interfere with normal speech.

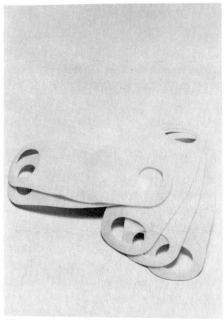

19

Disposable Garden Gloves, MODEL 5010, MELNOR, $1.15–1.30 (for 6 pairs) **(18)**

Green gloves of 1¼ mil. plastic with snug constricted wrists; one size fits all.

For temporary protection for sensitive or allergy-prone skin from gardening materials, disposable gloves come in handy, especially when using pesticides.

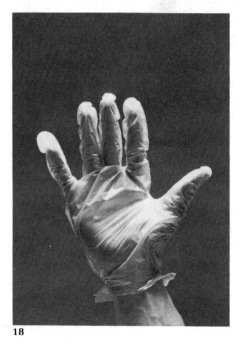

18

Respirator, MODEL 460968 WITH CARTRIDGE 464025, MINE SAFETY APPLIANCES, $10.50–12.50 **(20)**

Soft rubber face piece with adjustable straps fits snugly over mouth and nose; 4-point, floating yoke of formable aluminum; twin filter cartridges on either side take several different screw-in, chemical aerosol filters for protection against various vapors.

Respirators are not necessarily needed when applying pesticides outdoors, but using the proper filter can add an extra element of safety to any spraying operation. Although persons with heavy beards or long sideburns may find it difficult getting a tight seal, most people should find this unit gives good protection. The directions in the unit's manual are very clear and should be thoroughly studied before use. This respirator does not furnish oxygen and must not be used in atmospheres where the oxygen level is less than 19.5 percent. The filter included here protects against most nonorganic-based pesticides; but you should consult the pesticide manufacturer for advice on proper filter for protection against specific chemicals.

DUSTERS

Many pesticides can be applied as dust through applicators that project a short distance. These are appealing to gardeners for several reasons: they're inexpensive and simple to use, there's no mixing of liquids, and any excess can be stored until the next application.

The major disadvantage of dusters is that powder only travels a short distance, so they're useful only in small areas. Dust is easily blown off course, so accuracy is difficult. Dusters also tend to use more toxic chemicals than liquid sprays do to get the same amount of protection. Used with care in calm weather, dusters can help eradicate an infestation on a selected crop or a few plants, but in many cases, sprayers will do a more thorough job.

Duster, MODEL 6766, H. D. HUDSON, $12.65–13.85 **(21)**

Tin-plated tube painted yellow and green with red pump handle at rear and nozzle at front; 21-inch extension tube holds a swivel, fan-shaped nozzle.

Dust is forced out the tube with each stroke of this tool in a fine, uniform cloud. The extension tube keeps the dust away from the operator and on the plants, and the swivel nozzle allows you to dust at different angles, including the underside of leaves where many insects lurk.

Duster, "WHIRLY DUSTER," MODEL 913, ORTHO, $10.00–11.00 **(22)**

Dust tank and impeller housing of yellow plastic are about 4 inches across and 6 inches high; pistol-grip handle, with crank on right side; 14-inch extension tube and deflector.

This holds about ¼ pound of the dusts commonly used on vegetables, fruits, and ornamental plants. The dust can be applied at varying speeds, depending on how fast you turn the crank. This simple-to-use tool will give good coverage of most plants within about 2 feet of the operator.

20

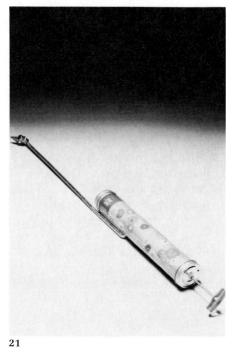

21

22

MANUAL SPRAYERS

All common sprayers are "manual" in the sense that they need an operator to start and aim them, but the ones in this section require continuous pumping in order to spray.

They don't all work exactly the same, however. There are small, one-hand types that you operate simply by squeezing the grip, two-hand "slide" or "trombone" sprayers, and some backpack types that require an up-and-down pumping motion with one arm. You don't need one of each type, but it's good to know about each one's special advantages and disadvantages.

The small hand sprayers make fine substitutes for the aerosol spray cans, many of which are now considered environmentally unsound. The hand sprayers usually hold about a quart of diluted spray and are used for routine and spot spraying jobs in gardens, or for selective weed killing. They're not the sort of sprayers you'd use for an apple tree. Get one with an adjustable nozzle and, as with any sprayer, clean it out after each use. These same sprayers are frequently used indoors as misters, but since they are so inexpensive, I'd advise getting two: one for indoor use as a mister and one to use outdoors with various chemicals. Mark each one clearly and keep them separate so that no chemical residues from outside get onto your houseplants.

Slide sprayers use a tubular-type pump that works by sliding one tube into another, like a trombone. This is a two-hand operation and some people find it a little difficult to control the direction of the spray accurately while pumping, since the spray nozzle and pump are all mounted on the same tube. As with any manual sprayer, this type tends to put out a pulsating stream, especially when the nozzle is set on coarse. This too can make for uneven coverage. Finally, there is no spray tank. Instead, a rubber hose is attached to the pump mechanism and dropped in a pail, which is an open invitation for insects and debris eventually to jam the filters and sprayer. So why have one? Well, the same pail that makes it easy for the solution to get dirty is also simple to clean. You don't have to fiddle with an awkward tank. It could be argued that a hose-end sprayer is as easy to clean as the slide sprayer but it is limited by the length of hose. The pail and slide sprayer goes anywhere. Finally, a slide sprayer is generally less expensive than tank sprayers of similar quality.

You have more control with backpack-type tank sprayers than with slide sprayers because one arm pumps while the other controls the spray wand. However, you still have the pulsating stream.

None of these backpack sprayers is for the infirm or out-of-condition gardener. When loaded with spray, they weigh as much as the pack carried by a veteran overnight hiker. Of course, you don't have to carry this weight around all day, and if you're working on a row of berry bushes or roses, it's more convenient than a slide sprayer unit that's set on the ground for one spraying operation, then picked up and moved to another location 15 seconds later.

23

Manual Sprayer, MODEL F-79, ILLINOIS B. & G., $1.49–1.65 **(23)**

Plastic bottle holds 8 ounces; squeeze-type pump with adjustable nozzle; bottle is 5 inches long, 1¼ inches thick.

This type of sprayer is frequently used as a mister for indoor plants, but it can also be used for applying pesticides outdoors. The same company has several larger models, but this one fits in your pocket and can handle those small, occasional spraying jobs where you might otherwise use an aerosol insecticide.

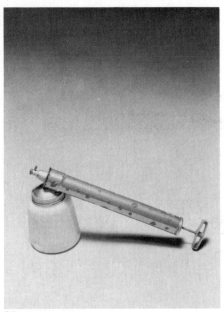

24

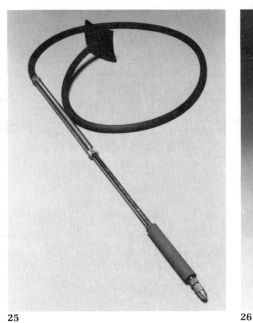

25

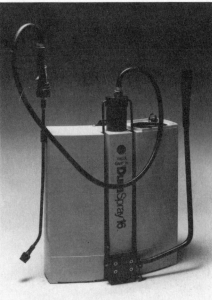

26

Manual Sprayer, MODEL 6428,
H. D. HUDSON, $9.50–10.50 **(24)**

Hand pump with chemicals in 24-ounce plastic jar; brass used in all areas where chemicals contact metal; nozzle has 2 positions for either a fine mist or a coarse spray; jar opening is 2½ inches in diameter; jar marked in 4-ounce gradations.

Although this isn't really a pressure sprayer, you will get a few seconds of fine spray after several strokes of the pump. The stream is less continuous when the nozzle is on a coarse setting. The wide-mouthed plastic jar is easy to fill and clean, and resists breakage and corrosion. The spray tube can be cleaned with a fine wire from the jar end.

Manual Sprayer, MODEL 216,
BURGESS VIBROCRAFTERS,
$17.00–19.00 **(25)**

Heavy brass sliding pump; 4½-foot green rubber hose with 3½-inch-square metal weight and screen at one end; adjustable nozzle.

I find the foot weight on this model more convenient than the more common clip arrangement for keeping the hose in the pail. The pumping action is slow and firm, delivering sprays from 2 to 20 feet, or a stream up to 30 feet long. The Model 202 is similar, but with a swivel nozzle on a 12-inch extension.

Manual Sprayer, MODEL "REDIMIX
16," BURGESS VIBROCRAFTERS,
$90.00–99.00 **(26)**

Plastic spray container, 22½ × 16½ × 9 inches, is concave to fit comfortably against back and holds 4⅓ gallons of spray; reversible pump handle for right- or left-hand operation; nylon reinforced hose with adjustable nozzle for mist, spray or stream; filter screen at fill opening. Weighs 8 pounds, 8 ounces empty, about 40 pounds full; adjustable padded shoulder straps.

You use the large muscles in your arm to pump this sprayer continuously in an up-and-down motion while aiming the spray with the other hand. No pressure builds inside the tank. Try to maintain slow, even strokes to discharge the liquid with a pulsating rhythm. I find this requires care when using the coarse stream, but when using the fine spray and mist, the pulsations are hardly noticeable. Since each stroke lowers and raises an agitator, this sprayer does a fair job of keeping wettable powders in suspension, although you should stir such a mixture thoroughly if you leave the sprayer idle for any length of time. The interior plastic surfaces are smooth and repel liquids, making cleaning easy.

Roller Applicator, "DRIFTMASTER,"
MODEL BP 27,
IMPORTED BY VANDERMOLEN,
$135.00–150.00 **(27)**

Metal framework holds 5½-gallon, black plastic tank, small diameter plastic tube with 14 tiny drip holes in it and 2 4-inch-diameter aluminum rollers with many small, sharp longitudinal ridges; other sizes available from importer.

This tool applies a liquid fertilizer or pesticide to a lawn or other relatively level surface without the wind's spreading it to adjoining areas. To use, fill the tank with the liquid and roll the unit over the area. A lever on the handle controls the liquid application — when it's squeezed, the solution travels from the tank to the drip tube and onto the rollers, where it spreads out uniformly over the area covered. A small wire on one end of the rollers scratches a soil guideline. How much this unit delivers depends upon the walking speed of the person doing the applying. It will vary from about 2,350 square feet to 3,420 square feet per 5½ gallons. The tank does not drain completely, and when cleaning, you must pour several ounces of the chemical solution out the fill opening.

When using the unit on a slope, be sure to walk up and down rather than across to get uniform application. The manufacturer's directions must be followed closely, for even small amounts of some chemicals applied to target plants can vaporize in very hot weather and damage nearby vegetation.

This unit does its job well and keeps the chemicals where they are supposed to be. However, it's the sort of item that calls for a large area with relatively frequent use to justify its cost.

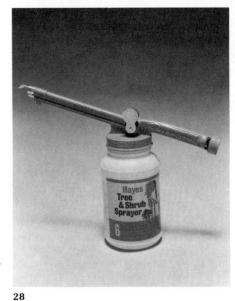

28

Hose-End Sprayer, MODEL H-6, HAYES PRODUCTS, $13.00–14.30 **(28)**

Plastic jar holds enough solution for 6 gallons of spray at a 24:1 dilution ratio; sprayer head is metal with deflector over nozzle serving to break up stream into a 3- to 4-foot fan; can be adjusted to deflect spray up, down, or to either side; thumb control on top turns sprayer on and off; with deflector removed, a coarse stream is delivered.

This is a fixed-ratio sprayer. To use, attach the spray head to hose, then fill the jar to the appropriate level according to the product used. If, for example, the product calls for one tablespoon of spray per gallon, put in six tablespoons of solution, or 3 ounces, then use the stream of water from the sprayer head to mix the solution, bringing the contents of the jar to the full point, a raised line near the top. Then screw the jar onto the spray head and you're set to spray. As with all such units, wash it thoroughly after each use. Although you'll get a coarse spray or a relatively fine fan spray from this nozzle and the fan spray can be directed to the underside of leaves, it isn't as versatile as the models with continuously adjustable nozzles.

27

HOSE-END SPRAYERS

When you're looking for a sprayer that's easy to use, inexpensive, and effective, try one of the hose-end units.

A hose-end sprayer is simply a spray head with a jar suspended from it which screws on a standard hose coupling like a regular hose nozzle. The chemical concentrate in the jar is drawn into the water stream and shot out the nozzle. The chemical/water ratio is usually determined by the manufacturer. (On some models, the ratio of water to concentrated chemicals is adjustable.) The main drawback of these is that they reach only as far as the hose does and their spraying power is determined by your home water pressure.

If neither of these limitations hampers your use, the hose-end sprayer is a good bet. I like the ones that provide different spray ratios, adjustable nozzles, and antisiphon devices. This last is a safety precaution. Suppose as you were spraying, a water main down the street broke, causing a sudden loss of pressure. Chemicals from the jar could then be sucked back into the hose and possibly the home water system. It's fairly easy to avoid this, either with special valves or other devices to break the reverse flow. At least two states already require antisiphon devices on all hose-end sprayers. Whether required by law or not, they're a good idea.

Other features I look for are a rotating hose coupling, making it easy to attach the sprayer without having to twist the entire unit, and a "fill" setting on the spray control mechanism that allows you to add water to the chemical concentrate while the unit is attached to the hose.

deflector for the direction you desire the spray to go in, and squeeze the handle. Removing the deflector gives a coarse stream of water that can reach up to 30 feet. When through, any unused concentrate can be returned to the original container.

This is a good unit for spraying with liquid concentrates. The tiny screen in the foot of the suction tube will keep the mixing head clean, but it will also prevent the efficient use of wettable powders that don't dissolve into solutions. The top of the suction tube slides into a short holding sleeve, unlike many similar tools where the tube simply slips over a short nipple and may stretch during long periods of use. The base of the handle has been drilled to provide an antisiphon device. Each time the faucet is turned off, a little water will squirt out these holes. This may get your hands wet, but it won't do any harm.

You'll find this precision tool too unwieldy to stand on its own, so after it has been cleaned and dried, store it lying down, or hang it up. Keeping it in a closed bag or box will prevent the mixing head's tiny air holes from plugging with dirt.

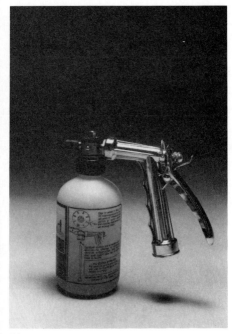

Hose-End Sprayer, MODEL 362-D, GILMOUR, $10.75–11.75 **(29)**

Chrome-plated zinc, pistol-grip handle, brass mixing head; adjusts for 16 different dilutions from 1 teaspoon of chemical concentrate per gallon (1:768 ratio) to 10 tablespoons per gallon (1:26 ratio); deflector in front of spray head provides fan pattern that can be aimed to spray down, up, or to either side; plastic jar holds 1 pint.

You can spray up to 96 gallons of diluted solution with this device. Just put a chemical concentrate in the plastic jar, adjust the black plastic dial to the desired dilution ratio, set the

29

COMPRESSED-AIR SPRAYERS

For generations compressed-air sprayers have remained the most popular tool for plant protection. When using a compressed-air sprayer, first you work, then the sprayer works. Your part of the bargain is to work the pump mechanism (usually a lever) a few dozen times until you have forced enough air in on top of the liquid to build up sufficient pressure to operate the sprayer. Then you aim the spraying wand and open a valve. For the next minute or two, the compressed air forces the liquid out in either a coarse or fine spray pattern, depending upon the nozzle.

Compressed-air sprayers come in two basic varieties, tank or backpack, and in two basic materials, metal or plastic. Tank sprayers are usually cylindrical and sit on the ground, although some also can be carried by a single strap thrown over the shoulder. Some are made of galvanized metal — stainless steel or brass — for corrosion resistance, an important consideration since they are subject not only to wear from moisture, but a variety of chemicals. Many newer ones are made of plastic, which is also corrosion resistant, strong, and easy to clean. The sprayers generally hold anywhere from 1 to 5 gallons of diluted chemicals. As water weighs about 8 pounds a gallon, these aren't exactly light, but you can carry them around to wherever the problem is and they don't always have to be filled to the top. In fact, you'll find many manufacturers give two figures when talking about the capacity of their sprayers, the larger being the actual size of the container. But since you usually have to leave space for air to build up, these containers aren't filled to the top, so the working capacity will be a bit less than the actual container size. I'm as interested in how efficiently a sprayer empties as I am in how much it holds. A poorly designed unit leaves several ounces at the bottom and if liquids can't be poured out through the top opening, you'll have to reach in and sponge them out — a messy but necessary procedure.

With the typical compressed-air unit, you'll have to build up air pressure at least twice before it is empty, and since there is more space to fill after some of the fluid has been used, it will take more pumping the second time to get up to spraying pressure. However, on the sprayers with an air-pressure chamber separate from the fluid tank, it always takes the same number of strokes to build to maximum pressure.

Be careful to release all pressure before opening the sprayer for filling or cleaning. You don't want a sudden stream of air squirting up some leftover solution in your face. It's a good idea always to keep your face and body away from caps and safety valves when building up pressure. And remember, never leave a compressed-air sprayer standing out in the sunlight; the extra heat can build up pressures to dangerous levels.

Compressed-Air Sprayer, MODEL 90, MELNOR, $30.00–33.00 **(30)**

1½-gallon operating capacity in translucent green plastic tank measuring 7¾ inches in diameter and 21 inches high; separate pump and carrying handles; 2 nozzles with one giving a finer mist and stream than the other; removable filter cartridge in handle; handle can be locked to prevent accidental spraying and will shut off automatically if dropped while spraying; built-in measuring spoon at end of pump; safety valve automatically vents excess air downward; spraying wand stores on or across handle.

There are several nice safety and convenience features in this compressed-air sprayer, some of which are obvious from the description. The carrying handles have three positions: straight up for carrying, tilted to one side for building pressure with the pump, and horizontal for filling. The pump handle can be pushed down into notches in the cap to make it easier to unscrew the cap. The spray adjustments for direction and fineness are away from the nozzle so you don't have to get chemicals on your hands while making a change. The built-in measuring spoon is washed with the sprayer, rather than left lying around with concentrated residue on it, as can happen with a separate measurer. There's a threaded home on the tank which keeps the nozzle that isn't being used out of the way. The funnel top means easy filling and the smooth, plastic sides make for easy cleaning. *One caution:* The hose is very close to the carrying handle, so be careful not to crimp or kink it with the handle.

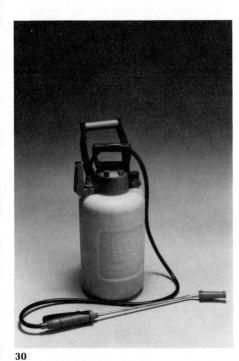

30

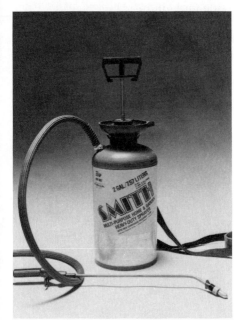

31

Compressed-Air Sprayer,

MODEL 23GP,

D. B. SMITH, $30.60–33.60   **(31)**

Galvanized tank with red trim has 1½-gallon operating capacity; black pump of nylon, polyethylene and polypropylene; 16-inch curved brass

extension with adjustable nozzle; padded carrying strap.

A comfortable carrying strap allows you to sling this unit over one shoulder. The stream reaches about 25 feet and will empty the tank in about 4 minutes of spraying with two sets of 40 pump strokes each to pressurize. It will take longer to use up the solution when the nozzle is set on the fine, 3-foot spray. The pump assembly screws into the tank thread with one complete turn.

Compressed-Air Sprayer,

MODEL 6335,

H. D. HUDSON, $55.00–60.50   **(32)**

Gold-colored epoxy finish on galvanized steel tank with working capacity of 2¼ gallons; 3 feet of black plastic hose; nozzle swivels in all directions and adjusts from fine to coarse spray; fill opening is oval shaped, roughly 4 × 5 inches; pump is separate from cover and set to one side; carrying strap of polyethylene is 1 inch wide.

You'll find the wide, oval mouth on this tank makes it easy to fill, easy to empty any excess, and easy to clean — all important features on a sprayer. The cover has a large gasket and when inserted in the tank is forced up against the top by the air pressure, forming a tight seal. Since the pump assembly is separate from the cover, it's not normally removed when filling, but you can remove it for repair or adjustment. The cover has a valve for releasing air pressure before removing it. This sprayer puts out a 15-foot stream or a fine spray, and you can empty the tank in about 4 minutes having pumped it twice using about 35 12-inch strokes each time. There's no lock on the spray lever, so you must hold it down throughout the spraying.

Compressed-Air Sprayer, MODEL

JETPAK-425,

IMPORTED FROM WEST GERMANY BY SOLO, $89.00–98.00   **(33)**

Backpack-style sprayer with a compressed-air chamber separate from the

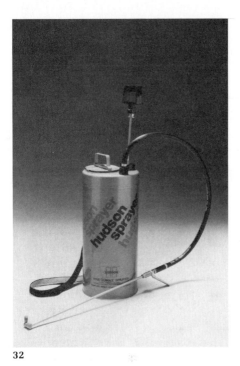

32

4-gallon tank; no metal or rubber parts come in contact with chemical formula; plastic is used throughout the sprayer (except for the aluminum frame and pump handle); padded leather shoulder straps; weight when empty is 9½ pounds, weight when full is about 43 pounds.

33

The separate air-compression chamber makes operation of this unit easier than other compressed-air sprayers. It only takes about 10 strokes to build up sufficient pressure in this chamber. However, while the pressure is high (about 85 pounds per square inch) and gives a fine spray, it won't last for more than about 1 quart of solution. (With other compressed-air sprayers, you typically use many more strokes to build up the pressure, but it lasts longer, emptying perhaps half the tank; to empty the second half, you may have to pump as many as 90 or 100 strokes.) With the Solo, whether there are 4 gallons or 1 quart of liquid left, the same 10 strokes will bring it up to pressure. What this means in practice is more or less continuous, slow pumping, as with a manual sprayer, never letting the pressure drop too much. But this pressure chamber will deliver a steady, even stream — an improvement over the pulsating stream of a manually operated pump. There are interchangeable nozzle inserts for fan sprays or a coarse stream that reaches about 25 feet. The pump empties all but the last few ounces of fluid, and these can be poured out.

POWER SPRAYERS

There's no doubt that using a power sprayer can be the easiest and best way to get the job done. The only question is whether or not it's worth the cost. Your decision will depend on the size of the spraying job you have to do and your pocketbook size. For the person with the small home orchard, it may well be worthwhile.

Power sprayers fall into two categories: "mistblowers" and those using hydraulic methods simply substituting machinery for muscle. The mistblower is distinctive because it generates a powerful airstream. Fluid is injected into this near the nozzle and broken into very fine particles, a foglike mist that penetrates even through dense foliage and will reach 20 to 30 feet (depending on the unit). It does an excellent job of covering the target with a very fine film of chemicals — using the least chemicals for the most protection. The primary disadvantage to a mistblower is that it must be used when the wind is less than 5 miles per hour. Although any spraying should be done in as calm weather as possible, this extreme calm isn't as necessary with a hydraulic sprayer.

Mistblowers use quite a lot of power to get air pressure up high enough to be effective. The electric model included here runs off standard 110 volt current and uses 625 watts, so you're limited by the length of the cord and the closeness of an electrical outlet. (The hydraulic sprayer uses a small gasoline engine, so it can go just about anywhere.) The mist from one of these blowers tends to be so fine that you may not see it reaching very far. Instead of looking for it, look for its effects — the movement of distant foliage as the airstream strikes.

Power Sprayer, MODEL 1026, ROOT-LOWELL, $150.00–165.00 **(34)**

White polyethylene tank with embossed filler markings topped by an electric motor that uses 625 watts to deliver 20,000 revolutions per minute; 10-inch, 3-prong, 110-volt cord; spray selector valve just above filler cap gives fine or heavy discharges; gray, flexible hose 2½ inches in diameter; discharge control adjusts for 1.5- to 5.3-gallons-per-hour rate for the fine sprays and 6 to 14 gallons per hour for the heavier discharge; metal carrying handle, black vinyl shoulder strap; weight when filled, about 20 pounds.

The efficiency of this sprayer will justify its cost and weight when there are large areas to cover. Using the shoulder strap leaves the hands free to operate the electrical switch and air pressure and discharge controls. The heavy spray will wet surfaces up to 5 feet away, while the fine fogging mist reaches up to 20 feet away, even through foliage. The air blast is so efficient in breaking up the solution into fine mist that it operates well with only a quarter of the amount of water needed for the more conventional hydraulic spraying. The sprayer uses nearly all the solution in the tank and the 3-inch opening makes cleaning and filling easy. I like this sprayer, because it uses fewer chemicals and conserves water and time. As a bonus, the airstream will do a fair job at such tasks as dislodging fallen leaves from among ground covers and shrub branches.

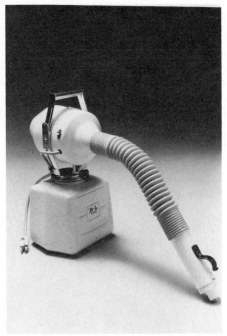

34

35

36

Power Sprayer, MODEL SG 17,
STIHL, $290.00–320.00 **(35)**

*Backpack unit with 2-cycle gasoline
engine of 3.42-cubic-inch displace-
ment, measures roughly 20 × 15 × 12
inches and weighs about 43 pounds
when full; fuel capacity is 3.18 pints
of 1:25 mixture of oil to gasoline;
spray tank holds 3 gallons of solution
that can be discharged in a mist at a
rate of 330 feet per second; discharge
from tank is through flexible, black
plastic hose, 3 inches in diameter; 3
interchangeable deflectors on nozzle
provide different air patterns.*

This will blow a fine mist about 30
feet either horizontally or vertically at
a variable rate of up to 1 gallon per
minute, permitting the operator to
reach practically any area except for
very tall trees (which should be handled by professionals with more powerful equipment). The 4-inch-diameter
fill cap with protective brass screen
permits easy filling and cleaning.
There are several other uses for a
mister such as this, some of them requiring special accessories. These
uses include dusting, spreading grass
seed, applying whitewash or oil for
treating concrete forms, sweeping

leaves and trash from an area (by just
using the airstream) or even melting
ice with a "flame thrower" attachment. In fact, it's reported that the air
blast from this mister has done a good
job of pollinating tomato plants grown
in a greenhouse.

Power Sprayer, MODEL 42025,
H. D. HUDSON, $427.00–470.00 **(36)**

*Galvanized steel tank holds 12½ gal-
lons and is mounted with 4-cycle,
2 hp Briggs and Stratton motor and
pump on 2-wheeled pushcart; tires
are 12 × 3–inch semipneumatic; 20
feet of ⅜-inch-inner-diameter spray
hose terminates with 13½-inch brass
tube and nozzle that is adjustable for
coarse to fine conical sprays of up to
35 feet; piston pump produces 20 to
150 pounds pressure for up to 2½-gal-
lon-per-minute output; weighs 97
pounds.*

If you have a large orchard or major
spraying to do, you'll find this sprayer
does a good job and is convenient and
easy to use. It's expensive, however,
so make sure your needs justify the
price.

Simply fill the large tank with
either a wettable powder (there's a
built-in agitator) or solution, wheel it
out to the trees to be sprayed, start the
motor, and go to work. You can adjust
the nozzle without getting your fingers wet with the spray.

Accessories include a "flower gun"
nozzle with 24-inch brass extension
and swivel nozzle; a root feeder for
feeding or watering trees directly in
their root zones; a 3-nozzle gun that
produces a 2-foot-wide swath of
spray; and a 4-nozzle boom primarily
for lawn work. Other models have
electric engines and trailer hitches for
use behind a large ride-on mower or
small tractor. The sprayer can also be
used for power cleaning, disinfecting,
or applying whitewash or stains.

GUIDING PLANTS AND
GARDENING IN SMALL SPACES

We Americans tend to be informal in our approach to gardening and landscaping and don't often aspire to the kind of strict control of plant life seen in such arts as topiary, espaliering, and bonsai. But this doesn't mean we shouldn't properly train our plants' growth. On the contrary, even if we prune and train them with an eye toward informality, the end result can be more and healthier growth, a better harvest, and more attractive plants that grow where we want them. Much work with pruning shears and plant ties is really just routine care. Dead branches should always be removed and if a scar 1 inch or larger is left, it should be protected with tree paint. When we see a young tree starting to grow with two leaders, the stronger should be selected and the other trimmed off. The candles of evergreens can be lopped off to produce bushier specimens. Many young trees should be staked with sturdy rope (old hose can be cut in short lengths and slid over such ropes where they touch the tree) for the first few seasons until they have developed strong enough roots to anchor themselves.

These are the types of chores we all should do. But our work with pruners and ties doesn't have to end there. We can change the growth pattern of our plants and trees by putting stress on certain branches at the right time. We can also shape fruit trees, not to fruit more, but to take up less space. Dwarf fruit trees, for example, can be trained to grow along the rails of a fence.

Training keeps the plants where we want them so they not only grow more attractively, but also make the most use out of limited garden space. Proper pruning and tying allows you to grow fruit trees much closer together than was once believed possible. In France, for example, they grow close rows of fruit trees espaliered and cordoned together as a commercial crop.

Certain ornamental plants need the most careful attention when you're staking. Many tall flowers, such as peonies or dahlias, will benefit from being tied to stakes or contained by supports so they don't droop. Several vegetables, too, such as tomatoes, beans, peas, and cucumbers, grow better when allowed to climb rather than sprawl.

The tools for these tasks are listed in this chapter. They are simple tools that only require keeping edges sharp and metal parts dry and oiled. Ties and plant supports should be cleaned at the end of each gardening season and stored where they can be easily found for the next gardening year. If you use small ties, especially ones that aren't made of biodegradable material, collect them from annuals and perennials and throw them out if they are too weather worn to last another season. Clean your containers at summer's end, also.

Finally, even if you have a very small gardening space, use it creatively. Train your plants up a wall, grow them in large pots, put them in hanging baskets or in containers on your rooftop. You don't need acres of land to enjoy gardening.

PRUNING SHEARS

Good pruning is as much an art as anything in gardening, but one thing's sure — you'll never do a good job unless you start with a good tool.

Now, while it's wise to get into the habit of always making a nice, clean cut right next to the trunk or large limb when you remove a branch, this won't be absolutely necessary except when pruning fruit trees and doing other fine work. Many times, we use pruners simply to snip off dead flowers, cut live ones for indoor bloom, or trim out dead wood.

Keep in mind these 2 broad categories of use — fine pruning and casual work — as you consider the 2 basic types of pruners, bypass and anvil. Bypass pruners work like scissors, usually with one fixed blade and a cutting blade. The fine, thin cutting edge gets in close so that a small branch can be snipped off right next to the larger branch.

With the anvil type, a cutting blade works against a flat anvil. This gives a little extra leverage and makes the work go a bit faster. It's also a more rugged design that isn't as likely to get seriously out of line, even when abused, as inexpensive bypass shears might. The drawback of this design is that the anvil won't let you get in tight to the branch, so the pruner always leaves a short stub. This means that the cut won't heal as smoothly, for the stub will always be present and disease is more likely. If you happen to trim water sprouts from fruit trees with an anvil pruner, the result is even more disheartening; the stub that's left simply sprouts several new branches. A bypass pruner cuts flush with the trunk, eliminating this problem.

A good compromise is to buy 2 pairs of shears: an inexpensive anvil type for casual everyday use, and a fine quality bypass type for the more critical jobs, such as pruning fruit trees, bonsai, and shrubs.

Whatever type of shears you have, don't abuse them. The most common mistake is to overload the shears with a size branch they simply weren't designed to cut. This can result in sprung shears and a torn and bruised branch, rather than a cleanly sliced one. Although many of the small hand shears can handle larger branches, I leave anything over ½ inch thick to loppers or a pruning saw.

And pay attention to the condition of the blades. The most common problem is sap buildup. Teflon-coated blades reduce this problem, but they don't eliminate it entirely. With any type of blade, clean it frequently and when you're through pruning, wipe your shears with an oily rag.

Sharpen the blade with a few swipes from a whetstone, trying to follow the original edge angle set by the manufacturer. I like pruners that can be taken apart for sharpening, as many times these small blades are hard to reach. Many of the better pruners have replaceable blades.

When purchasing pruners, pick them up and feel them. You're likely to use them for long stretches of time, and you want them to work comfortably in your hand. Special features such as shock absorbers and grooved blades designed to lessen sap buildup are useful, but not essential.

1

Pruning Shears, MODEL 119T, SEYMOUR SMITH & SON, $6.75–7.75 (1)

Anvil-type shears with Teflon-coated blades and aluminum handles; overall length 8 inches; cutting capacity about ¾ inch; red locking tab near pivot.

All parts are replaceable on these strong shears designed for gardeners with medium to large hands. Their rounded points make them convenient for carrying in a pocket without worrying about poking holes in your clothes.

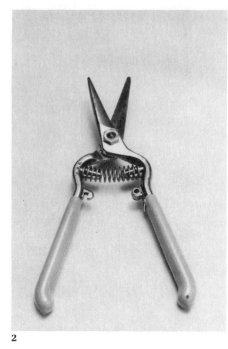

2

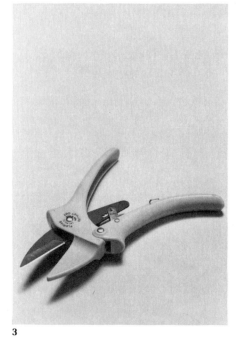

3

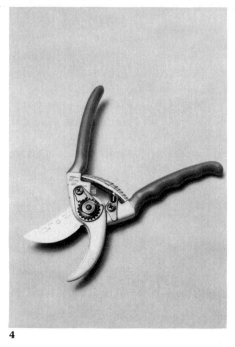

4

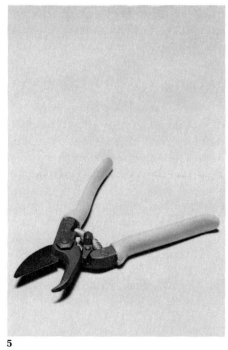

5

Pruning Shears, MODEL 21S,
CORONA, $9.00–10.00 **(2)**

*Bypass-type shears, 7½ inches over-
all, with 2 2½-inch-long straight cutting blades, coil spring, and plastic
handgrips.*

These are fine shears for doing delicate work on bonsai, thinning congested branches, and general light to
medium cutting work. The spring expands less than 2 inches, preventing
the shears from opening to their full
potential cutting angle. Blades and
handle are 1 piece, but the pivot bolt
removes easily so the blades can be
sharpened when necessary.

Pruning Shears, "SHORT CUT,"
MODEL RP701,
AMERICAN STANDARD, $13.00–15.00
(3)

*Ratchet action, anvil-type shears; ny-
lon fiberglass handles, Teflon-coated
steel blades; 7¼ inches long; weight, 4
ounces.*

You can use these lightweight shears
as you would any others, cutting
straight through with a single
squeeze, but the real advantage comes
in the ratchet action. When you give
several short squeezes, the ratchet toggle adjusts automatically along its 3
notches. As a result, it takes longer
but uses less strength to cut through a
piece of wood up to ¾ inch thick. The
manufacturer says the ratchet gives
this tool 5 times more power than
conventional shears of comparable
size. These shears are a special boon
to disabled gardeners who find pruning difficult.

Pruning Shears, "SHEAR MAGIC,"
MODEL 562-0,
HARDWARE & INDUSTRIAL TOOL,
$18.50–21.00 **(4)**

*Bypass-type shears; aluminum alloy
body and stainless steel blades; plas-
tic-coated handles; nylon shock absorber; overall length 8½ inches;
weight is 7 ounces.*

The handgrip is comfortable on these
strong, durable shears, which will
handle any pruning job intended for
hand shears. The blades are replaceable.

Pruning Shears, "PICA," MODEL N,
IMPORTED FROM SWITZERLAND BY
WAFLER FARMS, $20.00–22.00 **(5)**

*Forged steel, bypass-type shears; 7
inches overall, bright orange plastic-
sleeved handles, Teflon-coated blades,*

nylon shock absorber, and thumb latch that slides over the spring into a groove in lower blade.

The novel crooked tip on the lower blade, like a hawk's beak, is the secret weapon of this well-balanced, finely crafted tool. When you have to reach into a shrub to cut off thorny branches and twigs, this hook grabs the wood securely, allowing you to drag it free after cutting with a minimum of wasted motions and scratches. Comfortable and easy to use, these shears will make quick work of all pruning tasks.

Pruning Shears, "SCIMITAR"
MODEL W.58,
WILKINSON SWORD, $19.00–21.00 **(6)**

Chromed steel bypass shears; 1½-inch cutting blades; overall length of 6½ inches; nylon coated handles; weight, 5½ ounces.

These are lightweight shears that fit comfortably in any size hand to do light pruning tasks. They have a "flick"-type thumb catch for locking.

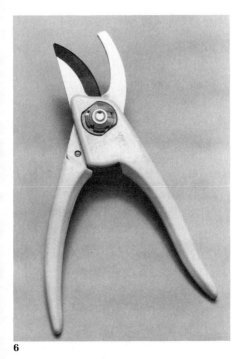

6

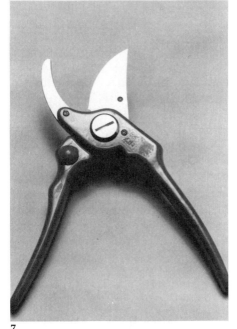

7

Pruning Shears, MODEL 75,
TRUE FRIENDS, $22.50–25.00 **(7)**

Forged aluminum handles on heavy-duty, bypass-type pruner, 8½ inches overall; beveled cutting blade of chrome-vanadium steel; green plastic-covered handles; coil spring entirely enclosed; wire cutter and sap groove.

These blades hold their edges well, but if you need to sharpen or replace them, they can be removed from the shears by turning a coin in the pivot bolt slot. A small rubber bumper absorbs the shock of repeated use and the sap groove is a nice feature that helps keep them operating smoothly when there's a lot of pruning to do at once.

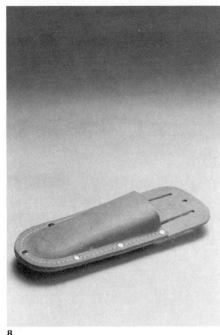

8

Scabbard, MODEL 81,
CORONA, $5.00–5.50 **(8)**

Heavy cowhide leather, 9¼ inches long, 3½ inches wide, with 2 slits for belt; made of 2 pieces stitched together with waxed thread and riveted.

When I go out in the yard or garden, I like to have my hand shears with me. Even if I don't have any pruning planned, I frequently spot something that needs to be done — a rose that should be pruned back if I'm to get maximum bloom, or perhaps some dead flowers to be trimmed so they don't go to seed, weakening the plant. Of course, you can carry shears in your pocket. In fact, some gardeners stitch up their rear pockets to make this a little easier. However, sharp, pointed shears can work their way through cloth. They won't work their way through the tough leather of this scabbard, though, which will hold most sizes of hand shears.

LOPPING SHEARS

Lopping shears are the big cousin to pruning shears. Where pruning shears take a one-handed squeeze action, these use a two-armed scissors action. Lopping shears take up where pruning shears leave off, cutting branches from ½ inch up to 2 inches thick.

The same general rules for anvil and bypass pruners also apply to loppers. If you want to do fine pruning of fruit trees or other plants, use the bypass type of lopper. The more rugged anvil types will do a credible job at pruning tasks which don't demand such precision.

As with the smaller pruners, lopping shears are easily abused by using them for cutting chores better handled by another tool, such as a pruning saw. Lopping shears, like all cutting tools, benefit from regular attention to the blades. Keep them clean and sharp and wipe down all metal parts with an oily rag after use.

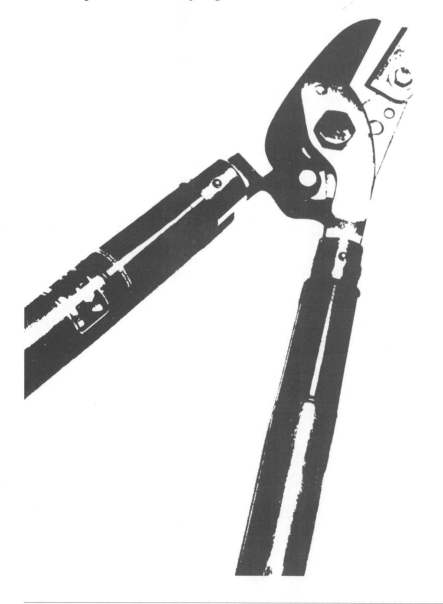

Lopping Shears, MODEL 23-020, AMES, $13.50–15.00 **(9)**

Bypass-type shears; 28½ inches overall; Teflon-coated blades, ash wood handle and rubber, impact-absorbing bumper.

These are well-balanced, heavy shears with the capacity for large and medium-sized wood. The Model 23-026 are similar shears, but have aluminum handles that are a little shorter and lighter.

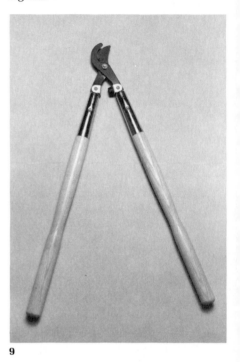

9

Lopping Shears, MODEL 25T, SEYMOUR SMITH & SON, $17.00–19.00 **(10)**

Brass anvil and Teflon-coated cutting blades, 27 inches overall; geared mechanism to add power; tubular steel handles; 6-inch plastic handgrips.

The gear drive on these shears gives them 3 times the power of similar conventional shears, the manufacturer says. Though the greater leverage makes hard work easier, the wide angle means they should not be used for fine pruning, since they will always leave a stub.

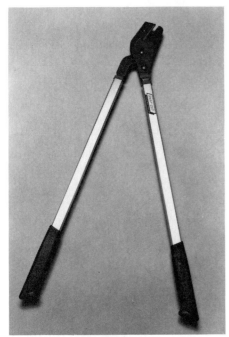

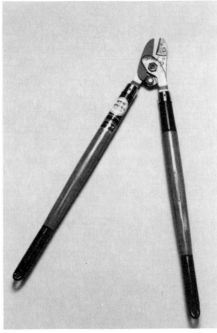

10

11

13

Lopping Shears, MODEL 2LAT, WALLACE MANUFACTURING, $19.00–21.00 **(11)**

28-inch anvil-type shears; unusual pivot system for greater cutting power; cutting blade coated with Teflon-S, wood handles with plastic handgrips, finger indentations and hanging tabs.

The leverage system on these shears has both blades moving in a slicing/shearing action during all parts of the cutting stroke. All cutting with these shears is done directly ahead of the operator. The tapered points of the blades make it easier to get in among small crowded branches, but, as with other anvil-type shears, they will not cut close enough for fine pruning.

Lopping Shears, MODEL 425, COLEMAN TREE PRUNERS, $25.00–28.00 **(12)**

Bypass shears made from chrome alloy steel; 25-inch-long handles (also available in a 30-inch model) topped by wooden grips.

12

The deep hook of these shears helps to hold the wood you're pruning for easier cutting. This durable model will cut limbs up to 1¾ inches in diameter. You can sharpen them with a file without taking the shears apart.

Lopping Shears, "RATCHET CUT," MODEL RL201, AMERICAN STANDARD, $57.00–63.00 **(13)**

Ratchet action, anvil-type shears, 27 inches overall; hickory handles, and soft vinyl handgrips.

If your age, size, or sore joints prevent you from doing heavy pruning, try these shears. The ratchet action may take a little more time to use, but the cutting is easier and you can get through a 2-inch branch. The angle and force of the cut is determined by the size of the branch.

PRUNING SAWS

A good pruning saw is one of those basic tools that should be in every tool shed whenever there are a number of trees or large shrubs on the property. You can use a pruning saw to do fine trimming on ornamental and fruit trees, remove storm-damaged limbs or dead wood, or even, with the larger saws, cut small- to medium-sized firewood.

If most of your pruning involves removing an occasional dead limb, one of the larger saws will probably be most useful. But if you have fruit trees, or other trees that need continuous attention, one of the small, hooked saws with a relatively narrow blade will probably be easier to use. (See "Clearing the Land" for more pruning and other types of saws.)

The curved blade saws have raked-back teeth that do more cutting when pulled toward you than when pushed away, giving good control. Unfortunately, sharpening these saws is a problem, since they don't fit in conventional sharpening machines. But the saw shouldn't need sharpening often enough to make this a serious problem, unless you have an orchard or large stand of trees and use it much more frequently than most homeowners.

A pruning saw on a pole allows you to get high into a tree without the risk of working on a ladder, but if there's a lot of treetop pruning to be done, it's best to call in the professionals.

Keep your saw dry and clean, giving a wipe with an oily rag after use. (Saws with Teflon blades may work a little more smoothly and won't need as much cleaning, but it's still worth it to take a few seconds to make sure they're clean also.)

Pruning Saw, MODEL 14, FANNO, $8.00–10.00 **(15)**

Gently curved pruning saw; 13-inch cutting edge, 7 points per inch; saw is of 19-gauge steel with 8-inch hardwood handle; 1¾ inches wide near handle; ¼ inch wide at tip.

Designed for cutting hardwoods such as citrus fruit trees, this saw is lightweight and well made. It will do general pruning tasks, and the small points allow it to cut cleanly through hardwoods without tearing the bark.

15

Folding Pruning Saw, MODEL 260ss, DISSTON, $11.00–13.00 **(14)**

10-inch cutting blade, 6 points per inch; 12-inch wood handle with button that will release or lock the blade in either folded or extended position; blade coated with Teflon-S.

This small-bladed saw won't tackle a large limb, but it will do a nice job on lighter pruning. The folding feature makes it simple to carry in a pocket. The Teflon coating helps keep the blade from becoming gummy.

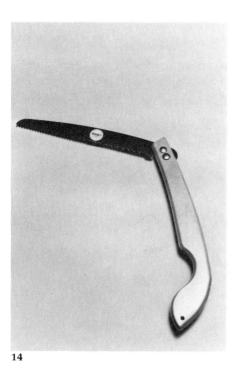

14

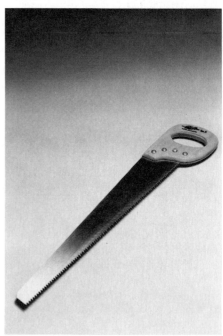

16

Pruning Saw, MODEL 8,
FANNO, $13.70–16.00 **(16)**

*22-inch, 18-gauge steel blade; 5½
points per inch; laminated wood
handle.*

This saw, designed for tree surgery
and general pruning, is especially
good for taking off large dead or damaged limbs. However, it is difficult to
maneuver into tight places for the
kind of delicate pruning often required on fruit trees. For a rubber-
handled version designed to withstand weathering, look at Fanno's
Model 8R.

Pruning Saw, MODEL 7064,
SKODCO, $17.65–19.50 **(17)**

*Curved blade, 26 inches long; 3½
inches wide at the base and 1 inch
wide at the outer tip; teeth about ⅜
inch deep spaced 4 to the inch; laminated handle held to blade with 3
bolts and sleeves.*

If you have heavy pruning to do, this
saw can handle it. The teeth cut fast
and clean, regardless of the position
of the saw.

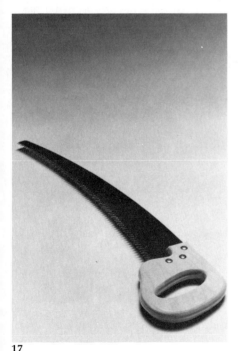

17

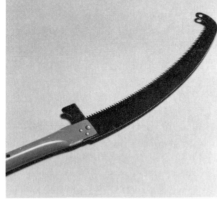

18

Pruning Saw, "LIMB MASTER,"
MODEL 385,
SANDVIK, $11.00–13.00 **(18)**

*Curved blade with 16-inch cutting
edge; 1½-inch hook at the outer end;
blade riveted to handle that is hollow
to receive a pole; at handle end of
saw is a 1½-inch-wide knife blade
with a hook on the back side.*

There are several good features to this
pole pruning saw. The hook on the
outer tip of the saw prevents it from
accidentally slipping out of the cut.
The knife blade allows you to cut the
bark and prevent ripping, which
leaves an uneven cut and leads to disease. The hook on the back side of the
knife blade allows you to snag a small
cut branch and pull it away from the
tree. It's easy to be enthusiastic about
the smooth operation of this pole saw,
as well as its special features.

Pole Tree Trimmer, MODEL 23-252,
AMES, $22.00–24.00 **(19)**

*Nonstick Teflon-S cutting blade; 12-
inch pruning saw; 8-foot wooden handle; heavy-duty nylon pulley; 8½-foot
rope with wood pull grip.*

Pole tree trimmers are not a gardening
necessity, but they're helpful for
reaching a limb that's impractical (or
dangerous) to trim from a ladder.
Here's how this unit works: place the
hook over the branch you want to cut.
Then pull down on the cord that's
connected to the cutting blade, and
the branch will be severed. Don't
stand underneath or the branch may

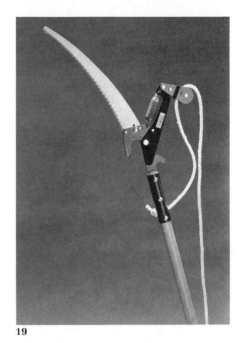

19

come crashing down on your head.
The trimmer also comes with a 12-
inch pruning saw blade for trimming
larger branches.

POCKET CALIPER

Caliper, "LEONARD PLASTIC POCKET
CALIPER,"
A. M. LEONARD, $1.50–1.65 **(20)**

Pocket caliper, 6½ × 3 inches, plastic.

When you need to know the width of
a tree for fertilizing, pruning, or fruit-
ing purposes, this caliper will come
in handy. It reads in ¼-inch increments, and both sides give the reading.

20

PLANT TIES

Plant-tying material should be strong enough to hold the weight of a mature plant, durable enough to last a season, and gentle enough not to bruise or cut tender growing tissue.

Bare wire is durable and strong, but it bruises, so you should select ties made of wire protected by plastic or paper. Twine is also strong and durable, but be sure you use a soft type such as jute, for a hard string can cut your plants in the same way that wire does.

When using any plant tie, my cardinal rule is that you want to secure it loosely to the plant and firmly to the support. Never wrap it around or tie it to a plant. Instead, gently form a "U"-shaped loop around the plant, then secure your tying material with one or more turns around the plant support. This will hold the plant securely without causing undue chafing, and it won't strangle the plant as it grows. Even after you've taken this precaution, you should check plant ties from time to time, especially on long-lived wood plants, to make sure they aren't girdling the plants.

The material you choose will largely depend on personal preference and availability. Any of the items included here meet the basic requirements of strength, durability, and gentleness.

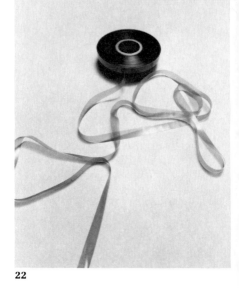

22

Plant Ties, "PLAS-TIES," MCHUTCHINSON, $4.00–4.50 **(23)**

Dark green plastic ties, ⅛ inch wide with wire center, on 25-foot spool with cutter.

You just pull out the length of the plastic ribbon you need from the spool, snip it off with the built-in cutter, loop it around a plant, and stake and twist the ends of the ribbon together. It's durable enough to resist weathering for at least a year, and is also available in 100-foot spools and packages of 8-inch strips.

21

Plant Ties, GREEN JUTE WRAPPING TWINE, LUDLOW, $1.10–1.40 **(21)**

Strong, soft 3-ply jute twine dyed dark green in ball containing 243 feet.

This wide, soft twine will hold stems of flowers, vegetables, vines, roses, and similar plants without damaging them. You can expect about a season's wear out of this twine, and it will weather to natural, neutral brown. I like this better than regular string, which is usually too narrow, too hard, or both.

Plant Ties, MODEL VT-405, DEXOL, $1.25–1.50 **(22)**

300-foot roll of ½-inch-wide green vinyl ribbon.

Use this tie, which stretches with growth, for basic plant support as well as for budding and grafting. The main advantage of using vinyl as a tie is that it's weatherproof and it won't rot, so you'll get more than one season's use from it.

23

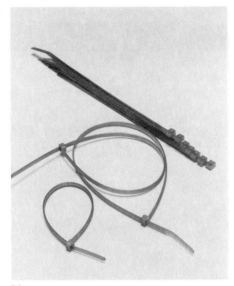

24

26

27

Plant Ties, MODEL NTP-01, DRIP GUARD, $.90–1.10 **(24)**

Package contains 8 ⅛-inch-wide ties, 8 inches long, and 2 ties about 14 inches long; made of dark green nylon, these ties are self-locking.

There's no twisting with this tie. You merely loop it around the plant and stake and pull the end through the locking head until the desired tension is reached, then snip off the excess.

Plant Ties, "STIK-N-TY," MODEL ST-4, DEXOL, $1.25–1.50 **(25)**

Clear plastic discs, ¾ inch in diameter and ⅛ inch thick; projecting eye

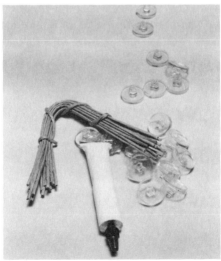

25

on 1 side to receive tie; tube of adhesive and several plant ties made of wire wrapped in soft paper.

These unobtrusive clear discs come in handy any time you want to train a plant (like a vine) up a wall. Just glue one to a plain, flat surface, then loop a regular plant tie through the eye in the disc and around the plant to hold it in place. Lock the ties by twisting the ends together.

Wall Nails, "FRANCIS WALL NAILS," MODEL 96-9198, E. C. GEIGER, $2.75–3.05 per box **(26)**

Steel nails topped by 1-inch-long pliable lead hook; each box has 20 nails, 10 of 1¼-inch length, and 5 each of 1 inch and 1½ inches.

Whether you want to secure ivy, climbing roses, espaliered fruit trees, or electrical wiring, you'll find these nails a convenient anchor. They'll work on brick, stucco, stone, or cement walls as well as wood and mortar. Sometimes their soft lead projection can be bent directly over the material being secured; in other instances, just form the lead into an eye to make a tie point for string or other material.

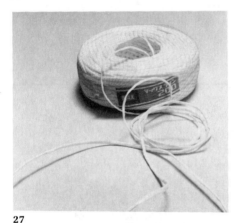

27

Plant Tie System, "MAX TAPENER," MODEL HR-F, IMPORTED BY L. E. COOKE, $14.20–16.00 **(27)**

Steel stapling device, weighs about 12 ounces and is 8 inches long; includes cutter blade and 5 spares; use with "Max" staples G1305M and "Max" line 200.

This soft line can be hung at your waist without tangling. Draw out what you need, wrap it twice around the plant and support, bring the two ends together, then staple and cut with this device. This is a good professional tying system, simple to use. You can carry out the entire process while wearing gloves, a boon when dealing with thorny plants or working in chilly weather.

PLANT SUPPORTS

Tomatoes, morning glories, peas, dahlias, gourds, cucumbers, hollyhocks, peonies . . . the list could go on and on. What these plants have in common is their need for support.

Providing that support can be quite simple. For peas, for example, I frequently take the dead branches and twigs of deciduous trees and shrubs and stick them in the soil right after I've planted the seeds, making a simple, natural trellis. Quite often your tool shed holds lots of materials for homemade plant supports. But there are times when a commercial plant support works better.

For years, most plant supports were wood (bamboo was a favorite), and this is still a good choice. But there are many simple, durable, wire, fiberglass, and metal supports now available that work just as well and last longer.

There are a few things to keep in mind when choosing such supports. First, consider the height of your mature crop. Nothing is more discouraging than watching your 5-foot-tall peas flopping over a 3-foot-high fence painstakingly put up at the start of the season. Once the crop has started to connect itself to one support, it's just about impossible to install another. Second, make sure your support is strong enough. When those first few vines engage themselves, there's not much to worry about, but as they grow and spread and develop fruit, they become quite heavy and can overpower a flimsy arrangement which has not been anchored securely in the soil.

When using any type of plant support (especially cages which go over a plant), install the support when the plant is young, then shape the plant to best fit the support, tying it gently when and where needed. (Remember not to tie anything completely around a stem, but loop it in a "U" instead. Save the heavy wrapping and knots for the support end.)

Finally, look at the plant supports, particularly cage and fence types, with some imagination. You should find more than one use for them. For example, you could get your tomato plants in the garden a week or two ahead of schedule by wrapping the cage in polyethylene and taping it in place. This would provide protection from winds, cutworms, and the worst of the cold for the young plants. Remove the plastic once the plants are well established and the weather has warmed. Some of these supports can also go under and around the branches of evergreen shrubs to help them deal with the snow loads during the winter. And, of course, some of the smaller ones can be used in greenhouses or for indoor plants.

For flowers, I like plant stakes, where possible, since they tend to be less obtrusive than the cages. But some flowering plants will benefit from a cage and an advantage of the cages is that you usually don't have to tie plants to them.

Whether you use a cage, stakes, fence, or net, give serious thought to supporting your plants. You'll be rewarded with cleaner fruits, better air circulation (which means fewer plant diseases), and far fewer broken stems and drooping flower tops.

Plant Support, GREEN HABIT ENTERPRISES, $3.00–3.50 **(28)**

Set of 3 galvanized stakes (7 inches, 14 inches, and 21 inches long), bent into horizontal loops at top with soft plastic coating; package includes 4 clips.

These stakes will last many years and can be used individually or attached together with metal clips as your plant grows taller. (Pliers are required for this.) For example, you may want to hook the 3 different-sized stakes together side by side so that loops are at 7, 14, and 24 inches, or you may want to stack them so you have a single support about 4 feet tall, with loops at different heights. The supports are also available individually.

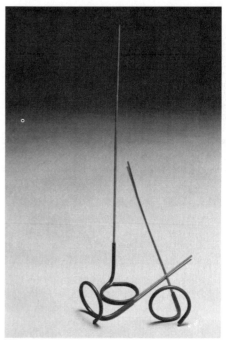

28

Above: Sugar snap peas growing on fencing.
Left: Cages supporting tomato plants.
Right: These beans will grow up the strings.

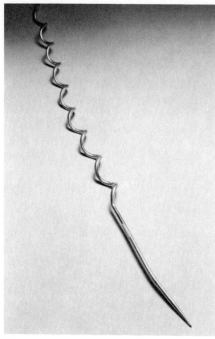

29

30

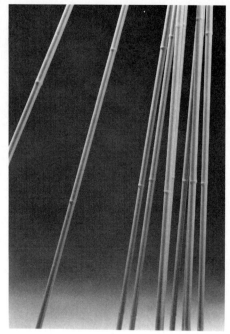

31

Plant Support, "ALUMINUM SPIRAL
TOMATO STAKE,"
MODEL 4-235BN011076-6,
IMPORTED FROM WEST GERMANY BY
GOOD-PROD SALES, $3.00–3.50 **(29)**

*Spiraled aluminum tube, ½-inch thick
and 5 feet tall, with straight length
about 15 inches at bottom for inserting in soil; also available in 6½-foot
length or in bundles of 6 at slightly
lower price per stake.*

The spirals on this stake provide a
gentle tunnel for a low-growing deter-
minate tomato plant to grow into,
holding it in place without ties and
with no danger of girdling. It's hard
to imagine when, or how, these stakes
could wear out.

Plant Support, "ANDERSON TRELLIS,"
AOW INDUSTRIES, $10.00–11.00 **(30)**

*4-foot-tall support includes vertical
pole section of white polyvinyl chloride pipe with 5 rings about 12 inches
in diameter made of black, 1-inch-di-
ameter polypropylene tubing; additional packages of 2 rings and 2 pole
sections available.*

This unusual, long-lasting support is
useful for many vegetables as well as
some high-climbing flowering vines
such as morning glories and clematis.

Plant Support, "LIFE-TIME STAKES,"
AMI MEDICAL ELECTRONICS, $.50–3.00
each, depending upon size **(31)**

*Steel tubing covered with a .2-inch
jacket of green polyvinyl chloride.
Plastic caps on both ends; lengths
shown are 4 and 6 feet; diameters are
⁵/₁₆, ⁷/₁₆, and ⅝ inches; also available
in 3- and 5-foot lengths in the ⁵/₁₆-
and ⁷/₁₆-inch diameters, and in 5, 7,
and 8 feet in the ⅝- and ¹³/₁₆-inch-di-
ameter units; available only in bundles of 10.*

The bamboolike ridges on these stakes
keep plant ties from slipping down
the stake. The color blends in nicely
with plants but the main feature here
is durability; the manufacturer esti-
mates their lifetime at 15 to 20 years.
These stakes are very strong and
won't warp or rust. If you're using a
¾-inch bamboo stake, you can feel
comfortable replacing it with the ⁷/₁₆-
inch steel tubing model. The price tag
might look high when compared to
bamboo or other similar materials, but

it really isn't when you consider how
long they'll last.

Plant Support, "SMALL PLANT
LADDER," MODEL PL-300,
NORTHERN WIRE PRODUCTS,
$1.40–1.60 **(32)**

*2 heavy-gauge galvanized wire rings
and 3 vertical wires form a conical-
shaped support, 30 inches high and
18 inches wide at top; the PL-250 is
the same height, but the top is 14
inches in diameter.*

This cage-type support will help keep
flowers such as peonies off the
ground, also preventing the plants
from being bent and broken by wind
and heavy rain.

Plant Support, MODEL TL-400,
NORTHERN WIRE PRODUCTS,
$4.00–4.50 **(33)**

*Square cage of heavy-gauge galvan-
ized wire, about 12 inches on a side
and 46 inches high (also available in
40-inch model); folds flat for storage.*

This cage was designed specifically
for tomato plants and other tall-grow-
ing vining plants. Stick the legs about
6 inches into the soil. If your ground

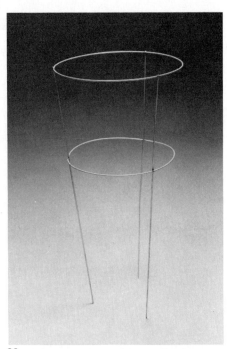

32

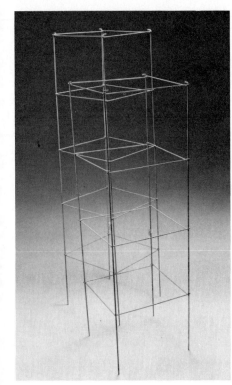

33

is stony, you may run into trouble getting all 4 legs in evenly, but since the cage is flexible, there's no reason why one leg can't be a little out of square.

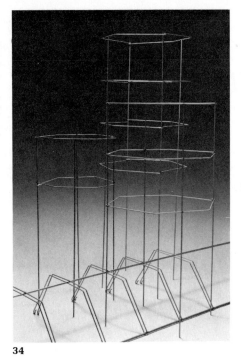

34

Plant Support, "SUPPORT-A-PLANT," MODEL 9430, FLETCHER, $.75–1.00 **(34)**

Heavy-gauge galvanized steel wire comes in 2 half hexagons that can be hooked together to form a hexagon 14 inches wide and 30 inches high; other models are 18 inches wide and 36, 48, and 60 inches high.

This is a flexible plant support. You can form 2 halves together to make a cage for tomatoes and similar plants, or you can hook several together side by side to make a low, long trellis, or a circle around evergreens and other shrubs to guard against breaking from snow loads. The units can nest together, saving storage space.

Plant Support, "VINET," MODEL VN-1, DEXOL, $1.50–2.00 **(35)**

Soft fabric netting, pale blue-green color, with a 4-inch mesh; 5 × 6 feet.

When you need a good, temporary trellis to provide a climbing base for flowers such as sweet peas or vegetables, this netting should last a full season.

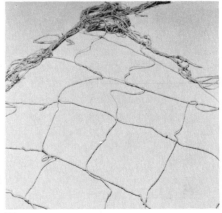

35

Plant Support, "FAN TRELLIS," MODEL 572, ROLLIN WILSON, $10.00–11.00 **(36)**

5 6-foot white fiberglass bars in fan shape.

This long-lasting trellis won't rust or rot. Be careful while assembling it, however, to avoid the burrs from the fiberglass.

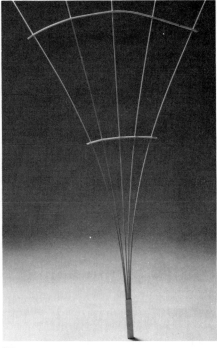

36

PLANTERS

Window boxes, outdoor flowerpots, and other special containers can make it possible for nearly anyone, on city rooftops or suburban lots, to grow flowers and vegetables in a small space.

The requirements for these containers are very similar to those for indoor use. However, remember that they are subject to damage from heavy rain and drying winds. The rains — which can be viewed as uncontrolled watering — mean that drainage is very important. While plants can be grown in sealed containers indoors by putting plenty of drainage material in the bottom of the container and by careful watering, outdoors, drainage holes are a must. The drying effects of full sun and wind mean that some containers, such as clay pots, might have to be watered twice a day. If you're not prepared to do this, consider the nonporous pots of fiberglass and plastic. Your plants won't dry out so fast in these.

Wood containers are pleasing, but they should be of a durable wood such as redwood, or else of wood that has been treated with a waterborne salt-type preservative which will not harm plants. Such preservatives can be brushed on or soaked in, but they are much more effective when applied by commercial pressure-treating methods. If you want to build containers yourself, pressure-treated wood can be specially ordered at most lumberyards. Container gardening not only allows people to grow vegetables, fruits, flowers — even dwarf trees — in areas where they could never be grown otherwise, but it also allows people with plenty of space to brighten up a patio, sun deck, or other outdoor living area.

Always keep in mind the weight of wet soil when attaching window boxes or other hanging containers, or else your decorations may prove hazardous.

Planter, "BO-KAY," MODEL 110-408, MOLDED FIBER GLASS TRAY, $8.00–8.50   **(37)**

Fiberglass indoor/outdoor flower box, 36 × 8 × 6 inches; available in white, green, avocado, lemon, brown, or clay colors; also available in 18-, 24-, and 30-inch lengths; optional accessory of zinc-plated steel wall bracket designed to fit under box and top lip.

This strong box should last indefinitely, whether mounted on a wall or set on the ground, patio, or deck. Indoors, it makes a fine planter. If you decide to place it outdoors, it would be a good idea to drill some drainage holes in it.

37

Plant Holder, MODEL PH-03, SILENT STEAM BLACKSMITHS, $22.00–25.00   **(38)**

Handwrought iron; 33 inches tall by 13 inches wide with 10-inch plate; weighs 3 pounds.

This sturdy plant hanger makes a handsome addition to a patio or looks attractive hanging by a window indoors. It's hand-forged by blacksmiths in New York State and is just one of a special line of planters, sconces, mobiles, and boot scrapers.

38

Planter, MODEL 2-101,
FILFAST, $29.00–32.00   **(39)**

*Polyurethane hexagonal planter, 8
inches high; outside diameter 23½
inches, outside depth 9¼ inches;
available in terra-cotta finish as well
as white or black.*

Even close up, this molded planter is
a dead ringer for the terra-cotta it imi-
tates. It's a good outdoor choice because it's lightweight and easy to
move around, leakproof, and durable.
Drill it for drainage or for bolting
down. This is just one of a custom
line designed by Filfast Corporation.

39

40

41

Strawberry Jar, MODEL 729,
ZANESVILLE STONEWARE,
$23.00–26.00   **(40)**

*Stoneware pot, 12 inches high with 8-
inch "pockets"; comes in white, forest
green, and sunflower.*

Here's a handsome pot from an old-
time pottery in the Ohio clay belt,
where the clay's high sand content
makes it possible to build large,
strong stoneware pieces. The best way
to grow plants in this jar is to plant it
in layers: put in some soil, then the
plant, firming the roots in toward the
center, then soil, plant and so on —
anchoring the plants so they grow
well. The pottery also makes several
jardinieres as well as hard-to-find
birdbaths. The strawberry jar is also
available in 5-, 16-, and 21-inch
heights.

Outdoor Planter, MODEL AP-542,
ARCHITECTURAL POTTERY,
$40.00–50.00   **(41)**

*White cast vitreous ceramic pot; 18 ×
10 inches. Available also in wide
range of decorator colors.*

If you have a spot on your deck where
you'd like to see a large cluster of ge-
raniums, this pot would be a good
choice. It's part of a custom line of
more than 200 sizes and shapes used
by architects and landscape designers
primarily for public areas where large
pots are needed. The heavyweight
pots of classic modern design should
last for years.

Planter, MODEL 841-2,
MOLDED FIBER GLASS TRAY,
$66.50–73.00 **(42)**

*White fiberglass container, 37½ ×
24¼ × 9½ inches; heavy-duty construction.*

This tray was designed for use in the
automotive industry, but would make
an excellent planting container for
rooftop gardening. Since it is waterproof, you'll want to put plenty of
gravel or other drainage material in
the bottom, if used in a sheltered area,
and drill some holes for drainage.
This holds nearly 4 cubic feet of
planting material and is deep enough
for most crops.

42

Planter, "VERTIGRO PATIO TOWER,"
MODEL 32,
DALEN, $43.00–47.00 **(43)**

*Kit of redwood with aspen wood base,
hardware and casters for assembling
24 × 24 × 48-inch terraced planter
with 1 gallon water and fertilizer reservoir in center; assembles with just a
screwdriver; holds 4½ cubic feet of
planting medium.*

This is an easy kit to construct and
once it's filled with a planting medium and plants, it provides what
amounts to 46 feet of garden row in 2
square feet of space. You could have
fun with this growing flowers, fruits
(such as strawberries), herbs, or vegetables. The manufacturer advises that
a soilless mix be used, which would
be lighter than soil and provide good
drainage. (See the Indoor Gardening
chapter for discussion of soilless
mixes.) Filled with a typical soilless
mix, wet, the planter will weigh about
115 pounds. The casters allow you to
move it about both for decorative reasons and to give the plants different
exposure to the sun. The interior
water reservoir provides a safe way
both to water and to feed the plants.
Directions for assembling are easy to
follow.

Though this is a fine way to make
maximum use of minimum gardening
space, I don't think it has to be limited to apartment gardeners. Even
someone with plenty of acreage could
enjoy this on a patio or deck. It's part
of a line of limited-space containers
including a redwood wall unit. (right)

43

43

POT WATERER

Waterer, "WATER BREAKER,"
MODEL 400,
DRAMM, $4.70–5.25 **(44)**

Aluminum nozzle, with many small holes in it; fits standard hose thread.

This provides a gentle stream of water suitable for plants in containers. Dramm also makes a series of aluminum extendors ("Handi-Reach"), 16, 24, 36, and 48 inches in length. The Model 148GB is curved to be especially useful in reaching hanging plants.

44

GROW BAG

Grow Bag, PATIO GROW-IN BAG, ANNAPOLIS VALLEY PEAT MOSS, $4.00–4.50 **(45)**

Plastic bag approximately 38 × 15 inches, containing 1½ cubic feet of growing medium.

City gardeners or gardeners plagued by soil-borne diseases will find these disposable growing bags convenient. The bags are filled with a sterile mixture composed of 30 percent sphagnum peat moss, 30 percent pine bark compost, 30 percent vermiculite, and 10 percent trace elements and slow-release fertilizers. The peat will hold up to 15 times its weight in water, while the slow-release fertilizers act over a 6- to 8-month period — a boon for gardeners who have long growing seasons. At the end of the year, put the contents in your compost pile and throw away the plastic bag. During the winter I use it to grow tomatoes in my greenhouse.

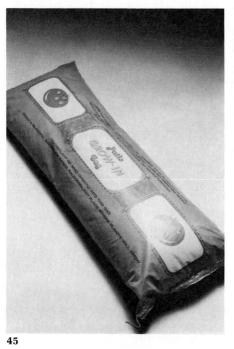

45

BOOT SCRAPER

Boot Scraper, MODEL 8043, WHITE FLOWER FARM, $44.00–50.00 **(46)**

Black iron handles about 33 inches high and ½ inch in diameter; wire brush at base; 2 fiber brushes on either side; 2 metal legs insert in the ground about 6 inches for stability.

One way a gardener can become unpopular is to track mud into the house. Here's White Flower Farm's way of avoiding that problem. They went to Connecticut blacksmith Lyle Lindsley with a few sketches and the result is this fine boot scraper. Since it's handmade, stock is limited. Brushes are replaceable with new units simply by loosening 2 screws.

46

HARVESTING AND PREPARING FOR WINTER

Harvesting probably involves more sheer pride than any other part of gardening. After all, who could resist displaying home-grown dead-ripe tomatoes, freshly picked tender sweet corn, multicolored strawflowers or fruit the supermarket doesn't bother to carry? What do you need to gather this bounty? Mostly your hands, some sort of container, and a few special tools professionals use.

Many people ignore their gardens after harvesting. But the garden year is a continuous process. Nothing better illustrates that than fall, which represents the end of one cycle and the beginning of another. Tools you haven't used since spring come back into their own. Cold frames once again are brought out for sheltering tender perennials, holding bulbs for forcing, and carrying lettuce and radish crops past the first frosts. Carts, wheelbarrows, forks, spades, rakes, and tillers all take their turns in fall garden chores.

You'll also be putting your native ingenuity to work, protecting newly planted evergreens or fruit trees from the sun, wind, and a few common critters. Rabbits who enjoyed your lettuce in the late spring will find pickings slim in December, so they may turn to the bark on your young trees. That's why I protect my trees from rabbits and mice with a loose-fitting wrap of ¼-inch-mesh hardware cloth or commercial wrap from ground level up to the first branches.

Evergreens, especially ones just planted, and some more tender types, such as azaleas, can take a real beating from the sun, wind, and snow. Wooden frames around them can keep the snow load from breaking branches, as well as supply some shelter from the sun. Burlap or polyethylene wrapped around such a frame, or around a few stakes surrounding the small tree or shrub, can help protect from bitter cold winds.

You'll want to gather a light mulch for rosebushes and some perennials, but don't make the mistake of too many home gardeners and think you're trying to keep the roots warm with this. What you're trying to do is maintain an even temperature. So, wait for the ground to freeze, and after several days of cold weather in a row, add the mulch. You simply want to avoid the constant freezing and thawing that will heave the ground and damage the plants.

Once you've looked to your plants, look to your tools that have served you so well. Now is the time to drain the gasoline from any small motors and to clean, sharpen, and oil hoes, spades, and other metal tools. When I notice rust starting to spot a tool, especially something such as the inside of a metal garden cart, I scrape it off, clean it, and dab it with a touch-up paint. I want all tools to be ready in the spring because when those first warm days in March hit, I don't want to be inside sharpening a spade.

HARVEST CONTAINERS

You could always go out to your garden, orchard, or flower border with whatever sack, bag, or bucket is handy. After all, a brown bag from the grocery store, a plastic bucket, or even an old pillowcase will hold the harvest. But there are some practical, as well as aesthetic, reasons for using the baskets and containers on these pages.

What's right for you will depend on such things as how much you grow, what you grow, and whether or not your orchard is comprised of full-sized or dwarf varieties. A basket is fine for picking cut flowers, collecting vegetables for the evening meal, or harvesting a few apples from dwarf trees. However, if you're going to harvest several long rows of corn for freezing, or climb a ladder to pull down fruit near the tops of trees, then you'll want a bushel basket or the special harvest buckets that can be worn on shoulder straps. The harvest buckets leave both hands free, which is a commonsense safety precaution, as well as a convenience. The buckets are gentle on the fruits, allowing the picker to empty a load by gently releasing the bottom into a larger container.

Although we use these containers for harvesting, don't overlook their other uses. They come in handy when planting seed potatoes, or broadcasting large quantities of seed, such as winter rye, or for carrying seed packets, gloves, or small garden tools.

Finally, I think using makeshift containers takes the fun out of what is the high point of the gardening year. A freshly picked head of lettuce can be a thing of beauty. So are those deep orange carrots, the green sheaths and golden brown tassels of sweet corn, and the multitude of colors, shapes, and textures found in other vegetables and fruits. When properly grown, they all radiate a sense of healthiness that enhances their other qualities. I don't want to hide them in a paper bag — I've worked too hard all season to grow them well. Now I want to treat them with care and take them back to the kitchen in a container that complements their beauty.

1

Garden Basket, MODEL 2, WEST RINDGE BASKETS, $12.00–14.00 **(1)**

Shallow basket with handle is woven of split ash and measures 18 × 12 × 4 inches.

Woven baskets were once a necessity in New England, and nearly every town had its weaver or basket factory. Mass production, imports, and inexpensive plastics have changed all that, and it's not so easy to find a woven basket here today. I did find some nice ones, though, manufactured in Rindge, New Hampshire. The model chosen is one of eleven sizes and styles ranging from a "porch mail basket" to a "miniature laundry basket."

This one is just right for carrying the evening's dinner or salad makings from the garden in the style well-grown produce deserves. It will also be useful for carrying cut flowers, supporting the long stems until you can get them into water.

These baskets are made of tough, northern ash, a hardwood you've probably met in the handles of axes, rakes, and other tools that benefit from both the strength and elasticity of ash. The hoops and handles are of oak. Much of the manufacturing is by hand, and no two baskets are exactly alike. The manufacturer gives each basket a final inspection, letting only the "perfectly sound" ones that "will serve at least two generations" go through. How many other things today are designed to serve "at least two generations"?

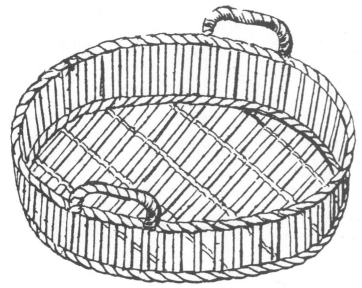

2

3

This durable container allows you to pick large fruits, such as apples and pears, while keeping your hands free. The bucket is larger at the bottom than at the top, to allow fruit to be released easily without bruising; the felt rim also protects against accidental bruising. Two cords keep the canvas bottom in place, but it can be easily released when the bag is suspended over a larger container.

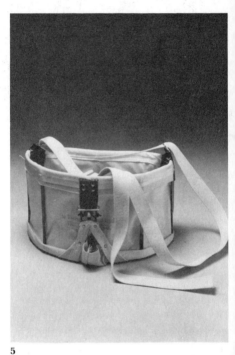

5

Garden Basket, CATALOG NO. 990, GARDEN WAY CATALOG, $12.00–13.00 **(2)**

Anodized aluminum basket with ¾-inch wire mesh, measuring 18 × 11½ × 8 inches; handles are coated with soft plastic.

If you object to running all the grit and clinging soil from various root crops down the sink, just put your crops in this basket, run a stream from the garden hose over them, and keep the soil residue outside where it will do the most good. It will also keep the sink a little cleaner, and how nice those glistening vegetables look when you bring them into the house.

Basket, MODEL 280C, HANDY FOLDING PAIL, $8.00–9.00 **(3)**

Nylon-laminated vinyl basket measuring 17 × 11 × 7 inches with heavy-gauge zinc-plated wire frame reinforced at weld points. Comes in blue, green, yellow, red and patterns.

Here is a basket widely used by farm stands and supermarkets because of its durability. The nylon-laminated vinyl covering can be wiped clean with a damp cloth or sponge and resists rot. It's just the right size for going out in the garden and picking enough vegetables for dinner, or for carrying

garden tools around. What's more, you'll find dozens of other uses for it throughout the year.

Picking Bucket, MODEL 2, WELLS & WADE, $14.00–18.00   **(4)**

Zinc-plated, metal bucket, oval shaped, 9 inches wide, 14 inches long, and 10 inches deep; 6-inch-wide piece of heavy felt stapled around rim; 10-ounce canvas bottom; adjustable shoulder straps of 1¾-inch webbing.

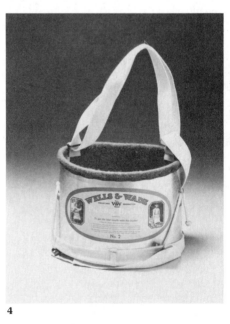

4

Picking Bucket, "APPEACH IMPROVED," FRIEND MANUFACTURING, $21.00–23.00 **(5)**

½-bushel bucket of canvas, protected by front stays and supported by web shoulder straps; bottom held by web straps closed in front with a toggle.

If you have nectarines, peaches, or other easily bruised fruit in your orchard, this canvas bucket will help you give them the tender handling they deserve. The front stays protect against the ladder, and the toggle arrangement for holding the canvas bottom in place means it can be released without raising the load of fruit, as is necessary with other systems. A "D" ring drops over the toggle to prevent accidental release.

6

Picking Bag, "ORCHARD KRAFT,"
FRIEND MANUFACTURING, $14.00–
15.50 **(6)**

White canvas bag, holds ⅞ bushel; 2-inch-wide webbing shoulder strap for one or two shoulders; bottom opens for unloading by the release of 2 heavy cords.

This is really a long, open-bottomed bag, folded up to prevent spilling. The wide straps spread the weight of the load quite comfortably. Picking can be done with the bag directly in front of the body or to either side. A practical container for reasonably firm fruits or sweet corn and a number of other vegetables from the home garden.

Harvesting Basket, CATALOG NO. 975,
GARDEN WAY CATALOG, $14.50–16.00
(12 ½-bushel baskets) **(7)**

Mixed hardwood splint wood basket; ½-bushel size measures 13 × 11½ inches, semi-tapered at bottom.

Wooden bushel harvest baskets are becoming hard to find in local garden supply centers. These baskets, available in both ½-bushel and bushel sizes, are roughly constructed of hardwood splints hand-nailed at the bottom. The hoops are secure. The ½ bushel is just the right size for harvesting tomatoes, beans, or cucumbers, while the bushel basket is excellent for carrying larger, less delicate produce such as squash or corn. *A note of caution:* Don't leave these or any wooden baskets out overnight sitting on the ground. If they are repeatedly wet, eventually the bottoms will weaken and rot out.

7

HARVESTING AIDS

When fruit is out of reach, as is often the case, you have two choices: either to climb or to extend your reach. The mechanical pickers shown here can be put on a pole of any reasonable length to let you get to fruit near the top of most trees. You may find this operation a bit slow if you have a lot of picking to do, in which case you'll want to try a ladder. The two I've chosen are designed for work in trees. They're not only sturdy, but they're built in such a way that it's easier to maneuver them among branches than is possible with a more traditional ladder, such as one designed for household chores.

9

Harvesting Ladder, "BASSWOOD ORCHARD LADDER," TOPPING LADDER, $28.00–32.00 **(8)**

Tapered, 8-foot-tall ladder, 15¾ inches wide at the base; 12 inches wide at the top, 7 white ash rungs with basswood rails 1⅜ × 3 inches.

The tapered design of this ladder accomplishes three things: it gives a wide base for stability, a narrow head to easily place between branches of trees, and a lighter weight than a ladder that is the same width over its entire length. These three factors add up to easy picking in tall fruit trees. This model is available in lengths from 8 feet to 22 feet.

Orchard Stepladder, TOPPING LADDER, $31.00–35.00 **(9)**

5-foot-tall, basswood stepladder with 36-inch-wide base on step side; brace side has 2 legs 10 inches wide at top of ladder which come together to form a single foot at the bottom; 5 steps, each about 4 inches wide.

The narrow brace allows me to set the ladder among or over small branches or thickets of plant stems. The very wide base flaring out on the step gives unusual stability. The rails and front edges of steps are beveled. It's secure and effective for harvesting from semidwarf or smaller fruit trees, or for pruning and general garden use on the home ground. Available in sizes from 5 feet to 12 feet.

Fruit Picker, MODEL 8, BARTLETT MANUFACTURING, $7.00–8.00 **(10)**

5-inch-diameter, galvanized metal ring about 3 inches high and ¹/₁₆ inch thick, with U-shaped "fingers" for guiding and twisting fruit stems; galvanized socket can be fitted on standard handles; attached white canvas bag about ½-peck capacity.

With this well-designed tool, fruit as large as grapefruit or as small as cherries can be picked with ease. Select

10

8

your fruit, then place the picker underneath with the fruit stem on the side of the picker rim. A slight lift of the picker, or a twist, will free the fruit from the tree and cause it to drop a few inches into the canvas bag. A number of fruits can be handled at one time before the picker is pulled down and emptied in a nearby box or basket on the ground. A handle may be purchased or made with a length that best matches the fruit tree height.

Fruit Picker, "LINDLAY" MODEL, DISTRIBUTED BY E. C. GEIGER, $5.00–6.00   **(11)**

Wire basket about 6 inches in diameter, 5 inches deep with a base socket into which can be fitted a 1¼-inch pole; wire tines extend about 4 inches above the basket on one side, curving over it slightly.

This is a strong, lightweight tool for picking larger fruits that are beyond arm's reach. You might want to add a small cushion of fabric or foam at the bottom of the basket. This cushion will help prevent bruises on the ripe fruits of soft skin varieties such as peaches. You choose, or make, a pole of a length appropriate to your needs. You might use the same pole for a pruning saw, since it's easy to remove from the picker.

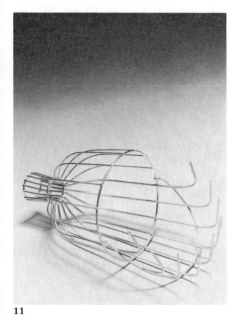

11

12

Picking Bag, "QUICKER-PICKER BAG," 1¼-QUART SIZE, GARDEN WAY CATALOG, $5.00–5.50   **(12)**

Waterproof bag made of 4-ounce orange nylon; wire rim, hand patch made of calf leather; three sizes: 1¼ quart, 3 quart, and 10 quart.

Grahame Dixie, a young Englishman, won the British Horticultural Brain of the Year Award in 1978 for inventing this harvesting aid which leaves both hands free to pick soft fruits and vegetables. A thornproof bag of heavy nylon suspended from a wire ring encased in suede is worn on either the right or left hand and is secured by elastic straps. The bright orange color makes the bag hard to lose. It's suitable for picking all bush berries, grapes, nuts, rose hips, flower seeds, beans, and tomatoes.

Apple Sizer, FRIEND MANUFACTURING, $5.25–6.00   **(13)**

Aluminum plate 6 × 8 × ¼ inches with five holes from 2 to 3 inches in ¼-inch increments.

Should you wish to prepare a fancy fruit basket for a friend, or want to sell some of your surplus fruit, this tool will help with the sizing. The edges of all openings are rounded and smooth so they won't tear or cut the skin of the fruit.

Potato Hook, MODEL 4BOL, TRUE TEMPER, $14.50–16.00   **(14)**

Head about 6¼ inches wide with 4 tines, 6¾ inches long, curved down at right angles to the 4½-foot handle.

This tool can be used for hooking out potatoes, but you'll also find it is a help in several other tasks, such as spreading manure, or picking out roots and stones after plowing.

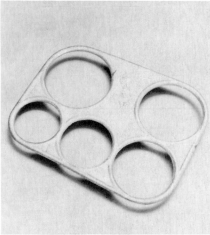

13

14

15

Gloves, "PIGSKIN FRUIT PICKERS," MODEL 05120, WOLVERINE WORLD WIDE, AVAILABLE IN MEN'S SIZES S-M-L, $9.00–10.00 **(15)**

Green domestic pigskin with 5-inch brown cotton gauntlet, fused with rubber; palm is constructed of 1 continuous piece of leather with no seams; lock stitch construction.

These are the gloves you'll want if you're gathering fruit or nuts in trees that are thick with twigs, or even thorns. Pickers in Florida orange groves wear them because citrus branches are sharp and citric acid makes cowhide gloves stiff and brittle. These pigskin gloves resist the effects of citric acid and stay soft and supple. They can be laundered in soap and water. The long gauntlet protects the wrist and arm, and will prevent most twigs and leaves from falling inside the glove.

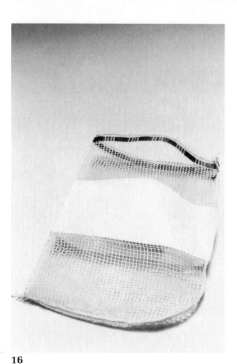

16

Storage Bag, CATALOG NO. 165, GARDEN WAY CATALOG, $2.00–2.25 (for 5 10-pound-capacity bags) **(16)**

Plastic mesh bag measuring 11 × 17½ inches; plastic ribbon closure at top.

Air should circulate around your storage onions, and that's possible with this mesh bag patterned after the larger sizes used by commercial growers. The bag, formed of nonrot plastic ¼-inch-square mesh, also comes in 25 and 50 pound capacities, useful for storing potatoes as well as onions. The 10-pound size shown here is ideal for storing winter-tender bulbs.

STORAGE

Don't let your gardening efforts go to waste. Obviously, the compost heap is one place where excesses can be recycled, but also remember that many crops can be stored without any elaborate canning, freezing, or drying. Apples like to be stored at about 45 degrees; for potatoes, parsnips, beets, carrots, cabbage, celery, salsify, turnips, and winter radishes, a 35- to 40-degree area that's a little on the humid side is fine. Squash and pumpkins prefer to be on the dry side at temperatures between 40 and 60 degrees. Without a special root cellar, these conditions may be a bit difficult to find, but certainly not impossible. Use a maximum/minimum thermometer and check the temperatures in a cellar bulkhead, different corners of the garage, or a sun porch. Even your tool shed might do for beans, which like it dry and near freezing.

FLOWER SHEARS

You can use your kitchen scissors or a household knife for cutting flowers, but chances are they won't be sharp enough to do the job well. If you want flowers that will last, you must start with a good, clean cut that doesn't destroy the water-carrying cells. Remember, you're cutting the flower (or foliage) off from its normal water supply, but if done right, the plant will continue to take up water through the stem and the leaves and flowers that have been cut will last longer. So, your primary consideration is for a sharp cutting blade of high-quality steel that will take a good edge and hold it through long use. Once you have such a tool, dry it after use, occasionally apply a little light oil, and don't abuse it by asking it to do other cutting tasks that might dull the blade.

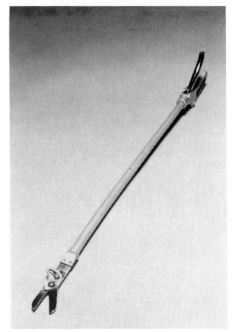

18

Flower Shears, MODEL FH4, WISS BY TRUE TEMPER, $7.50–9.00 **(17)**

6½-inch-long metal-plated shears with stainless steel blades; 1⅝-inch cut.

For quick harvesting of annual flowers and protection from thorns, these old-time cut-and-hold shears will come in handy. The fixed blade surfaces hold the flower until you can put it down. If harvesting roses, be sure to recut the rose stem on a slant before putting it in water.

Flower Shears, "CUT AND HOLD FLOWER GATHERER," IMPORTED FROM ENGLAND BY EQUIPMENT CONSULTANTS AND SALES, $14.00–16.00 **(18)**

1½-inch Sheffield stainless steel blades are controlled with aluminum handle and extension tube 31½ inches long; one blade has a holding groove for keeping flowers erect after they've been cut.

Many gardeners will find this tool useful, but it will be especially helpful to those who have difficulty reaching long distances to gather flowers and fruits. Anyone who has tried to reach across several feet of rosebush to cut a particularly beautiful blossom will see the handiness of these shears.

Flower Shears, "BARONET FREEHAND SNIPS," IMPORTED FROM ENGLAND BY EQUIPMENT CONSULTANTS AND SALES, $6.00–8.00 **(19)**

1-inch-long cutting blades of Sheffield stainless steel are attached to over-sized, oval handles covered with red plastic grips; small notch at base of blade will cut wires.

These shears were developed primarily for the gardener who has lost manual dexterity due to arthritis or similar ailments. The large hand opening means they're easy to use by any gardener, even with gloves on.

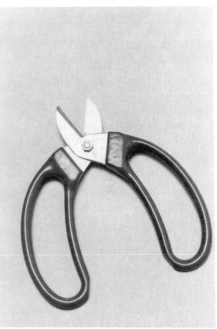

19

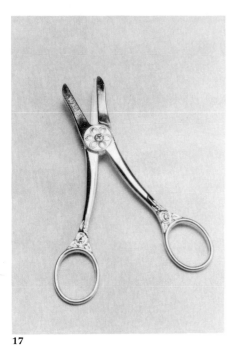

17

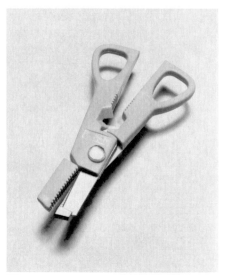

20

Flower Shears, MODEL 81,
TRUE FRIENDS GARDEN TOOLS,
$6.00–8.00 **(20)**

6-inch orange plastic shears with nut-and-bolt construction; removable single razor-type blade; thorn remover and stem squeezer.

These inexpensive shears will give you a quick cut on most flowers. The thorn remover is particularly good for stripping thorns off roses, and the stem crusher should be used on woody plants such as lilacs, forsythia, and pussy willows. They are small, and the ends are blunt, so you can easily drop these shears into your pocket. Should you leave them on the ground, their bright color will make them instantly noticeable.

Pruning Shears,
CUT-AND-HOLD PRUNER,
TELESNIP, CHEYENNE, $35.00–38.00
(21)

Pruning shears with stainless steel cutting blades opening to ¾-inch; plastic handles with strong coil spring; attached to the cutting blades is a patented device with small notches for holding the stem of the cut off plant portion; packed separately from the shears is a telescoping ⅞-inch aluminum tube, 3½ feet to 6 feet long, with enclosed cable ac-
tuated by an easy-working 4-inch hand lever.

Although these are pruning shears, they are very handy for harvesting single pieces of fruit or tall, old-fashioned roses. Note that when cutting upright flowers, the plastic holding blades must be upward; when cutting fruits with appreciable weight, hold the blades downward. When the shears are attached to their telescoping handle, they will be adjustable to any angle and they will cut and hold flowers, fruits, or prunings as far as 7 feet beyond the operator's hand. The attaching mechanism is simple and strong. The Telesnip makes easy work of gathering roses, bougainvilleas and other flowers, as well as camellia and gardenia flowers from large conservatory plants.

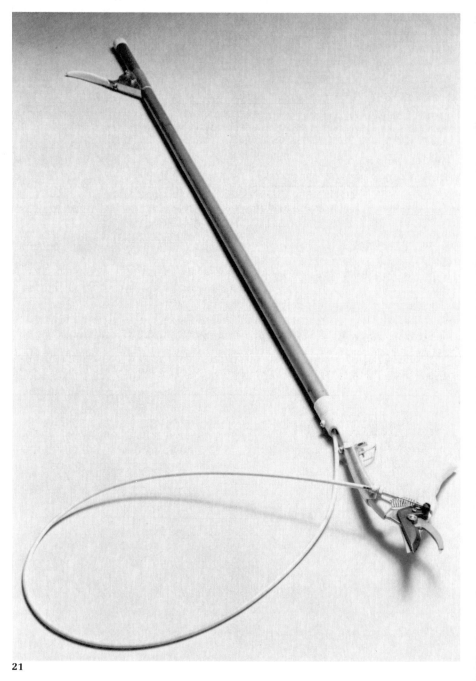

21

FLOWER SHEARS

FLOWER ARRANGING

You don't have to be an artist to make a beautiful, long-lasting display of cut flowers. Nature has already done most of the necessary artwork. But don't go out and lop off your flowers carelessly. Just as a seedling needs to be "hardened off" to help it adjust to outdoor conditions, a cut flower will last longer if it's properly prepared when making the move indoors.

The steps florists recommend when cutting most annual flowers can be used by almost anyone. First, cut in the early morning. Recut under water (a running faucet will do) at least ½ inch above the initial cut. This keeps the water-carrying cells in the stems from being blocked by air bubbles. Immediately plunge the flower stems into warm (75 to 95 degrees F.) water. If you wish to add a preservative, do so at this point, or make your own by using half water and half sugared, citrus-flavored carbonated soft drink, to which you've added ½ teaspoon of chlorine bleach per quart. That way you'll have flowers to enjoy in the garden and flowers in your home that last much longer than those that have not been treated properly.

Florist-supply companies carry dozens of items that the dedicated flower arranger would find helpful, such as preservatives to lengthen the life of cut flowers, foam bricks to hold bouquets, and sticky tape to anchor flower holders even under water. These products and others listed below should give you a hint of what's available.

23

This is an item for making flower arrangements in a shallow bowl, or on a mat or wood plaque. The pin holder portion can be removed easily from the cup for cleaning, or to use separately.

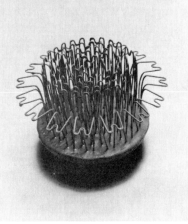

22

Hairpin Flower Holders,
MODEL JPA-435,
DOROTHY BIDDLE SERVICE, $6.50–7.15
(22)

3½-inch round lead base, holding rustproof brass "hairpins."

After preparing cut flowers properly, you won't want to crush or clog the water-carrying cells in the stem ends. This flower holder has no sharp pins to prick your fingers. The brass flower supports are flexible and ingeniously shaped to hold stems of fresh, dried, or artificial flowers at any angle without damaging them. Nine different sizes are available.

Flower Holder, MODEL 338,
BEAGLE MANUFACTURING, $2.40–3.00
(23)

Brass-colored, 2¾-inch diameter cup, 1¼ inches deep, holds slightly smaller flower holder with many ½-inch pins.

24

Flower Bowl, MODEL 50-0496,
ROSEVILLE FLORALINE DIVISION OF
NELSON MCCOY POTTERY,
$5.20–5.70 **(24)**

Ocher-colored oval bowl, 9 × 5⅜ × 2¾ inches.

Because of clay readily available in the region, the area of Ohio around Roseville where this bowl was made has been a manufacturing center for pottery for many years. Nelson McCoy is just one of several companies in the area that make products for the florist trade.

Floral Foam Brick, "FLORALIFE
QUICKEE," MODEL 4036,
FLORALIFE, $.90–1.10 (no photo)

*Plastic foam brick, 4½ × 4½ ×
3 inches.*

Transporting flower arrangements is
easier if you don't have to worry
about spills. Foam bricks, soaked with
preservative solution and anchored
with tape of floral adhesive provide
nourishment and support for your display.

Flower Drying Compound,
"CHERISH," MODEL 257,
FLORALIFE, $2.50–2.75 (for 1-pound
box) (no photo)

Moisture Barrier, "CHERISH,"
MODEL 281, FLORALIFE, $4.00–4.50
(for 13-ounce aerosol can) (no photo)

These items, sold separately, can be
used together for best results. The
drying compound, a reusable nontoxic
material, replaces the silica dust used
in the past to preserve and dry flower
blooms. Complete instructions guide
you through the process of making
permanent stems, "embedment," air
curing, and quick-dry techniques. One
1-pound box will embed and cover 8
flowers in individual cups or 18 dai-
sies in a flat box. You can dry flowers
within 24 hours using this drying
compound and your oven. Directions
come with the product.

Cherish Moisture Barrier is a spray
sealer that protects dried flowers from
humidity and dirt. Statice can be
dried and preserved in about 4 days
using these products.

Flower Picks, MODEL QA-553,
DOROTHY BIDDLE SERVICE, $.70–.80
(no photo)

*Package of 60 2½-inch or 25 4-inch
(Model # QA-554) green wood picks,
each wired with a 6-inch coated non-
rust wire.*

Flower picks are used like splints on
the ends of particularly small or flexible flower stems to facilitate flower arranging. When arranging in clay, the
slightly extended picks go into the
clay, leaving the stem free to draw up
moisture.

Florist's Wire, MODEL JQA-524,
DOROTHY BIDDLE SERVICE, $.70–.80
(no photo)

*Package contains 100 pieces of 12-
inch-long green enameled medium
wire; also available in finer, heavy,
and heaviest weights.*

These straight wires are used for floral
arrangements, corsages, and decorations. They're useful for winter dried
flower arrangements as well.

Floral Adhesive, "SURE-STICK,"
MODEL 5017,
FLORALIFE, $1.00–1.20 (no photo)

*60-inch roll of ½-inch adhesive
backed with paper.*

A floral adhesive used in flower arranging to anchor flower holders, styrofoam, and so forth, this tape holds
tight even under water.

WINTER PROTECTION

These products will help protect your trees and some other plants from the ravages of winter.

The large areas of soft bark on the trunks of newly planted trees can suffer sunscald or winter frost cracks the first year. Damage first appears as longitudinal cracks on the southerly or southwesterly side of the trunk exposed to the strongest sun. The tree wraps will protect against that, as well as repel wood borers which may attack new trees.

The other accessory you'll find here is a screen to hold in place insulating mulches around roses and other choice landscape plants. If you have some of that "Instant Greenhouse" material recommended for making cloches (see the Preparing and Planting chapter) left over, it could be cut and used for the same purpose, although it would probably last only a single season.

Tree Wrap, SMALL SIZE, WALTER E. CLARK & SON, $1.00–1.10 (no photo)

Roll of 2 layers of crinkle paper, bonded with asphalt, 3 inches wide and 50 feet long.

Whether you plant in fall or spring, it's a good idea to give the bark on the trunk of a young tree the protection of this wrap through its first winter. To apply, start by wrapping the bottom of the trunk and spiral upward, with a one-half overlap, to the branch head of the tree, and secure with string. This wrap is also available in a 4-inch-wide, 150-foot-long roll.

Winter Protection, "ROSS TREEGARD," ROSS DANIELS, $2.50–3.00 (25)

Package of 3 rolled plastic tree wraps, each 24 inches long; also available in 36-inch length.

To guard young trees against sunscald, winter wind, rabbits and other rodents, simply wrap the trunk in this plastic material. It snaps on or off in

25

seconds, needs no taping or tying, can be reused, and will expand as the tree grows. As the tree matures, it will reach a point where this is no longer needed, but it is particularly useful for the first full season. It will also help protect the tree from insects or an accidental bruise from a lawn mower.

Winter Protection, "SLIP-ON ROSEBUSH WINTERIZER," F. & R. FARRELL, $1.00–1.15 (26)

Fiberglass screening, ¼-inch mesh, formed in flexible, flat cylinder, 12 inches high and 13, 15, or 18 inches in diameter.

At about the time of your first killing frost, tie the canes of your hybrid tea roses and others into bundles, slide on this protective cover, then fill it with peat moss, corn cobs, pine needles, peanut shells, or some similar insulator. Be sure to firm the insulation into position and take the time to mound it a little higher near the plant stems. These winterizers are guaranteed to last 3 years, but you should get at least 5 years' use out of them if you store them properly. They won't mildew, rot, or rust.

26

YARD CLEANUP

For some people, the smell of burning leaves is a nostalgic reminder of fall, but as a gardener, I'd rather burn dollar bills! That's because the roots of trees forage deep, bringing up to the surface many trace elements of substances plants need in small quantities. These end up in the leaves and the leaves end up in either my compost pile, or a separate wire bin I've set aside for making leaf mold.

All I really want when it comes to leaves is a way to gather them. To me, this is just another harvest. The rakes that will do this job best will be found in the maintenance chapter. You can use a wheelbarrow or cart, such as those in the Preparing and Planting chapter, to carry them to your compost bin, but some of these may not have the desired capacity, and you'll be making many weary trips. You'll find here a few simple, large-capacity carrying devices that can make that task much easier.

Incidentally, if you do use leaves in the compost bin with other materials, be sure to put in thin layers or small amounts at a time, mixing them with the other materials. They tend to compact otherwise, slowing the decaying process. Making leaf mold takes 3 years, but the end result is worth it. That's why a separate bin of wire fence, out of the way somewhere, is ideal for this process.

You'll also want to clean up the yard — getting rid of paper or plastic wrap that has drifted around. You don't have to bend to use the cleanup tools found here.

28

Clean-Up Caddy, MODEL 3400, RINGER, $13.00–15.00 **(28)**

Wire frame about 2½ feet wide, flat at the bottom and rounded up to the handle, which is about 2 feet above the ground and supports a bright yellow coated woven bag about 3 feet deep.

This tool will carry small weeds, grass clippings, trash swept from the patio and driveway, and small prunings. When the caddy is placed level with the ground, you can easily use a rake or gloved hands to sweep the trash into the large opening without any lifting. It will take two hands to carry the caddy when it has been filled with trash, but only one hand will be needed to carry lightweight loads. If you are careful not to puncture the bag, it should last for several seasons.

Leaf Carrier, "MCGUIRE'S BURLAP TOTE," MODEL 66, GEO. W. MCGUIRE, $5.70–6.50 **(27)**

Square sheet of burlap (about 9 threads to the inch) measuring 6 × 6 feet, and having 4 large, yellow loops at the corners.

Here's a simple way to pick up leaves and other lawn debris. Rake them onto this burlap sheet, pull the corners together, and sling it over your shoulder. In some cases, you may want to drag it, but be wary of rough ground, which could tear it. Be sure it is clean and dry before folding for storage. Another model (88) measuring 8 feet per side is also available.

27

29

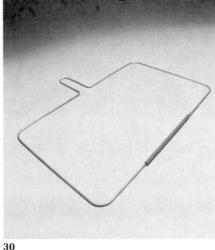

30

Clean Up Caddy,
A. M. LEONARD, $8.00–9.00 (32)

Aluminum tubing, 34 inches long, plastic hand grips, 1 pound.

This lightweight, out-sized "tweezer" allows you to pick up debris without bending over, even bottles and cans. Brambles and other thorny brush can also be kept at arm's length.

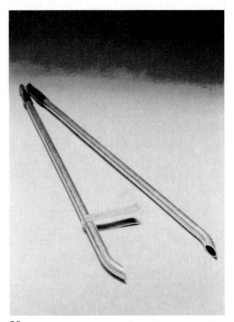

32

Hoop, "HANDY HOOP,"
DYNAMIC FORM SYSTEMS, $2.00–2.25 (29)

Plastic hoop, 19 inches in diameter; tubular yellow plastic insert with red plastic snap-on rim.

This tool will clip on the open end of plastic trash bags or canvas or burlap containers. With the hoop holding the bag open, it will be much easier to put leaves, grass clippings, small prunings, and light garden and household trash into the container. The hoop can also be used on plastic bags as a temporary protection to tender plants against frosty nights or hot sun immediately after plants have been set outdoors. Indoors, hang it in your tool shed with a bag attached to hold trash.

Yard Bagger, MODEL YB-100,
NORTHERN WIRE PRODUCTS,
$2.00–2.40 (30)

Heavy wire rectangular frame 23 inches wide, 14 inches deep, with a convenient handle 2 inches wide and 5 inches long. Ends of wire are joined with a green plastic sleeve.

This frame is designed to fit the opening of most large trash bags which can be filled very easily by sweeping or raking the trash or grass clippings, leaves, small prunings, plant waste; it's also useful for picnic or cookout cleanup. It can also be fastened to a

wall to hold the bag open for ordinary trash collecting. When the bagger is not in use, it will hang in any one of several positions flat against a wall.

Yard Arm Weeder, MODEL LG,
HALL INDUSTRIES, $3.60–4.00 (31)

36-inch wood handle with 2½-inch double spike tip with barbed points.

This is a multipurpose tool used easily with one hand to stick, twist, and pull out most weeds from the lawn or the garden. It may also be used to pick up twigs, paper, and other trash. There is a small hanging hole near the sharp points so the tool may be hung safely away from people walking near it.

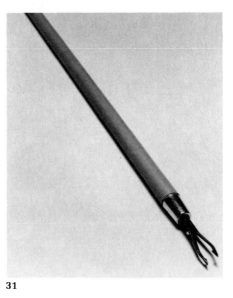

31

Manure Fork, MODEL 054,
TRUE TEMPER, $16.00–18.00 **(33)**

*4-foot straight wooden handle with
10-inch-wide head and 5 12¼-inch-
long sharp pointed oval tines.*

This well-balanced long-handled tool
will find many uses other than cleaning or loading manure. Use it to pick
up sod, light brush, matted leaves, or
accumulated trash around the home
landscape. The handle is long enough
so there is good leverage, and the
loaded fork can be swung to throw its
load quite a distance.

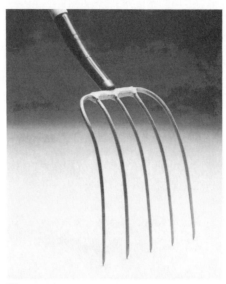

33

Shovel, MODEL A50A,
TRUE TEMPER, $6.30–7.00 **(34)**

*Aluminum shallow scoop shovel, 11½
inches wide and 13½ inches deep;
heavy metal blade is riveted to lightweight double tubular handle with a
"D" grip at the top; blade is enameled
bright red, handle reinforced with a
flat plastic support.*

This is a lightweight edition of the
shovel that I called a "scoop shovel"
for years. Its job is to pick up dirt,
trash, and other materials on a smooth
surface. It is not intended to be used
for digging in the soil and will only
be effective where piles of trash can
be picked up off level surfaces. I find
it invaluable for fall cleanup work.

34

SHARPENING STONES

My last gardening chore in the fall is to clean, oil, and sharpen my gardening tools and put them safely away for winter. Gardeners in more temperate zones should remember to select a tool-conditioning period as well. Here are a man-made sharpening stone and an Arkansas oilstone I like.

Sharpening Stone, MODEL 87745-7, NORTON, $2.70–3.00 **(35)**

Stone, 9½ inches long, ½ inch thick, tapering from 1⅜ inches wide in the center to about ¾ inch at each of the rounded ends.

This is a top-quality sharpening stone, large enough to hold in the hand and to use either on curved or flat surfaces in sharpening many tools. This stone is heavy enough to sharpen the cutting blade of turf edgers, hoes, mattocks, shovels, and spades, and small enough to do a good job of sharpening grass whip weed cutters, grass shears, and the larger type of pruning shears. It should always be used with either the type of oil furnished by the manufacturer or another type of household oil. The stone does not have a handle. Its color is dark gray, and it should have a shelf of its own where it will not be dropped on the floor or have large tools thrown on it carelessly.

Arkansas Oilstone, MODEL STC6, HIRAM A. SMITH WHETSTONE, $11.00–12.50 **(36)**

Natural oilstone, 6 × 2 × ½ inches, comes in cedar box.

There's no point in having good tools with fine blades if you don't keep them sharp. Soft Arkansas is a general-purpose whetstone, an excellent choice for a wide variety of garden tools. Hold the blade at a 20-degree angle and pull it toward you across the oiled stone 2 or 3 times, as though you are trying to carve thin slices off the stone. Repeat with the other side of the blade. The oil protects the natural stone and is good protection for your blades as well.

35

36

TOOL HANGERS

I think pegboard has done more to keep home workshops and garden tool sheds in order than any other invention. It's probably saved a lot of tools from abuse, rain, weather, and a shortened life, too. If your tool shed is built so you can easily attach pegboard to walls or the back of a door, by all means do so. Then use one of the many arrangements available for hanging tools on it. One of the hangers shown here is a multiple unit that can be used with pegboard. For others, a simple 1 × 2 can be nailed across rafters. As long as they're sturdy and tools aren't placed so someone is likely to come in contact with a sharp cutting edge accidentally, it doesn't matter that much what kind of hangers you use. The point is, you want some way to store your tools so they will be clean, protected from the weather, safe, and easy to find when you need them.

37

Tool Hanger, "GREEN THUMB,"
MODEL GHH-1P,
UNION FORK AND HOE, $2.75–3.00
(37)

Heavy metal rods, 2½ inches apart, bent at the rear for installation in standard ¼-inch pegboard; sheet metal mounting bracket with two screw holes and sockets for hanger.

You might have seen larger versions of this bracket supporting tools in stores. Each arm of this hanger has welded to it two metal balls to separate the two or three tools which may be hung on it. The hanger may be used on a pegboard, or the special bracket included may be attached to any flat surface you can get a screw into. This is especially handy where wall space is at a premium.

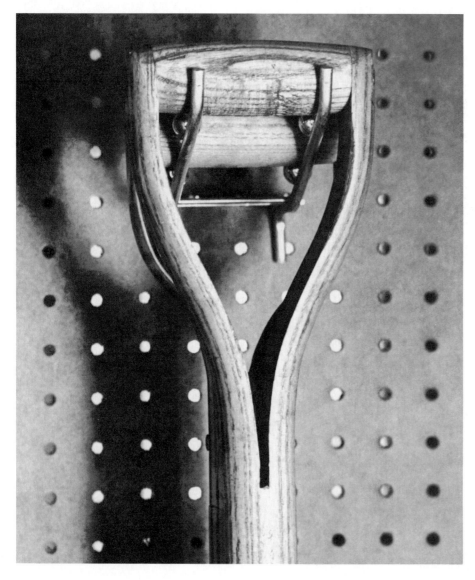

38

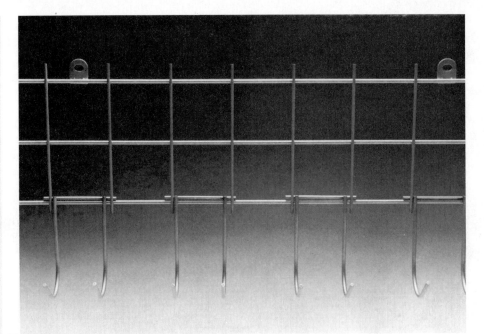

39

Tool Hanger, MODEL TH-600,
NORTHERN WIRE PRODUCTS,
$3.00–3.50 (for 3)   **(38)**

*Galvanized sheet metal pressed to
form a pocket between 2 forward-
jutting arms 2½ inches long with a
space of 1½ inches between them;
hooks hang over a horizontal 1 × 2,
or other width lumber with a finished
size ¾ inch thick; the 1 × 2 can
be nailed across exposed studs, or
⅛-inch spacers can be used to set it
out from a dry wall or other flat surface.*

These hooks are strong and large so
they will hold all but the very heaviest of garden tools. Since they hang
on the mounting board, you can move
them to different positions to adjust to
varying tool needs.

Garden Tool Rack,
CATALOG NO. 6-102EN01477-5,
IMPORTED BY GOOD-PROD SALES,
$8.00–9.00   **(39)**

*28 inches long, 6½ inches high,
welded wire mesh of 2½-inch squares;
2 tabs for hanging on nails or screws;
7 wire hooks that can be used on any
one of the 3 horizontal framework
wires.*

This lightweight rack can hold many
light and medium-weight tools. Rakes,
shovels, shears, and many of the other
awkward-to-store tools can be kept
safely on the wall and away from the
floor or other places where they could
be bent or broken or cause accidents.
This is very practical for many tools
found in garages and garden sheds.

INDOOR AND GREENHOUSE GARDENING

What I enjoy most about indoor gardening is, in a word, control. Indoors we handle essentials such as soil, heat, water, humidity, and light on our own terms. Capillary watering systems, artificial lighting, plant-hanging accessories, and small tools to make gardening more enjoyable all relate in some way to control of the indoor gardening environment.

Several tools you use outside are equally helpful indoors. Soil testing can be done with the same soil test kit used outside. Some of my favorite watering cans are just as useful indoors as outside. Some aerosol sprays and insecticides used outdoors can also be used indoors, but be absolutely sure that they're safe to use inside — and remember that you're dealing with a closed environment. There's no wind to blow away excess spray or fumes.

Elaborate greenhouses aren't necessary for growing plants indoors, nor are artificial-light gardens, but they both can make the hobby much more enjoyable (see the special feature on selecting a greenhouse). If you're contemplating building a new home, consider including a greenhouse, or one of the attractive window greenhouse units available from several manufacturers. Also, give a little thought to the width of your windowsills. The narrow sills of today's windows may be attractive, but they're frustrating to the gardener. Sills 4 to 6 inches wide are much better for holding houseplants and present no problem to a contractor.

Light gardens deserve some forethought, especially if you design a very large one. A few artificial lights won't strain the electric circuits, but if you want to install a full-scale garden, it's best to confer with an electrician. Separate lines may be needed.

It's easy to become so fascinated with the mechanics and horticulture of growing plants that we forget their decorative effects. While I appreciate nice, neat benches filled with healthy plants, I think the key to making your plants a joy to everyone is to find a way to make them appear to be a natural part of the indoor environment.

You can get started in indoor gardening with a very small investment in plants, tools, and accessories. From there, let your interest be your guide. But don't let initial enthusiasm run away with you. A few well-grown, effectively displayed indoor plants are always nicer than a large collection of straggly, tired, diseased plants.

POTS

You can grow a plant in just about anything, so long as you know the properties of the container and the needs of the plant. But most of us, most of the time, will be using two basic types of containers — clay and plastic.

For most plants I prefer plastic. Plants in plastic pots have to be watered about one-third as frequently as those in clay pots. Less-frequent watering means that less fertilizer is washed through the soil and lost, so less fertilizer is needed. Plastic pots tend to be easier to clean, and you don't have to soak new ones overnight before using.

All these advantages result from the basic difference between clay and plastic. Clay is porous. Water and air seep in and out through the sides and bottom. Plastic is impermeable, so the water remains inside the pot.

This doesn't mean clay pots are useless. With cacti, orchids, and other plants that prefer a fast-draining soil, clay is a boon. There's one other useful characteristic of clay: it's heavier than plastic. Try putting a tall, night-blooming cereus cactus in a plastic pot, and it's likely to end up on the floor. The extra weight of clay keeps tall plants from tipping over. This extra weight does become a disadvantage, however, with hanging containers. Here a light weight is usually desired, which means plastic.

Cleaning pots is simple and absolutely critical if you want to keep a healthy plant collection. The method I prefer is to scrub them clean, then soak them in a solution of 1 part household bleach to 10 parts water for 10 minutes. This should kill off harmful organisms that may still remain in the pot after a simple washing. Clay pots may be more stubborn to get clean, but in most cases they'll surrender to a large dose of elbow grease.

The clay pot's porousness deserves a little more attention. If you buy a new clay pot, soak it in a pail of water overnight before using it. The same is true for a clay pot that has been unused for a long time. Otherwise, it will steal water from the soil around the roots of the plant. Second, be wary of clay saucers. Water will seep through them, so they can't be used to protect windowsills or other surfaces from moisture. (If, for decorative reasons, you want to use a clay saucer this way, shellac the inside of it thoroughly, then test it before using to make sure it really is watertight.) Finally, while there are some attractive clay containers for outdoor use on patio and porch, I stay clear of them. The added drying power of the sun and wind makes it far easier to grow plants outdoors in plastic or other less-porous containers. With clay, you'll have to water twice a day in some cases.

Pot sizes sometimes confuse people. While there are many variations, the standards are simple. Pots are described by the diameter of the top. With the standard pot, this closely matches

Some of the many varieties of pots available.

the height. The "azalea pot," which is also used by many growers for African violets and similar plants, is about three-quarters as high as its diameter. The "bulb pan" is about half as high as its diameter. These shallow pans are excellent for forcing bulbs and are also useful for seed starting.

Glazed pots are attractive and are fine so long as you treat the plants just as if they're growing in plastic, for the glazing makes the sides impervious to water.

You can grow plants in containers without any drainage holes. Use plenty of pebbles, old crockery, or other drainage at the bottom, however, and be very careful about watering. A little activated charcoal added to the soil will also help sweeten it.

Wooden containers make particularly attractive outdoor planters. You'll find that the plants grown in them need more water than those grown in plastic, however. Obviously such containers have to be highly rot resistant. Some growers get around this by using the wood container as a jardiniere, putting a plastic pot inside it. Others line the wood with plastic, fiberglass, or galvanized steel. If not protected in this way, containers should be made of cypress, redwood, or some similarly long-lasting wood. Don't overlook pressure-treated lumber for window boxes and other plant containers you build yourself. As long as the chemical used to treat it is a water-borne salt, such as chromated copper arsenate, there won't be any harm to the plants. (Creosote and similar oil-borne treatments do give off fumes that are toxic to plants, so stay away from them for garden applications.) Pressure-treated lumber has a protective chemical forced all through it, so this is far more effective than applying similar chemicals by brush or soaking. You can paint it, just as you would other lumber, and it should last for decades. There are different degrees of pressure treatment: one for exposure to air; one for material that will be in contact with the ground; and one for material to be immersed constantly in water, such as the pilings of a dock. For plant containers, get lumber treated for "in-ground" use.

Choosing pot color and decorative containers is an art form in itself. I follow a few basic rules, the primary one being that the pot shouldn't overshadow the plant. I do find that pots with a floral design look best with a foliage plant and that plain white or green pots look well with almost anything. (Don't be alarmed, incidentally, by the bright orange color of new clay pots. They'll mellow with time to a subdued old brick or dull orange color.) There are now several clear pots on the market, and it's interesting to be able to see the root growth in the plants, but be careful when you use them. There is some research that indicates plants don't do as well in a clear pot because of the growth of algae in the soil, which is stimulated by bright sunlight. So I use such pots only with plants grown in subdued light.

PLANT HANGERS, HOOKS, AND WINDOW EXTENDERS

Plants tend to land around windows, especially south windows, like moths around a porch light in June. And why not? Every plant needs light and most want more light than we can provide easily — particularly in winter.

Window space quickly becomes at a premium, and with the narrow sills in many modern homes, it can be very restricted space indeed. The problem has challenged gardeners and designers alike, and some of the new solutions are both attractive and useful.

In looking at fixtures, I always consider usefulness, strength, ease of installation, and the ability to fit in with different decors. Will a device hold plants of several different sizes? Is it strong enough to hold the plants under consideration? Can it be installed with common small tools? (Anything here can be installed with a screwdriver and drill.) Will it permanently mar window, wall, or ceiling surface, or just leave a small scar that could be repaired by the average handyman? Is it subtle, blending in with the decor? You don't want a hanger that's so fancy it actually overshadows the plant.

If brackets are going to break, it would most likely be at a joint. Inexpensive ones which are held together with rivets are not as strong as solid weld styles (which are also more attractive). Brackets that swivel or adjust in other ways obviously offer more flexibility, but they usually cost more. They're handy for mounting alongside a window, since they allow you then to swing the plant closer to the light. Finish on metal brackets can vary tremendously, even on those by the same manufacturer. Many brackets are now packaged in clear plastic, which, because of light reflections and air bubbles, makes it difficult to recognize a really good finish. It can also hide flaws such as rough areas, scratches, and excess accumulations of the finishing material. Make a thorough inspection of the product in the packet. Many times these rough spots will be out of sight when the bracket is in place and no harm is done, but it would be a shame to pay between $5 and $10 for a bracket, only to get it home and notice it is poorly finished.

Try to find out the maximum weight a bracket, hook, or shelf is designed to hold, then make sure you're within that weight limit. There's no simple guide to plant weight. While it is the rare hanging plant that exceeds 12 pounds, the weight will vary with container, hanger, soil type, size, and moisture content. The best guide is to weigh your plants with the soil freshly watered. I've had a range of weights from 2½ ounces for a seedling in a peat pellet to 8.4 pounds for a spider plant in an 8-inch clay pot with saucer. To keep hanging plants on the light side, use one of the new "soilless" mixes and plastic pots. This combination can cut the weight by more than half.

Finally, keep in mind that any holder is only as strong as its weakest link — which may not be the holder itself, but the surface to which it's attached. Whenever possible, put screws directly into wall studs. Studs are nearly always located on 16-inch centers and can sometimes be found by tapping the wall and listening for the point at which the hollow sound disappears. (You can also buy a stud locater at most hardware stores.) If you're screwing into plaster or plasterboard, especially with a ceiling hook, use an expanding toggle bolt.

The products below can be used to hang or hold anything within their weight limits. Link some of these hangers with imaginative use of artificial lights, and some very attractive effects can be achieved anywhere in the home.

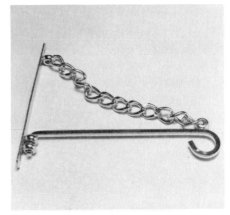

3

All are steel, but they come in several finishes, including brass, antique brass, white, gunmetal, chrome, and pewter. The brackets are sturdily made with welded joints, and are designed to hold up to 15 pounds.

Bracket, "THE SUSPENDER," SOUHAN DESIGN, $4.00–4.50 **(4)**

Hexagonal wall bracket made of Lucite plastic, available in clear, chrome, red, yellow, green, and brown; rod is ⅝ inch in diameter and projects 11 inches from wall; holds up to 10 pounds.

With the exception of the chrome finish, all of these are transparent, giving attractive reflections of light. There are three different mounting holes drilled for each of the two 2¼-inch mounting screws supplied. This means the bracket can be mounted either to the left or right of a window so that it projects both away from the wall and toward the window. In the third position it projects straight out from the wall.

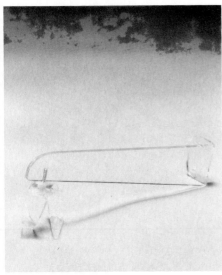

1

Bracket, MODEL 748, AKKO, $5.50–6.25 **(1)**

9-inch-long bracket of clear Lucite plastic, ¼ inch thick; holds up to 20. pounds.

This clear bracket will be unobtrusive and, if properly attached, sturdy. Two 1-inch wood screws are supplied for attaching to wall or window frame. The end of the bracket is an unusual double hook of the same material. It turns, so plants can be rotated for balanced growth.

Bracket, "NATURAL WOOD HANGER BRACKET," INTERDESIGN CRAFT, $3.50–4.00 **(2)**

Curved, laminated wood bracket, clear lacquer finish, ⅝ inch thick, extends 12 inches from wall; holds up to 50 pounds.

Here's a natural-looking bracket that is simple and strong. It is one-piece, laminated construction bent at a 90-degree angle in a graceful curve. It at-

2

taches to the wall with two screws and there's a notch almost ½ inch wide and ³/₁₆ inch deep at the top near the end to hold a hanger loop.

Swivel Bracket, MODEL HB-42G, COUNTRY PLANTER, BLACHER BROTHERS, $7.30–8.00 **(3)**

7¼-inch-high wall plate of flat, cold-rolled steel ¾ inch wide, with a 9-inch-long bracket arm of ¼-inch-square steel; brace portion is 9-inch chain; finished in chrome, gold, or gunmetal; holds up to 15 pounds.

The bracket arm sits in two large "eyes" and, when mounted on a wall or window frame, will swivel a full 180 degrees. This is strong enough and extends far enough from the wall to hold most large plants.

Note: Other Country Planter brackets range in cost from $.79 to $8.40.

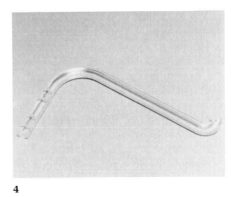

4

5

Plant Holder, BUZZA, $15.00−16.00
(5)

Shelves 30 inches long, 9 inches wide, height adjustable in 3-inch increments starting at a point about 27 inches from the sill, constructed of ½-inch, ¾-inch, and 1⅛-inch dowels; supports 25 pounds.

This is an unusual approach to the window shelf problem, designed by an architect who got tired of moving his plants every time he opened a window or pulled down a shade. The Buzza provides 2 shelves, with 2 screw eyes the only permanent connections needed. The 4-foot-tall unit leans into the room a maximum of 16 inches from the window casing. The dowels should be glued for permanent installation.

The height and distance between the two shelves is adjustable, as is the width. Although it's designed for a 30-inch window, the shelves could be assembled to work with a window several inches narrower. If you feel you're approaching the 25-pound limit of this unit, weigh each plant with wet soil. Since the shelves themselves are made of several ½-inch dowels, they won't block light to plants beneath them and plants may be hung from them as well as set on them.

These shelves come unfinished and unassembled. You'll probably want to stain or paint them to match your decor. Plan on spending about an hour assembling and installing.

Window Suction Hanger,
THE DESIGN FACTORY, $3.00−3.50
(6)

Clear plastic hanger 6½ inches long, 1 inch wide; suction disc is 1½ inches in diameter; holds up to 8 pounds.

This is a rugged (³/₁₆ inch thick) hanger with a different approach. The suction disc can be attached to a glass window, sliding glass doors, or other nonporous surfaces. The hanger portion can be attached or removed simply by pulling it from the suction disc, which remains in place. (A fingernail or knife underneath the edge will remove the suction disc quickly if desired.) Pots used with it must be

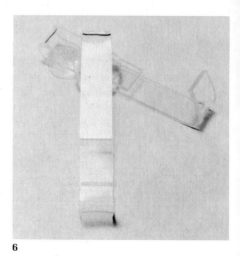

6

between 2½ inches and 4½ inches tall. The bottom of the pot rests on the bottom of the hook. A 4-inch portion of the hanger is bent down, similar to a paper clip or old-fashioned clothespin, and goes on the inside of the pot, extending into the soil.

7

Window Shelves, "HANGING WINDOW
GARDEN II," MODEL 627,
OPUS $12.00–13.00 **(7)**

*21-inch-long metal brackets with two
clear plastic plant trays; top tray measures 22 × 3¼ × ¾ inches, bottom
tray measures 22 × 5³/₁₆ × ³/₃₂ inches.*

Designed to hang from the top of the
lower half of a standard window, this
unit includes two metal brackets and
two clear plastic plant trays. The top
tray will hold up to 4-inch pots while
the bottom tray will hold up to 6-inch
pots. Both trays can be filled with
pebbles or coarse sand to increase the
humidity around plants.

The trays are attached by screws
that go through holes in the top of the
brackets, which hang over the window frame. There are 10 inches between trays. For many windows, the
bottom shelf will be so close to the
sill that it will be impossible to use
the sill for plants. However, if your
sill is too narrow to hold plants, or if
the window is tall enough so that the
bottom tray of this unit hangs well
above the sill, then this is a fine way
to get additional space for plants.

The metal is painted either white
or black and the design is simple and
sturdy.

8

Window Shelves, "EXTENDA-SILL,"
MODEL 626,
OPUS, $8.00–9.00 **(8)**

*2 metal brackets and clear 22 ×
5³/₃₆ × 1³/₃₂–inch plastic tray.*

Here's a simple way to get some additional plant space when your windowsills are too small. This unit includes a couple of metal brackets (in
white or black) which are attached by
two screws to the trim beneath a windowsill. The brackets hold a clear

plastic tray, deep enough to hold
some pebbles or coarse sand so your
plants can have additional humidity
around them.

I like this arrangement, not only
because it allows plants to grow near
windows with narrow sills, but because it extends into the room from
the window, which means there is
more space between the plant and
the window for full development of
foliage.

Plant Hanger, "THE HANG-UP,"
SOUHAN DESIGN, $2.00 **(9)**

*Clear plastic platform suspended on
monofilament fishing lines 24 inches
below a 1½-inch-diameter plastic
loop; platform is 2¼ inches square
and ⅛ inch thick; can hold up to 25
pounds.*

Plants seem to float in midair when
suspended by this clever, but simple,
device. The platform is large enough
to hold easily a 6-inch or bigger pot,
but with the 24-inch lines, a 4-inch
pot looks best. However, the "Hang-
up" comes in 36-inch or 48-inch
lines, a good length for larger plants.
A 1-inch-long clear plastic tube slides
over all four lines, pulling them together and thus making adjustable the
point at which the lines spread out to
embrace the pot.

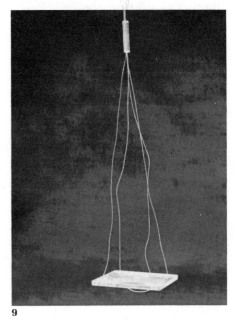

9

11

install as a stationary hook. Both a
1¼-inch wood screw and a 2-inch
toggle bolt are supplied, so it can be
fastened to wood or plaster ceilings.
The screw goes through a clear plastic
disc. The hook then slips over this
disc in a fashion that makes it secure
to any downward pull, but still allows
it to turn in a full circle.

10

Ceiling Hook, "HOOK-UP," SOUHAN
DESIGN, $3.00–3.50 **(10)**

*1¼-inch-long clear Lucite hook on a
1⅛-inch-diameter base of same material;
holds up to 25 pounds.*

A metal screw socket is molded into
the base of this hook and the package
includes a 1¼-inch threaded wood
screw, and a 2-inch toggle bolt. The
toggle bolt is for mounting in plaster
or plasterboard ceilings and requires a
½-inch-diameter hole, which will be
hidden by the fixture.

Ceiling Hook, MODEL LH2, HOLD-ALL
MANUFACTURING, $.80–1.00 **(11)**

*Rotating hook of clear Lucite; hook is
1½ inches long; base is 1¾ inches in
diameter; rotates 360 degrees; designed
to hold up to 50 pounds.*

The swivel feature of this hook means
plants can be turned regularly to receive
even lighting and thus grow in
a balanced fashion. It is as simple to

Plant Hanger, MODEL V731,
STANLEY HARDWARE, $4.00—4.50 **(12)**

3-foot-long, 1-inch-wide steel track with white enamel finish and clear plastic end caps; four 1½-inch-long white enamel metal hooks and sufficient hardware to install with wood screw or three 3-inch toggle bolts; holds up to 40 pounds total.

This track looks like the more familiar tracks used for curtains, but is sturdier and is designed to hold up to 10 pounds per hook. It could be used to hang plants inside the window frame portion of a window greenhouse, or perhaps from a ceiling as the upper portion of a room divider. Other possibilities include in front of windows, doors, or over the railing of a stairway. You might also try combining a pair of 40-watt fluorescent tubes at the same level as the rack, hidden from sight by wood trim. This way a pleasant divider could be created with plants growing well away from natural light.

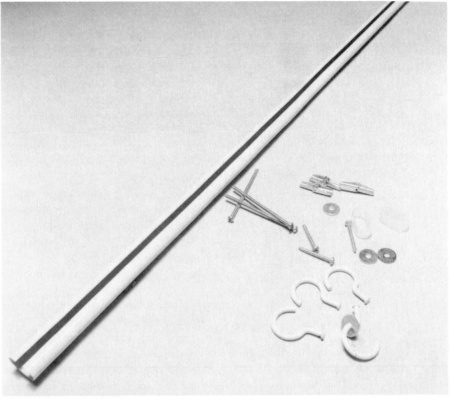
12

Plant Hanger, Wall Track System,
STANLEY HARDWARE, $12.00—13.00
(13)

Black-finished steel strip, 32 inches long and ½ inch wide is attached to the wall; on it are mounted 4 gracefully curved hooks of the same material and from these hang small plant hooks, 6 inches from the wall; holds up to 32 pounds total.

This is a flexible system, since the hooks can be slid along the mounting bar to any desired position and the small hook that actually holds the plant can swivel to give the plant a balanced light diet. The system can be mounted on a wall near a window, or in some other location where it can take advantage of either natural or artificial light. The hardware includes three 1¼-inch wood screws for mounting to the walls, as well as some black rubber pads, which can be placed behind the large, curved plant hooks to make sure they don't mar the wall. Each hook will hold up to 8 pounds.

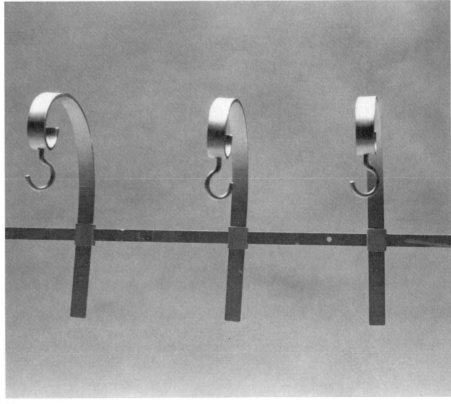
13

SOILS

Nongardeners look on soil as dirt, which it isn't. In fact, to many indoor gardeners, it isn't even soil, but a mixture of sterile substances that sound like they belong in a chemistry set rather than in a garden.

But, before exploring in detail those apparent contradictions, let's think about soil itself. Soil is a living substance, filled with healthy, active, useful bacteria with a natural mixture of ground stone and organic matter. The size of the stone particles and the amount of organic matter are what interest the indoor gardener.

Coarsely ground stone becomes pebbles. From there the continuum moves to sand, loam, silt, and clay. Clay is the finest. In this the particles are all very small and they pack together tightly. It is nearly impossible for anything to grow in such a medium. We need organic matter (decayed leaves, sawdust, peat moss, etc.) to lighten a clay soil or help a sandy soil hold water.

I look for a high organic content in my gardening soil, but it is a fortunate gardener indeed who can simply scoop up some soil from the outdoor garden and successfully grow houseplants in it. In most instances, even good soil from the outdoor garden will soon become nearly as hard as concrete when it is subjected to repeated watering in the confines of a pot or greenhouse bench.

This doesn't mean you have to forgo using the outdoor garden soil indoors, but that you have to add organic matter to it. There are several ways of achieving this, but I like the formula developed in 1939 at John Innes Horticultural Institute in England. It calls for 7 parts loam, 3 parts peat moss, and 2 parts sand. (Perlite can be substituted for the sand.) Different nutrients can be added, but the crucial point is the good soil structure achieved with the mixture of loam, peat moss, and sand.

Mix your own potting soil by this formula and it will be suitable for houseplant culture or greenhouse benches. Pasteurization (sterilization) isn't absolutely necessary. The major advantage of pasteurization is in seed starting, where a sterile medium avoids damping-off fungus, which kills many seedlings in their first few days. If you do want to sterilize soil, it can be done by baking in a 180-degree oven for 30 minutes, or over a charcoal grill at the same temperature for 30 minutes. (If done indoors, prepare for a strong odor!) There are also chemical means of pasteurization, and of course, if you wish to be sure, you can buy commercial potting soil that is already sterilized.

If you have relatively few houseplants, these commercial mixes are the easiest route. Although some are made for specific plants, one formula will do for just about everything except orchids and cactuses. (Some people grow orchids in pebbles. Although this works, I prefer fir bark or ozmunda fiber.) There are many good varieties of commercial potting soil, and in

*many regions local greenhouses bag their own. Such local prod-
ucts will be fine and are likely to be less expensive simply because there's little transportation involved. Whatever you buy,
get the largest bag possible — you'll pay a premium for small
bags.*

*What about soilless mixes? I think these can work well, espe-
cially for seedlings. Keep in mind, however, that they usually
contain few nutrients and so they'll need fertilizing right from
the start. These mixes are light, fluffy, and well-balanced for
providing both good aeration and water retention. You can buy
them packaged, or make your own from individual ingredients.
The key ingredients are sphagnum peat moss, vermiculite, and
perlite.*

*Sphagnum peat moss comes from a family of bog plants by
that name (sphagnum) and is found in Canada and several European countries. Michigan peat is finer, darker, and has different origins. It isn't quite as useful for our purposes. While virtually sterile and devoid of nutrients, sphagnum peat is an
organic substance that can absorb between five and fifteen
times its weight in water. Its fibers are not only spongy, but
longer than most soil particles, and thus help resist compacting.*

*Vermiculite is simply natural mica that has been heated to
about 2,000 degrees. At this temperature it puffs up like pop-
corn. The result is a fanlike particle with many empty spaces
that can hold water, nutrients, and air. It is approximately 30
percent magnesium and 6 percent potassium, both of which are
used by plants.*

*Perlite is a natural volcanic ash. The small white particles,
like sand, are good for adding drainage to a mix and are sterile. It is not a substitute for vermiculite. While it is a slightly
better drainage agent, it can hold nutrients only when they are
dissolved in water. I've found vermiculite alone a handy medium for starting cuttings, and when used with a top dressing of
finely milled sphagnum peat moss, it is good for starting seeds.
(For fine seeds, fill a pot nearly full of a good, pasteurized
houseplant formula, then add about ½ inch of milled peat to the
surface.)*

*You'll find soilless mixes easiest to work with if they've been
moistened first according to directions on the bag. In fact, many
commercial growers wet them moderately 24 hours before they
are to be used, then wet them again when planting the seeds.
The trick to wetting sphagnum peat moss is to use very warm
water — it will be absorbed much faster.*

*The other planting medium you'll find handy is unmilled
sphagnum moss. Its long fibers are spongelike, and excellent for
retaining moisture. It can be used to fill in the spaces in some
wood or wire-mesh containers; to wrap around the cut in an
air-layering, where it provides a moist medium for the new
roots; or to keep a graft in the outdoor garden moist. In these
last two cases, the moss is sealed in a piece of thin plastic.*

ELECTRIC SOIL STERILIZERS

Electric Soil Sterilizer, MODEL SS-5, PRO-GROW SUPPLY, $130.00–145.00 **(14)**

500-watt, 120-volt electric soil sterilizer with 1-cubic-foot capacity; heavy gauge, aluminized steel; sides and top are insulated and 1 inch thick; outside dimensions are 15¼ × 14¼ × 13¼ inches; thermostat control with settings in 10-degree increments from 140 to 200 degrees Fahrenheit.

If there's one quick way for a gardener to offend the other members of the household, it's by attempting to sterilize soil indoors. The odor is extremely strong. If you use this sterilizer indoors, it won't solve that problem, but the advantage of this unit is it's portable. It will go anywhere there's a three-prong power outlet. (Any extension cord must be heavy enough for the 4½ amperes this draws.) There's no bottom to this unit.

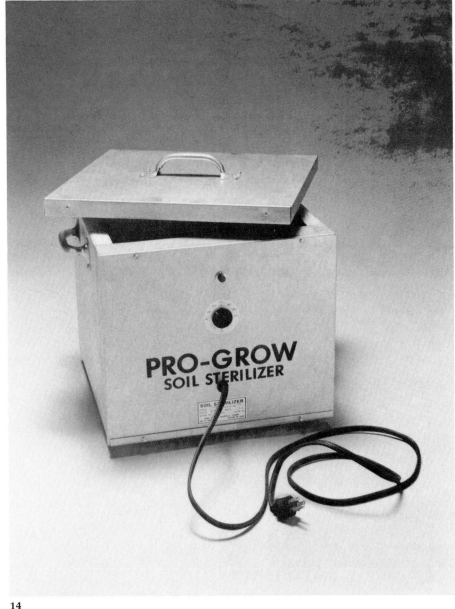

Set it on a greenhouse bench, load it up with soil, and turn it on. A red pilot light goes off when the temperature on the thermostat is reached. Do not let the soil cool too much in the sterilizer. After the thermostat lights goes out, wait a few minutes, then remove the top. When soil has cooled enough so it can be touched without discomfort, grasp the handles on both sides of the unit and lift it up. The soil should slide out the bottom. It can then be bagged for later use. In good weather the operation may be done outside, in the garage, or at any other convenient location. The 1-cubic-foot capacity is small, but it's enough for most hobby greenhouse and home operations. When I last used the unit, I took soil from a compost heap that was barely unfrozen. Its temperature was 36 degrees. The "Pro-Grow" cooked it up to 180 degrees, enough to kill most soil-borne diseases and weed seeds, in about 1½ hours. Time should be shorter if you start with soil at room temperature, or if the air around the sterilizer is already warm.

The manufacturer also suggests that you start with a setting of 160 degrees. The actual soil temperature reached should be higher than this, since it will keep heating for a while after the thermostat shuts it down. Use soil that is slightly moist, yet dry enough to work. (You should be able to make a ball of it without leaving mud on your hands.) Too dry soil takes longer to sterilize. Soil that is too moist sticks to the sterilizer and is difficult to get out.

This is certainly not for everyone, but for the greenhouse owner with benches to fill, it is worthwhile.

SMALL TOOLS AND OTHER ACCESSORIES

There are really very few tools needed for indoor gardening, but they do become helpful in special areas such as terrarium gardening and bonsai. Look closely at the tools mentioned here. In some cases, you'll find they're also useful for other gardening tasks. The rules for choosing indoor tools are simple. Look for tools with small working portions but large handles. That way they'll be the right size for houseplant culture *and* your hands. Aside from that, use the same guidelines given elsewhere in this book for larger tools designed to do similar tasks outside.

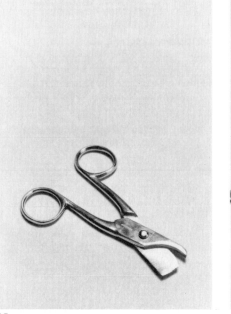

15

Flat-end Scissors, MANUFACTURED FOR BROOKSTONE, CATALOG NO. E.2040, $5.65–6.25 (plus postage) **(15)**

Stainless steel scissors, 4 inches long, with flat-end blades and ¾-inch cutting head.

This lightweight tool can be dropped into any pocket without poking its way through the fabric, because the outer end is flat across, ½ inch wide. One blade is a hook and the other is thick, slightly convex, with fine serrations. The tool will cut plants, string, ties, fabric, and other small objects. The blades keep closed with tension, so the scissors can be stored among other small tools in the work basket or tray, without being dulled or sprung by their environment.

16

Scissors, "COMBI-SNIP SHEARS," MODEL 48, IMPORTED BY GOOD-PROD SALES, $9.95–10.95 **(16)**

Stainless steel; plastic-covered handles; 7½ inches long overall; safety catch.

These excellent German-made steel shears will cut wire, sheet metal, cardboard, fabric, and leather as well as woody plant stalks; it's a tool so versatile that it just may replace your favorite pocket knife. The shears are also available in a smaller size (Model 47).

17

House Plant Tool Set, IMPORTED FROM ENGLAND BY ALLEN SIMPSON MARKETING AND DESIGN, $5.00–6.00 **(17)**

Two-piece, 7-inch-long stainless steel small shovel and fork.

Unlike many other indoor gardening tools, these stainless steel implements are not simply copies of common outdoor tools. The tools are sturdily made with easy-to-grip handles. The houseplant set includes a small shovel and fork.

I know many gardeners who (often to the irritation of other family members) reach for a good kitchen knife, fork, or spoon when transplanting seedlings or when faced with a stubborn potted plant that they can't remove from its container. These sturdy tools will do those jobs and several others — loosening soil, cutting around the edges of a tight root ball, or delicately prying out a seedling for transplanting. Made in England, they should last a lifetime.

18

Magnifying Instrument,

"MAGNA-LITE," MODEL 100,
MANNING HOLOFF, $4.50–5.50 (18)

Black plastic, 4¾ × 1½ inches,
weighs 1½ ounces, uses 2 AAA pen-
light batteries, 4X unbreakable plastic
lens.

Through an ingenious design, a tiny
magnifying bulb projects a strong
beam of light at just the right angle
for you to look through a 4X lens and
see what's bugging your plants. Even
red spider mites are clearly visible.

Bonsai Trowel, MODEL 46L,

HAND-CRAFTED KANESHIN TOOLS
IMPORTED FROM JAPAN BY CRANE
PRODUCTS, $6.75–7.50 (19)

2-inch triangular trowel of copper on
4½-inch wood handle; also available
in a smaller size.

This is an unusual trowel that is
shaped rather like a flatiron. For bonsai, it is used to shape and tamp into
place the soil around the trees. The
copper eliminates soil clinging, a feature that is important to bonsai where
very small changes can ruin the appearance of a planting. You may also
find this tool helpful in some seed
starting and transplanting operations,
as well as for loosening the soil

19

around the edges of a pot when transplanting a mature plant.

Four-Piece Bonsai Tool Set,

MODEL 200,
IMPORTED FROM JAPAN BY CRANE
PRODUCTS, $73.50–80.00 (20)

Four hand-crafted steel bonsai tools:
 # 2 branch cutter, # 22 wire cutter,
 # 33 thinning shears, and # 27 pliers
in 5 × 9½–inch soft, folding case with
zipper. Tools are also available indi-
vidually from the importer.

These fine, hand-crafted Kaneshin
tools have comfortable, long handles
and cutting edges designed especially
for bonsai work. The branch cutters
are 8 inches long with a 1-inch cutting blade that leaves a concave cut.
This kind of cut will heal over
smoothly, leaving little or no visible
callus. The wire cutters are also 8
inches long with just ¼-inch cutting
blades. This design allows you to snip
a wire that is very close to a branch or
other surface. The leverage is so great
and the cutting surface so true that
there is no difficulty in snipping a
18 wire that is lying flat on a ta-
ble. The thinning shears are 7 inches
overall with a 2-inch blade. A spring
holds the blades 2¼ inches apart at
the tip, but it takes very little pressure

to squeeze them together. A leather
loop, attached to one handle, holds
them together when stored. The
blades are flat on the sides that go together and, when completely closed,
overlap one another. These are fine
small shears for a variety of indoor
trimming, as well as for pruning the
roots and foliage of bonsai. The pliers
are 7 inches long with about a ⅝-
inch-long gripping surface. This surface has a waffle pattern to make it
easier to grip wire. It is about ⅜ inch
wide and comes to a rounded tip.

The manufacturer recommends the
tools be cleaned and wiped with a
light oil after use. To sharpen the
blade, they recommend using the Kaneshin stone rather than a grinder or
other substitute. These are the kind of
precision tools that are built with care
to last a lifetime. As such, they are a
complement to the spirit of bonsai.

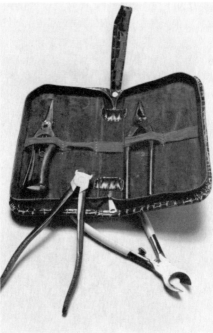

20

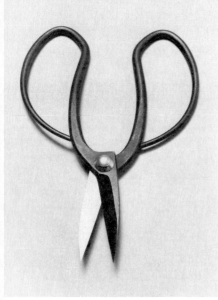

21

Scissors, MODEL 118,
IMPORTED FROM JAPAN BY CRANE
PRODUCTS, $17.50–19.00 **(21)**

Handles 4½ inches long, with more
than 1 inch of space to slip fingers
through; light gray finish; 2¼-inch-
long blades.

Although these hand-crafted Kaneshin
Koryu-style scissors are sold for bonsai use, they are really good for trimming any indoor plant, or for cutting
outdoor flowers for decorating. Even a
gloved hand can fit through the over-
sized handle to get a firm, comfortable
grip. Clean and wipe with a light oil
after use. (You can keep a soft, lightly
oiled cloth on hand for this.) The scissors may become loose after much
use, but can be tightened by hammer-
ing the rivets on both sides.

Terrarium Tools, MODEL 3057-1,
MADE IN JAPAN FOR GREEN GARDE,
$17.00–18.00 **(22)**

4-inch wood handles top these 4 dif-
ferent 13-inch tools for use in bottle
gardens and other hard-to-reach con-
tainers; metal parts are stainless steel.

The tools include a tiny 1-inch-wide
shovel for planting, a 1-inch-wide, 4-
prong cultivator for loosening hard
soils or moving plants and accessories, a 1-inch-wide pair of tongs and
¾-inch-long pruning scissors. The
tongs and scissors are worked by pulling or pushing a large ring near the
end of the handle. These are well-
made tools, but they will need care
and lubrication for smooth work, because a sharp impact can jam the sliding rods of the movable tool heads.
For the bottle garden or the large and
congested terrarium, these tools will
make planting and maintenance easy.

22

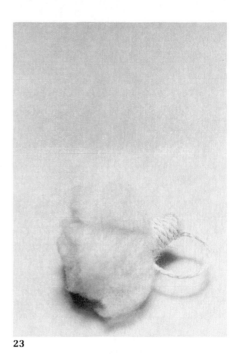

23

Leaf Cleaner, "THE DUST BUFF,"
NANCRAFT, $1.00–2.00 **(23)**

Fist-sized ball of lamb's wool tied at
the top with heavy cord, which is also
formed into a loop to make a small
handle, convenient for hanging.

Plants have to breathe and, in the
house, the greatest deterrent to this
can be the dust that gathers on leaves,
closing the tiny pores. The "Dust
Buff" is one solution to that problem.
It's gentle, picks up dust well, and
once it gets soiled, it can be rinsed
and left to air dry. (Of course, it's also
nice to give your plants a bath once in
a while under the kitchen faucet or
bathroom shower.)

Plant Support, "THE PLANT SCULPT,"
GREEN INK, $3.50–4.00 **(24)**

*24-inch green plastic stake with holes
drilled at selected locations on all
sides for feeding two 6-foot lengths of
⅛-inch flexible plastic tubing through
in unusual designs.*

Volunteers at the Krohn Conservatory
in Cincinnati originally designed this
vine support system as an educational
feature. The unit was so popular that
it's now sold to raise money for the
conservatory. Here's how it works: a
stake goes into the soil in the pot. The
thin tubes are then threaded through
it in whatever patterns your imagination can devise. Plants such as ivies,
wandering jews, philodendrons, and
others will climb the supports and
can be trained into the pattern set by
the stakes. Also available in clear
plastic.

25

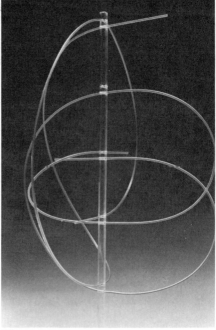

24

Window Plant Unit, "NATURE BUBBLE,"
FEATHER HILL INDUSTRIES,
$60.00–66.00 **(25)**

*One-piece cast clear Plexiglas, ⅛ inch
thick to mount outside a conventional
window; outside dimensions are 27½
inches wide, 17½ inches high and 16
inches deep; with filler panels,
screws, and foam self-stick weather-
stripping along with a black plastic
base tray, 25 × 14½ × 3 inches.*

The lower sash of many windows can
be opened in full or part to permit
this one-piece "mini-greenhouse" to
be screwed in place, projecting out
from the house. Insulation has been
supplied for the edge of the bubble
and for the space between the raised
lower sash and the upper sash of the
window.

The bubble becomes part of its
room, using heat from the room at
night, and from the sun during the
day. Directions are given for filling
the tray with soil for planting directly.
Most indoor gardeners will prefer to
spread gravel or stones on the tray
and to set pots or flats of plants in
place. The design of this unit is pleasing, its planning makes it practical,
and it can be used for a variety of indoor plants up to 14 inches tall, as
well as starting seedlings. As with
any greenhouse, a southern exposure
is preferred, with east, west, and
north following in that order.

INDOOR WATERING AND MISTING

Getting water to dozens of plants scattered all over a house or greenhouse can be a problem. In the greenhouse, I prefer to see a faucet installed and a full-sized garden hose as standard equipment. In the house, this isn't practical.

I've looked at dozens of indoor hoses through the years. There are several on the market, but most develop problems at one end or the other. Some worked at first, but after repeated connections and disconnections to a faucet, they leaked, or the threads on the connector became stripped or corroded. Others developed leaks at the nozzle end. I suspect the basic problem lies in going from a ½-inch or ¾-inch pipe in the house to a ¼-inch hose. This is bound to put pressure on the connection to the small hose. If you find one of these that really works over a period of time, that's fine. There's no doubt that it is more convenient than making several trips back and forth to the sink. For now, however, I'll stick with the watering can.

Here's what I look for in a watering can:

1. Enough capacity (say, 2 quarts) to keep the trips back and forth to the sink at a minimum. However, it must be shaped in such a fashion that it will still slide under the kitchen or bathroom faucet.

2. Good balance so that when it's full of water I can comfortably hold it and control a stream of water directed to the pot of an overhead plant (Some of the squat, longer cans I've seen are difficult to hold because they lack this balance.)

3. A long spout with a relatively small opening (about ¼ inch) so that it can be tucked underneath foliage and deliver a gentle stream of water to the soil without wetting leaves or disturbing the soil too much. Be wary of pots with spouts made in two pieces. Unless the connection between them is very well made, it's likely to leak and drip water onto furniture. The spout should end at a point 1 inch or more higher than the level of the water in the can. If it doesn't, water will spill out of the spout as you walk.

4. A design that allows you to walk around the house with a full can of water without its spilling as it sloshes about. The Haws cans are particularly good in this respect because of a tall, oval mouth. Other cans accomplish the same thing with more subtle design.

5. A rose, which attaches to the end of a spout and breaks up a single coarse stream into many small gentle ones, is a useful accessory, especially for watering seedlings. It should be designed to accept water evenly and distribute it in a series of fine streams of roughly equal intensity.

26

Watering Can, MODEL 2637Y, VITRI PRODUCTS, $2.60–3.00 **(26)**

Yellow (or green) plastic can, about 6 inches in diameter at base and about 9½ inches high (to highest point on handle); spout is 11 inches long; about 2½-quart capacity.

This is a simple, inexpensive can of attractive and functional design. The front of the can is about ¾ inch higher than the rear, which, combined with an overhanging lip, prevents water from spilling as the can is carried. The end of the spout is about 2 inches above the water level in the can, so there's no problem of spilling there, either. The mouth of the can at the highest point is about 7 inches, so it should slide nicely under most faucets for easy filling.

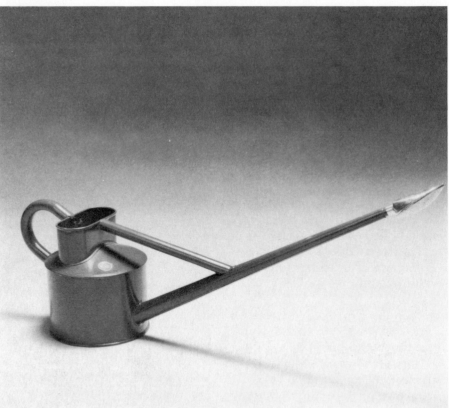

27

*Clear plastic saucer, 3 inches in di-
ameter and ¼ inch deep with 1¼-inch
tube, 3 inches deep.*

Here's an unusual item that really
works if you have this particular
problem. It's designed to catch the excess water that goes through the center drainage hole in the bottom of a
hanging planter that has no saucer. If
your planter has a built-in saucer, or
you've already placed one under it,
there's no need for this. But if you
have no saucer, or if for reasons of
weight or aesthetics you don't wish to
add one, this will do the job for you.
It simply slips under the plant and
catches the excess water. You can
leave it in place permanently, or just
leave it for a few minutes after each
watering. If it's in place permanently,
you can empty the Drip Guard without removing it simply by pulling a
small plug at the bottom and letting
water drain back into the watering
can. With a sling-type hanger that

Watering Can, HAWS,
IMPORTED FROM ENGLAND BY WHITE
FLOWER FARM (OTHER HAWS STYLES
IMPORTED BY GOOD-PROD SALES),
$32.00–35.00 **(27)**

*1-gallon-capacity can made of steel
plate undercoated for rust protection
and deep red lacquer finish with 27-
inch spout and oval-shaped rose.*

Here's an excellent can, for greenhouse or outdoor use, that should last
a long time. Its wide mouth and low
profile made it easy to fill (it will even
slide under a kitchen faucet), yet the
design makes it difficult to spill water
accidentally. The brace that goes to
the spout also doubles as a convenient
carrying handle, while the large, comfortable handle at the back is used
when watering. The rose is of excellent design, giving dozens of very fine
streams of water. This rose is a bit
large for typical houseplant use, but

it's very good in the greenhouse,
where a little water spilled on
benches or floor just adds to the humidity. There are several other styles
of Haws cans, starting with one that
holds just 20 ounces.

Watering Can, THE ROUND WATERER,
SOUHAN DESIGN, $5.00–5.50 **(28)**

*2¼-quart watering can of either clear
or white plastic, 6½ inches tall, with
7-inch spout.*

The handle of this design is molded
into the rear with indentations in the
container to leave plenty of room for
your knuckles. The spout is about 1
inch higher at the tip than the water
level when filled nearly to the top.
The filling hole is just 1½ inches in
diameter, so even when filled nearly
to the rim of this hole, there's little
room for any to splash out. Well balanced, it's easy to use with just one
hand, even when tending overhead
plants.

28

This sprayer can be used to add humidity to the air around plants, or to spray insecticides that can be mixed in water. As with all pressure sprayers, the air pressure should be released (simply twist the top) when the tool is not in use, and it should never be left in the sun when pressurized. The manufacturer advises that it be rinsed clean with water after it's been used for pesticides; water also should run through the sprayer to clean the nozzle. Nearly all parts on this sprayer are plastic, and there are no directions for disassembling and replacing pump parts.

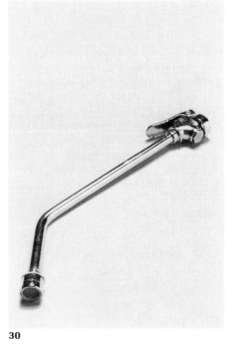

29

30

31

goes around a plant container, you install this by lifting the plant a little and slipping the drip guard between plant and sling. If you have a pot that's attached to the hanger by its rim, then you'll have to use the rubber bands and hooks supplied with Drip Guard.

Pot Waterer, FOGG-IT NOZZLE, $12.50–14.00 **(30)**

1-pound, 14-inch watering device with thumb lever shut-off valve and two interchangeable heads; attaches to standard garden hose; both spout and valve are chrome plated and valve has brass moving parts.

This handy device allows the greenhouse owner three choices for watering his plants. Without attaching either nozzle, it can be used to fill watering cans or pails. Attaching the bubble aerator dissipates water pressure for a splash-free stream, similar to what comes out of a kitchen faucet. Then, by placing the small nozzle on

the waterer, you'll get a superfine mist particularly good for orchids, seedlings, and delicate flowers. It's easy to reach inaccessible overhead plants with the long spout that comes in both 14-inch and 17-inch sizes. Come summer, you'll find many uses for it outside — such as watering your hanging baskets and container plants.

Sprayer, ''MIST-A-MATIC,'' MODEL IL, MANUFACTURED FOR E. C. GEIGER, $7.00–8.00 **(31)**

1-liter (about 1 quart) compressed-air sprayer, white, translucent plastic container with green plastic spray head.

The pistol-grip handle on this sprayer is simple and functional, making it easy to use with one hand. About 30 strokes of the pump will put enough pressure in it to empty a little over one-third of the contents in about 1½ minutes of steady spraying. The spray is turned on and off by depressing a trigger with your thumb. The spray can be made into a fine mist reaching just a few feet, or into a thin stream reaching about 20 feet, by twisting the nozzle.

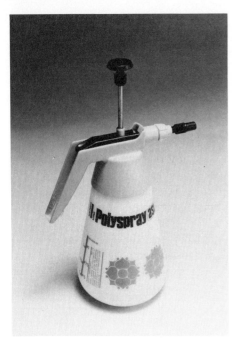

32

Sprayer, POLYSPRAY, MODEL ASL, IMPORTED FROM ENGLAND BY E. C. GEIGER, $16.00–18.00 **(32)**

1-quart compression sprayer of translucent plastic; sprayer head is orange and black plastic.

At first glance, this one looks like several less-expensive plastic sprayers, but some of the differences are important in the long run. For example, there are simple, detailed instructions with drawings that show how to take apart the sprayer for routine maintenance and cleaning, as well as for replacement of worn parts. There are also more small metal parts in this unit than in some of the less-expensive ones.

The spray is adjustable from a fine mist with a range of just a few feet, to a thin, steady stream with a range of more than 20 feet. The sprayer can be held in one hand and is triggered by depressing a black plastic lever with the thumb. Twisting the nozzle determines the type of spray. Another use for this sprayer is to knock red spiders and other pests from the leaves of houseplants. Just take your plants to a sink, put the sprayer on a medium to coarse setting, and thoroughly wash both sides of leaves.

Of course, the sprayer can also be used for applying pesticides in the greenhouse or the outdoor garden. The smooth plastic sides make it relatively easy to rinse clean. As with all compressed-air sprayers, you must be careful not to leave compressed air in it, especially if it is sitting in the sun or near some inside source of heat. Simply twist the top about half a turn and you'll hear the air escape.

Plant-Tray, MODEL 1020W, BEH HOUSEWARE, $7.00–7.50 **(33)**

⅛-inch-thick white plastic tray, 10 × 20 × 2⅛ inches, with ⅜-inch-high ribs on bottom.

The main feature of these sturdy trays is the ridges on the bottom. Potted plants can be set on these ridges, and water can be poured beneath them. Evaporation from the water, which need not touch the plant pots, provides added humidity around plants. Additional evaporative surface can be created by filling spaces between the ridges with perlite, vermiculite, coarse sand, or fine gravel.

The trays are deep enough to be used for growing seeds or cuttings of many plants if a layer of coarse drainage material is used in the bottom of the tray. Trays are available also in square and round models, as well as a 5-inch-wide unit suitable for windowsills.

Windowsill Plant Tray, MODEL 242, CARE FREE GARDEN PRODUCTS, $1.00–1.10 **(34)**

White plastic tray, 3½ × 22 inches.

This is a reasonably sturdy plastic tray that is also handy for starting seedlings. The bottom has a sort of waffle pattern to it, making it possible to leave about ¼ inch of water in the tray without soaking the plants. The tray can also be used to hold small plants, but for a permanent unit, I'd like something stronger and wider. As a seed starter, it will hold fifteen Jiffy-7 peat pellets. There's a clear version of this tray which some might find more attractive, but the price is almost double.

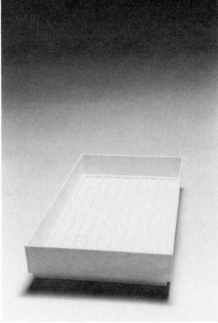

33

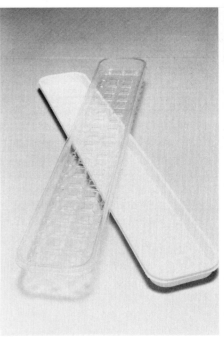

34

Window Tray, MODEL 620,
OPUS, $3.50–4.00 **(35)**

*Clear plastic tray, 22 × 3½ × ¾
inches.*

These trays will go with any decor
and can hold pots up to 4 inches. You
can put pebbles, marble chips, or similar material in the bottom of the tray,
then set plants on these. This way you
don't have to worry about water stain-
ing woodwork, and the added wet
surface means evaporation and in-
creased humidity.

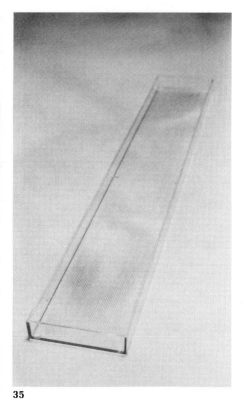

35

HUMIDITY

*Houseplants seem to thrive on company — particularly the
company of other plants.*

*That's why when gardeners start talking about too little
humidity, I first ask how many plants they have and whether
they're grouped together. Several plants on a windowsill will
usually do better than a single one because water is given off
from both the leaves and the soil, making the air more humid.*

*Even in a greenhouse loaded with plants, however, the
humidity can be lower than desirable, especially in winter
when heaters are on full blast, warming and drying the air.*

*There are several steps that can be taken to add moisture to
the air. In a house with old-fashioned radiators, a few pans of
water on top of the radiators can help. Grouping plants together
helps. Even more evaporative surface can be supplied when
saucers, or trays, filled with wet pebbles are placed beneath
plants. (Don't set the plants in water. Keep the level just below
the top of the pebbles.) I like some handy windowsill trays
designed just for this purpose.*

*Mist sprayers are also useful for adding moisture to the air.
Unfortunately, many people think these are intended for
wetting plant leaves. Sadly, they think they're treating their
plants well by faithful spraying each day, when in reality,
direct spraying may be creating conditions that increase the
chance of both sunburn and disease. Remember as a general
rule to mist the air around plants, not the plants themselves.
Such sprayers are difficult to use in the home where they can
damage furniture, but in a greenhouse or artificial-light garden
environment, they can help the dry air problem.*

*Since humidity is also desirable for people, there are several
small electric humidifiers on the market that also help a plant
room or small greenhouse. Vaporizers, such as people
frequently use in a bedroom, especially during the head-cold
season, can serve this purpose. Of the ones I've tried, the cool-
mist variety seems to work best for plants.*

*Humidity shouldn't be as difficult to maintain in a
greenhouse. First, the large group of plants helps. Second,
wetting down walks and other surfaces on a warm day creates
a large evaporative area. But if these methods are insufficient,
or if an automatic system is desirable, there are both
evaporative coolers and large humidifiers, adequate to handle
the typical home greenhouse, which cost in the $200 to $400
price range. Such specialized equipment is beyond the scope of
this book, but most greenhouse manufacturers can point their
customers toward equipment that would be suitable for the
small greenhouse.*

HUMIDITY INDICATORS

My friends in the north complain of too little humidity, especially in winter. Friends to the south complain of too much, particularly in summer. But whether your problem is too much or too little, it's good to know just what the relative humidity is at any instant; for that, it's hard to beat the simple, direct-reading hygrometer.

True, sling psychrometers are still a more reliable way to measure humidity very precisely. But they're more of a bother to use than they're worth. The instrument must be wetted, whirled about in the air, and then the readings checked against a table. I just don't feel the extra measure of accuracy this affords is necessary to the typical gardener.

Most dial-type hygrometers have a hair or spring mechanism and many of these can be damaged by freezing temperatures or by an accidental spraying with the greenhouse hose. The Lufft hygrometers included here can take freezing temperatures and won't be damaged if, by chance, the hose does play on them. (It is still advisable to mount them out of the way where they won't be subject to such accidents.) Incidentally, don't expect two hygrometers in the same room to read the same unless you've stacked one on top of the other — the relative humidity can vary significantly from one section of a room to another.

37

The comfort range of 40 to 75 percent relative humidity is indicated by the shaded portion of the dial. It can be calibrated by wrapping it in wet cloth for 30 minutes, then adjusting the calibrating screw on the back to indicate 95 percent.

Hygrometer, WET/DRY BULB HYGROMETER, IMPORTED FROM ENGLAND BY E. C. GEIGER, $20.00–22.00 **(38)**

Two tubular thermometers registering from 20 to 120 degrees Fahrenheit (Celsius scale also) set side by side in 2¾ × 8½-inch white plastic case; a 2-inch-deep plastic water reservoir screws into the bottom of case, and the wick extends from it to wrap around the bulb of the "wet" thermometer.

The basic idea of a wet/dry bulb thermometer is to determine relative humidity by noting the evaporation of moisture from a wet bulb thermome-

36

Hygrometer, LUFFT MODEL 4004, IMPORTED BY WATROUS, $38.00–40.00 **(36)**

3¾-inch-diameter, brass-cased instrument, with range of 20 to 100 percent.

The normal comfort range of 40 to 75 percent relative humidity is set off by a plain white band on the scale of the hygrometer. The unit can be calibrated by wrapping it in a moist strip of cloth covering all holes for 30 minutes, then adjusting the screw on the rear to read 95 percent. (The manufacturer advises calibrating twice a year.) A hole in the back allows for simple mounting to a wall by a single screw or nail.

Hygrometer, LUFFT MODEL 4041/1, IMPORTED BY WATROUS, $20.00–22.00 **(37)**

2⅜-inch diameter, black plastic case, 20 to 100 percent range on silver-colored dial.

Here's a handy, relatively inexpensive instrument designed to be suspended on a wall by a single nail or screw.

ter. The faster the evaporation, the greater the temperature difference between the two thermometers. (Evaporation cools the wet bulb thermometer.) Thus, in dry air there will be rapid evaporation and the temperature difference will be greatest. The larger the temperature difference, then, the lower the relative humidity. However, a numerical determination can only be arrived at by consulting a table. One comes with the instrument, of course, and should be kept nearby for convenient use. It's helpful to cut the table out, mount it on a piece of cardboard, then cover it with clear plastic to keep moisture and dirt from it. Then it can be hung or set next to the instrument. The basic difference between this and a sling psychrometer is that the sling psychrometer is whirled rapidly about to cause evaporation. This instrument isn't quite as precise, but your readings will be truer if you fan it vigorously for about 1 minute prior to reading the wet bulb temperature.

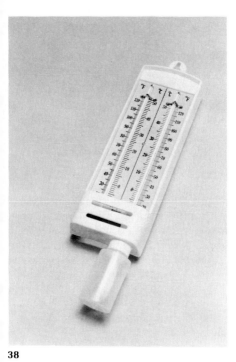

38

CAPILLARY WATERING

Gardening adds a note of constancy, of long-range consistency, that doesn't always mesh with our modern life-styles. I have a friend who loves to grow vegetables, and he likes to start his annual garden indoors under artificial lights. Unfortunately, his work calls him out of town for days at a time and this has led to some frustrating experiences with young seedlings which need regular attention to make sure they don't dry out. His frustration ended when he discovered capillary watering.

Capillary watering is no more mysterious than the action of a sponge. The beauty of it is that it can deliver just the right amount of water to plants. While not drying out, they won't get so much water that the roots will become oxygen-starved and rot.

Capillary watering is relatively new to America, but it has been used successfully for years in Europe, and there are now several items available, ranging from single pots to large systems designed to handle dozens of plants at one time.

Here's how it works: a large water reservoir is kept near the plants. Water is constantly fed in small amounts to either a wick or mat, which works like a sponge to soak up small supplies. The wick goes directly into the plant container, or the pots are set on the matting. In either case, the soil in the pot soaks up the continuous supply of water it needs. This can go on as long as there is water in the reservoir. How long it will last depends on the plants and other environmental conditions, but it should be several days (even a few weeks) before the plants need attention. At any rate, it will mean that care can be withheld for much longer than is normal. When you go on vacation, you won't have to ask someone to baby-sit for the plants. The most you'd have to request is that someone come in just once a week and fill a large water reservoir.

My only quarrel with these systems is that most have a utilitarian appearance. This isn't true of the single-plant containers, but it is of larger units. Still, they're very useful in a working light garden, home greenhouse, or other area with a concentration of plants, and there's no reason why you can't set them up just to get through a vacation period, moving all your plants onto the mats.

A few things to keep in mind:

1. Capillary watering works only with a well-aerated potting soil mixture. This means one that uses a mixture of soil, peat, perlite, vermiculite, and so on, as most mixtures do. The idea is to have uneven particles.

2. Plastic pots set on a capillary mat won't need any special attention, but clay or thick fiber pots will need wicks inserted.

3. When using wicking in pots, put about half the wick inside the pot, splaying the ends, and about half outside. Cover the inside part with a layer of fine soil and don't use any drainage.

4. If a capillary system is to be used over vacation, you'll have to set it up well beforehand to make sure you know how long it can go without needing additional water.

continued

An occasional brief drying-out period will be healthy for your plants. So will an occasional top-watering which will wash salts, gathered near the surface, back down into the soil.

The major difference in the systems now commonly available is in the use of a plastic cover over the matting. I think it's a toss-up as to which approach is best. Those with a plastic cover are not as likely to get algae growth in the matting, which requires cleaning with a solution of chlorine bleach and thorough rinsing. However, the added evaporation from the uncovered mat increases humidity around the plants, which is an advantage.

You can make your own capillary system using waterproof trays and a cheap blanket of a synthetic material.

Capillary Waterer, Water-Rite,
"MASTER SYSTEM," MERKLE INDUSTRIES,
$40.00–42.00 **(39)**

6-gallon polyethelene reservoir unit, 4 heavy-duty black plastic trays, 18 × 24 × 1 inches, constructed with raised sections to support mats and channels for water to flow in; 6 cloth "bridging" strips; 4 capillary mats, and 12 plant wicks.

This is a complete system for capillary watering sufficient to handle anything from 280 seedlings in 2-inch pots, to 48 plants in 5-inch pots. To use, fill the water reservoir and set it so the spigot extends into one of the trays. Wet the mats and set them on the raised portion of the trays. Two small capillary strips are used to bridge from one tray to another, keeping the water level constant in all trays.

This is a good system for baby-sitting plants when you're on vacation, or as a permanent watering device for

39

plants under artificial lights or in a greenhouse. One requirement: The trays must be placed on a level surface, or you'll have water where you don't want it. When I first set this up on a bench, I soon found I had water running on the floor (not desirable!); but a little time spent leveling the trays solved the problem and the water from the reservoir shut off automatically, as it should, when the trays were full. One feature I especially like is that this is a modular system. You can purchase smaller units to start with, or if you buy the master unit you can add on later.

Capillary Waterer, GROSFILLEX SELF-WATERING PLANTER, IMPORTED FROM FRANCE BY LONDON GARDEN ASSOCIATES,
$17.50–19.00 **(40)**

8.2 × 8.2–inch cube; overall height 9½ inches, with a planting depth of 6½ inches; 7¼ inches high; sits on 2-inch-thick round base, 7 inches in diameter.

This is one of a handsome line of fine self-watering pots and planters in several colors, sizes, and shapes. Included in the line are 17.7-inch square pots on casters, and rectangular, round, and bowl shapes. The smallest is a 4-inch octagonal pot.

But in this case, sizes and shapes mean little compared to what's inside. This is a well-engineered self-watering planter suitable for a tremendous variety of plants indoors, or on a patio, and built to last a long time. You plant directly in the pot, on top of a large wick and a plastic grating with slots in it. This grating allows air to reach the base of the root ball. The water reservoir is at the base of the container, beneath an air reservoir. Thus your plants are assured a continuous supply of both moisture and air. An added feature is a simple, float-type indicator visible near the top of the container that tells you when additional water is needed.

The water reservoir holds a supply sufficient for 3 to 5 weeks, depending on the plant and growing environment. Once dry, the container should be left empty for another 10 to 15 days. As with other capillary watering systems, a solution of fertilizer can be put into the reservoir. In short, a plant in one of these containers can go without watering for at least a month. Unlike the more utilitarian capillary watering systems, these planters, winners of the Beaute-Industrie design award, should fit comfortably in a variety of home decors.

40

PROPAGATING

The easy way to keep your plant collection growing is to start your own young plants from cuttings.

Different plants show varying levels of tolerance to this procedure. Some, such as Swedish ivy, root very easily if a stem is clipped off and dropped in a glass of water. For these, there are several special rooting containers that can be hung near a window. (Don't put them where they'll get direct sunlight, or it will be too much for the plants at this early stage.)

Other plants are more sensitive and need greater care. The main problem is that when you take a cutting, you eliminate the plant's source of moisture and food — the roots. The secret is to provide an environment in which the plant loses very little water and roots have a chance to form and grow. Look for a container that is watertight and that can be covered to keep humidity high, yet uncovered when humidity gets excessively high. (Too much condensation will fall on the leaves and may lead to various diseases.)

The devices I've included here can in some cases be used as seed starters or as containers for growing full-grown plants in water and nutrient solutions.

This is simple to use and as near as I can tell, foolproof. The only problem that might develop is a salt build-up on top of the soil, a problem that can occur any time extensive bottom-watering is used. The manufacturer says this hasn't happened in their trials. They do advise sparing use of fertilizer (every second or third time the water reservoir is filled) and suggest that if the top of the soil does turn white with salts, you should simply scrape off this top layer and replace it with fresh potting soil.

40

Plant Propagator, "ROOT SHOOTER,"
MODEL 121,
AKKO, $8.00–9.00 **(41)**

Clear plastic planter about 5 inches tall and wide in a convoluted pattern; 4 strands of clear nylon and clear plastic ring for hanging; can also sit flat on tables or shelves.

Some will be fascinated by the convoluted design of this planter, but the elaborate curves actually serve a purpose by effectively holding in place cuttings being rooted. This makes a good choice for that use, but the "Root Shooter" can also be filled with soil, stones, or water for planting, displaying cut flowers, or other decorative purposes. There's about 2½ inches of depth to hold drainage and rooting medium.

41

Plant Propagator, F. & R. FARRELL, $15.00–16.50 **(42)**

*Heavy, dark gray plastic tray 21 ×
15 × 4½ inches with 3 adjustable
metal bows that curve to 11 inches
above the top of the tray; tray is covered with clear plastic film (two
sheets supplied) secured around tray
with vinyl tape; plastic screen mesh
covers the more than 200 drainage
holes in the bottom.*

This is a sturdy, functional flat that
should last for years and be useful for
many tasks. The metal bows fold
down out of the way when not holding the plastic cover. You can place
individual pots in the tray, or fill it
with a planting medium. In either
case, it's very handy for germinating
seeds or rooting cuttings. The clear
plastic keeps the humidity high, but
it's no problem to lift a corner and let
in some fresh air. You can also use
this as a miniature cold frame for
hardening young plants before putting
them in the garden. Set it outside in
an area protected from high winds
and raise the cover a bit more each
day until the plants are accustomed to
outdoor growing conditions. You will
need a tray or piece of plastic underneath this if used in the home, since
the drainage holes do let water out.

42

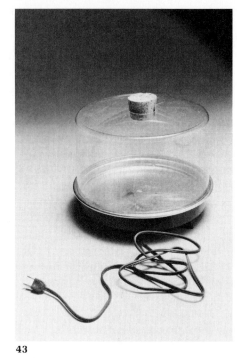

43

Plant Propagator, MODEL PP2000,
KAZ, $18.00–20.00 **(43)**

*Round metal base, 11 inches in diam-
eter, stands on 3 plastic legs about 1
inch high; base has heating element
and thermostat enclosed to provide a
constant temperature in the 70- to 75-
degree range; clear plastic cover, 6
inches high, with 2-inch-diameter
hole in the center sealed with a large
cork; also included are 12 2-inch
plastic pots and a strip of vinyl edging to increase effective depth of base
for direct planting.*

Here's a propagator that's simple to
use, practically foolproof, and the
right size for typical home use. The
gentle bottom heat provided by the
heating element is ideal for both seed
starting and rooting cuttings. The
plastic dome lets in plenty of light
while providing a good seal to keep a
humid atmosphere. If the atmosphere
becomes too humid, take out the cork.
If this isn't enough ventilation, remove the cover for a while, or prop it
open.

The inside of the propagator is
only about ¾ inch deep, but the vinyl
collar supplied brings this to 2 inches.
With the collar in place, fill the propagator with coarse sand, vermiculite,
or some other propagating medium,
and plant cuttings directly in the
propagator. Whether you use it for
seeds or cuttings, place the unit in
good light, but not direct sun. With
the cover in place and sealed, direct
sun would bake the young plants.
Once the seedlings or cuttings have
gotten a good start (the first set of true
leaves for seedlings, or roots ¾ inch
long for cuttings), remove the cover.
Seedlings should go into bright sunlight. Cuttings should be moved to
permanent containers and put in light
appropriate to the particular plant.

Incidentally, this unit probably
won't feel warm to the touch. Your
body temperature is at least 20 degrees warmer, but the propagator
gives the kind of steady bottom heat
that most plants love.

Hydroponic Grower, "SQUARE ROOTER PLUS," MODEL 655, OPUS, $7.00–8.00 (44)

Watertight clear plastic cube, open at the top; measures 4 × 4 × 4 inches; thirty 1⅛-inch clear plastic balls; bracket with 2 suction discs.

Here's a good way to get your roots wet, so to speak, in hydroponic gardening. Complete systems for gardening in water can be quite elaborate, but this heavy-gauge, clear plastic container is an easy way to get started. It can be mounted on an east, west, or north window, and is large enough to grow a mature begonia, philodendron, spider plant, or other plants suitable for this kind of culture.

Complete directions for transferring a plant from soil to hydroculture are included. Of course, many gardeners will use this simply to root cuttings. Many plants, such as Swedish ivy and wandering jew, root quickly in water. The kit includes several large plastic balls which not only hold plants or cuttings in place, but also make an attractive display in themselves. I found the suction cups held firm, even on a sliding glass door subject to much vibration and a wide variation of temperatures.

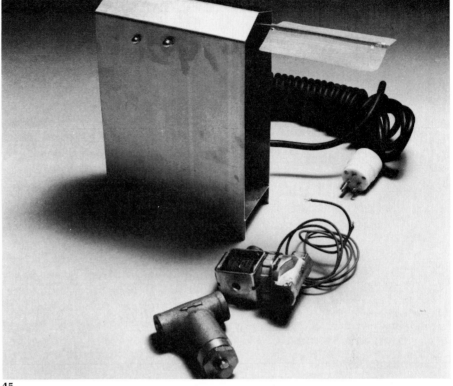

45

Propagator, "MIST-A-MATIC," E. C. GEIGER, $130.00–145.00 (45)

Control box measures 7 × 10 × 3 inches with stainless steel screen, 3¼ inches wide, projecting about 5 inches from the rear like two feathers on an arrow; inside is a level and a mercury switch, along with related mechanical parts.

Although aimed primarily at the commercial grower, a hobbyist intensively interested in rooting cuttings, especially of hard-to-root varieties, will find this automatic misting device both interesting and useful. This is essentially a control system for turning on and off a misting nozzle, or series of nozzles, that will provide a fine spray to a bed of cuttings or seeds.

A misting nozzle covers a circle about 6 feet in diameter, providing a fine mist to keep leaf temperatures low and humidity high, conditions that are conducive to good rooting. (If used to germinate seeds, it should be turned off as soon as the seeds germinate.)

You can't simply turn a mister on and leave it. The constant fog would be too much for the plants. It's also difficult to set up a timing system that is appropriate for turning a mister on and off, because the proper amount of moisture varies with weather conditions, particularly cloudiness.

The key to the "Mist-A-Matic" system is that it lets the humidity and weather conditions vary the cycle. It does this with a very fine mesh screen that extends from the unit on a rod. This rod has a weight on one end (a counterbalance) and the screen on the other. The screen is placed so that it collects a portion of the mist. As it does so, it becomes heavier until it finally tips the rod, opening a mercury switch which shuts off the misting system. The switch remains open while the screen dries. Obviously, the rate of drying will depend on humidity and weather conditions. Once the screen is dry, the counterbalance weight pulls the rod back up, switching the system on again. The whole cycle may take just a few minutes on a sunny day.

44

ARTIFICIAL-LIGHT GARDENING

Many gardeners despair of growing under artificial lights because it sounds so complicated. It's easy to become overwhelmed by the technical jargon that can surround artificial-light gardening, and that's unfortunate. Using artificial lights can be a productive and easy way to grow annuals for the flower or vegetable gardens, cuttings from favorite houseplants, or just about any mature plant you can think of, including orchids and salad greens.

If you want a simple, inexpensive way to get started with artificial lights, try this:

1. Purchase at a discount store an ordinary, workshop-type fluorescent light fixture designed to hold two 40-watt fluorescent tubes. It should include a reflector and chains by which it can be suspended. ($10–15)

2. Place in this fixture one "cool white" and one "warm white" fluorescent tube. (About $2 each)

3. Suspend this about 2 feet above a growing area. An old table in the basement would be fine.

4. This will effectively light a strip 1½ feet wide and 4 feet long directly beneath the lights. Most plants should have their foliage 6 to 12 inches below the lamps. Vegetable and flower seedlings can be placed as close to the lamps as you can get without touching them.

5. Purchase an ordinary timer, such as those used to turn lights on and off when away from home, and plug the fluorescent fixture into it. A grounded, three-pronged unit is preferable. ($7–12)

6. If growing seedlings for the outdoor garden, African violets (they do beautifully under lights), or summer-blooming plants, set the timer so that the lights are on 18 hours a day. If growing other houseplants, set it for 14 hours a day.

This is sufficient space for about 100 seedlings, or about 12 mature African violets. To maintain the artificial lights, merely wipe the tubes and reflector clean once a month. Mark the dates on the tubes with an indelible marker and replace after two years, even if they still work, since their light output will have dropped too much by then to be effective for plants. (Output drops about 10 percent the first year and about another 15 percent the next year.)

If you wish to be a little more complete in your approach to artificial-light gardening, here are some more details that will help you choose appropriate light fixtures and lights.

Natural light is a mixture of colors. The exact mix changes with time of day, season, and weather conditions. Artificial lights are also a mixture. None exactly matches sunlight. Several manufacturers emphasize blue and red — colors plants appear to use the most. (The blue end of the spectrum encourages foliage growth; the red end, flowers.) This is why some plant-

growth fluorescents give a pink or purplish glow. The visible color on others is less apparent, however. Engineers vary the color of a fluorescent light by using different phosphors in the tube. The common fluorescent light uses inexpensive phosphors, and is a very efficient user of energy — far more efficient than the incandescent light, which gives off much of its energy as heat. Since most plants respond well to a combination of two common fluorescents, "cool white" and "warm white," I recommend using a balanced mix of those two. These are far less expensive than the special plant-growth lights, which give different color balances. If you wish, experiment with the plant-growth lights. For plants under certain conditions, they may do well for you. But don't expect miracles. Be especially wary of claims for special plant-growth incandescents. They develop heat that can be damaging to plants placed too close to them, and they do not give the kind of wide spectrum beneficial to plant growth that you can get from individual ordinary, or special, fluorescent tubes. They can be useful as spotlights accenting an individual plant and supplementing what may be a meager sunlight diet for that plant.

The simplest approach to fixtures remains the ordinary workbench type with reflector. However, you may wish to use artificial lights in a bookcase, or home-built cabinet. Here, industrial strip lights without reflectors are fine. Do, however, paint the insides of the cabinet flat white for best light reflection. This will increase the total light reaching your plants.

There are also special 4-lamp fixtures, useful in some instances for more intense light, and fixtures with accompanying trays designed expressly for the artificial-light gardener. These have the virtue of convenience or, in some cases, are more appealing to the eye. They are also more expensive.

For a working light garden, go the longest length light you have space for. A 4-foot, 40-watt tube is more efficient and gives more light than two 2-foot, 20-watt tubes placed end to end. An 8-foot, 75-watt tube is even more efficient. The smallest unit generally recommended is the 4-foot one, but if all you have space for is 2-foot tubes, these will grow plants.

A plant's response to light, as well as invisible energy, is an extremely complex subject still being explored and debated by plant researchers. Part of the fun of gardening under electric lights is that it gives you control over the quality of light (by choosing bulbs that emit with varying intensities in different parts of the spectrum), the quantity of light (by varying the distance between lights and plants), and the day length (by turning lights off and on at predetermined intervals). What's more, you never experience cloudy days, or smog. But if the scientific end of this hobby becomes overpowering, go back to the simple formula at the beginning of this section. You achieve a green thumb through common sense and by watching the response of
continued

---

your plants under different conditions. In the end, they'll tell you what they like, or don't like, by how they grow.

For more information on artificial-light gardening, send a stamped, self-addressed envelope to the Indoor Light Gardening Society of America, Inc., 128 West 58th Street, New York, NY 10019. Ask for information on membership and a list of their books. They have a wide variety of inexpensive, small books that will be helpful to the beginner, and they publish a bi-monthly magazine.

Some sources for special artificial lights for gardening include:

Duro-Lite Lamps, Inc., Horticultural Division, 17-10 Willow St., Fair Lawn, NJ 07410 (Natur-Escent, Vita-Lite)

General Electric Company, Lamp Marketing Division, Nela Park, Cleveland, Ohio 44112 (Plant Light Gro and Sho, Gro and Sho Wide Spectrum)

GTE Lighting, Sylvania Lighting Center, 100 Endicott St., Danvers, MA 01923

Verilux, Inc., 35 Mason St., Greenwich, CT 06830 (TruBloom)

Westinghouse Electric Corp., 100 Westinghouse Plaza, Bloomfield, NJ 07003 (Agro-Lite)

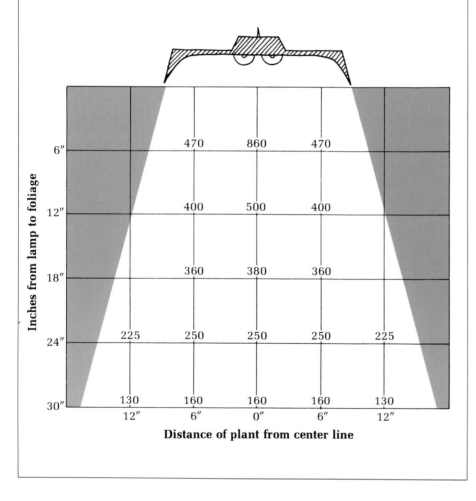

LIGHT AND MOISTURE METERS

Light and Moisture Meter,
INSTAMATIC DUO,
AMI MEDICAL ELECTRONICS,
$15.00–17.00 **(46)**

4 × 2⅝ inches; meter face 1 × 2 inches; white plastic case holds easily read meter and light/water switch; moisture and light scale divided into 8 color-coded sections; 8¾-inch metal moisture probe is attached to the meter by a 25-inch insulated wire; probe clips to case for storage; 50-page direction book with minimum light and watering requirements for more than 200 houseplants.

There are several simple moisture meters on the market. This one was chosen because the detachable probe is a little easier to use with overhead hanging plants than the type that has the meter attached to the end of the probe. It would take a truly meticulous gardener, however, to check a moisture meter and plant list every time he wanted to water a plant. But you can use it as a self-teaching tool. Test a plant with the meter, then feel the soil with your fingers. Pretty soon you'll be recognizing moisture content in soil without a meter as if you had been doing it all your life.

The light meter portion of this unit has a chromatic filter so it reads those wavelengths of light most important to plant growth. Unlike some others, it is still readable when placed close under artificial lights. (In some designs, the angle of the meter face in relation to the sensing portion makes this difficult.) The major disadvantage of this light meter is that it shows a

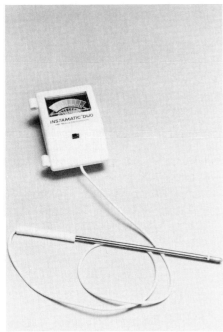

46

47

maximum filtered foot-candle equivalent of about 1,400. That means it is effective for checking to see if you have the minimum light requirements for a particular plant, but it won't tell you if there is too much light. Some tropical plants, for example, burn when the light gets above 4,000 foot-candles.

Still, you'll find the light meter handy for checking near windows to make sure you're giving your plants the minimum light needed, and it will also help you locate plants in an artificial-light gardening arrangement, as well as tell you when the fluorescent tubes are getting too weak for effective light output.

Light Meter, MODEL 214,
GENERAL ELECTRIC, $37.00–40.00
(47)

Hand-held meter in plastic case 2 × 3 × 1¼ inches with 1¾ × 1¼–inch meter face; reads in foot-candles on three scales, from 0–50, 50–250, and 200–1,000; a perforated metal cap slips over the light sensor unit on top of the meter (with this in place, the readings from each scale are multiplied by ten); soft vinyl outer case included.

Light meters are not infallible, but when used with knowledge of their limitations, they can be helpful in several gardening situations. For example, while using this meter, I learned that a second layer of fiberglass glazing on a pit greenhouse had weathered to the point that it was cutting light by more than 20 percent. While I was checking the light coming through a south window that held an African violet all winter, I noticed that the intensity there now had climbed to 9,000 foot-candles. That's high for African violets, but it was good to learn this from the meter before the plant showed signs of damage from too much light.

As is typical with small, inexpensive meters, this one has an accuracy of plus or minus 10 to 15 percent. The meter is color corrected to respond to the yellow-green wavelengths (colors) of light the human eye is most sensitive to. Plants seem to prefer the blue-red region. What this means is that the meter will give relatively low readings when checking light below special plant lights designed to give off most of their energy in the very blue and red regions the meter isn't sensitive to.

But even if you are measuring the light from such plant-growth lamps, the relative foot-candle readings will be of value. If this meter shows 200 foot-candles at one location and 100 at another, you can assume there's half the light at the second spot as at the first. So it's useful in determining where to locate plants and in checking the output of such lights over a period of months. Just don't treat these foot-candles as absolute and comparable to foot-candles read in natural light, or perhaps listed in a book as proper for a given plant.

In using the meter, hold it near your plants and line up the white, light-sensing portion on the top so that it's parallel to the plant's foliage. This meter has a wide angle of acceptance so it will read reflected light as well. In fact, you can falsely influence the reading simply by wearing a white shirt and standing in such a way that light reflects from it to the meter. While reasonably rugged, the meter should be treated with the care given any sensitive instrument.

SELECTING A GREENHOUSE

It is mid-January in New England. Snow has drifted 4 and 5 feet deep across the vegetable garden, perennials are frozen solid, the thermometer says 14 degrees, and a brisk, northwest wind is swirling powdery snow into sharp crystals which sting the face and eyes. In short, it is an ideal gardening day — if you have a greenhouse.

For it always seems that the day after a storm, temperatures drop and the winter sun shines brightest. Your greenhouse gathers that sun, stimulating both you and the plants. When you enter, you're met by a rich, humusy smell topped by the delicate fragrance of a newly opened cattleya orchid. All is vital and alive, for in the greenhouse, you hold sway over temperature, water, nutrients, and to some extent, light. A greenhouse can become an extension of the activity that too often is limited to outdoors during much of the year.

Are greenhouses out of the reach of the average gardener? Hardly. Perfectly functional hobby greenhouses can be built and equipped for less than $1,000. In fact, even the renter can have a small temporary greenhouse that could be dismantled in a weekend and moved to another location.

However, most people are going to want a permanent greenhouse built in a style that complements their home. To achieve this, the cost rises. A realistic minimum is probably around $2,000, while a truly first-class installation with professionals doing all the work can be obtained for about $5,000. Even at those prices, a greenhouse can be the least expensive addition to a home, and it will provide space that the whole family can enjoy, even if they're not all gardeners.

I admit to a northern bias which tends to make me think of greenhouses first in terms of keeping out the cold weather. But they are really much more than that, which is why you'll find greenhouses even in near-tropical climates such as Florida and Southern California. The reason is simple: a greenhouse is an environment which you control. Most gardeners I know think of a greenhouse as providing extra light for their plants, which it does. But it also means you can supply more humidity than is normal in a house and you can let nighttime temperatures drop into the 40s, a feature many plants, but few humans, enjoy, even in these energy-conscious times.

In fact, a greenhouse is an excellent solar collector. Connect one to a south-facing wall, and you'll be able to gather significant excess heat. We used to vent that heat to the outside because even on the coldest winter day, if the sun is shining, the greenhouse temperature can rise to 90 degrees or more, which is too high for most plants. Today, many people use small fans to draw extra heat into the house. Some even pump it to solar heat storage bins of rocks or water. You can now even buy a system that will take the excess heat from high up in a greenhouse and pump it into gravel beds beneath greenhouse benches for storage and release after the sun goes down. A greenhouse doesn't have to be a liability from an energy standpoint. It's possible to design it in such a way that it adds only as much to a heating bill as any other indoor space of a similar size.

It's beyond the scope of this book to go into detailed descriptions of greenhouses and greenhouse accessories. I have included some specific greenhouse items on these pages because I thought they were unusual, especially effective, and in some cases have applications to other aspects of gardening. I've also included answers to the questions I most frequently hear regarding home greenhouses. I hope these will give you a start in finding a hobby greenhouse that most fits your needs.

The exterior of a lean-to greenhouse.

Q: *I can't decide. Should I buy a free-standing greenhouse, or one that attaches to the house?*

A: **This depends on your property. If either would look all right, I prefer the attached. It's easier to heat, allows a heat exchange between it and the rest of the house, and is far easier to use. Do you want to put on a hat, coat, and boots every time you go to the greenhouse? If you decide on an attached model, be sure to include an outside door. (You'll know why the first time you need to carry in a large bag of soil, fertilizer, or flat of young plants — through the living room isn't the best way!) You'll also find that it's easier to extend your home heating system to cover an attached greenhouse. The same is true of electric and water lines.**

Why would anyone want a free-standing greenhouse? Temperate zone gardeners may prefer it. Or, frequently there's no good place to attach one. A free-standing greenhouse can usually be oriented so it takes full advantage of the winter sun, with possibly some protection by evergreen shrubs from the north and west winds. You can also fumigate a free-standing greenhouse without worrying about fumes getting into the home.

Q: *We want to attach a lean-to greenhouse to our home. We have it all picked out, but we can't decide whether to put it on the east side, or the west. Don't they both get the same amount of sun?*

A louvered window ventilation system.

A: **Yes, for all practical purposes, they do. But the sun hits a greenhouse on the east side in the morning after the plants have had a cool night's rest and are ready to start back to work manufacturing food. Other things being equal, the east side is a better choice. You'll also find that the west-side greenhouse is subject to more winter winds, increasing heating problems. My first choice would be south. But if I had no option but north, I'd**

A window greenhouse.

still have a greenhouse. The heating problems would be greater with this exposure, but African violets, some orchids, and many foliage plants would do beautifully in a northern exposure.

Q: *My husband's pretty handy with tools. He built a large deck last summer. This year, he'd like to build a small greenhouse. I'm not sure. Would we be better off with one of the prefabricated kits?*

A: *No, not if you're careful. Don't make the mistake of thinking that a greenhouse is just a shed with clear sides and roof. You must consider air circulation for proper ventilation and such realities as condensation dripping on plants. The key for the do-it-yourselfer is to first obtain good plans. There are several books published, and many agricultural extension services offer greenhouse plans at very low cost. Next, be sure to use materials that can take high humidity. Presuming you'll use wood, it should be cypress, heart redwood, or pressure-treated lumber. The latter doesn't cost any more than heart redwood, will last as long, and won't require painting. Finally, either cut in condensation gutters, or go to a greenhouse supply firm and buy wood milled with these gutters in place. Otherwise, you're likely to have moisture condensing on the inside of the glass, then dropping on leaves, a situation that can lead to plant disease in a hurry. There's a real satisfaction in building something yourself. But many people will find sufficient challenge in putting together a greenhouse from a precut or prefabricated kit, rather than building from scratch.*

Q: *I saw a plastic-covered greenhouse for just $240. It didn't need any foundation, the ad said, and the plastic was good for two years. Is this possible?*

A: *Yes, but this is a buyer-beware market. Most greenhouses are purchased by mail, and, even if there's a money-back guarantee, it may not include shipping expenses; and two-way shipping could amount to a significant percentage of the greenhouse cost, certainly no bargain. Plastic film, usually polyethylene, is subject to deterioration by the ultraviolet rays of the sun. Most film is good for just one season, while Monsanto 602 may last two or three years before it needs replacement. Commercial growers frequently choose polyethylene because they can put large areas under cover with very little capital investment. In many communities, such a structure is not considered permanent, so there are no building taxes. They can be built without a foundation because if there is some twisting and pulling from frost heaves, the plastic film is flexible enough to take it without breaking. The main reason plastic houses haven't caught on in the home market is that they simply aren't as attractive as glass ones. Don't be misled by photographs that make a polyethylene-covered greenhouse look clear. The film is milky. It lets in plenty of light, but you can't see clearly through it. Some vinyl films are clear, but they're also more expensive, subject to deterioration with the sun, and tend to have an electrostatic quality that attracts dust.*

Q: *My neighbor built a greenhouse and covered it with fiberglass panels. They looked fine the first few years, but now they're beginning to fray and turn yellow. Is there anything that can be done?*

A: *Yes, fiberglass can be restored by applying a special coating. Contact the panel manufacturer or distributor for information. A good grade of panel made especially for greenhouse use may last up to ten years before any restoration work is needed. But with all fiberglass, ultraviolet rays of the sun are the enemy and eventually deterioration takes place. This is both unsightly and cuts down on the light reaching the plants. The best grade of panels are covered with a Tedlar film made by Dupont and are guaranteed for twenty years. Glass should last at least forty years without deterioration, which is why it's still favored. The main advantage of fiberglass is that it comes in large sheets and is virtually shatterproof. (It will burn rapidly, however.) In areas where hail is a problem, you may want to use fiberglass in the roof and glass on the sides. Another alternative is acrylic, such as Plexiglas, which is strong, difficult to shatter, won't deteriorate in the sun, can be bent in a variety of graceful curves, and has good heat retention and light transmission. Unfortunately, it also costs more than glass or any other common covering.*

Q: *We're thinking about adding an 8 by 14–foot lean-to greenhouse to the south wall of our New Hampshire home, but the prospect of high heating bills has us worried. Is there any way to conserve on heat?*

A: *Certainly. Your first conservation measure is to choose plants that like cool nights. There are several that can tolerate a nighttime minimum of 45 degrees, including bulbs, chrysanthemums, and many popular cut flowers and vegetables. By opting for a 45-degree minimum rather than a 55-degree one, you'll save about 20 percent on heating. The next move is to storm window the greenhouse. You can add a sheet of polyethylene to the inside of a glass greenhouse, taking it down after the worst of winter is over. Sealing it tight so you have a dead air space between the plastic film and the glass could cut the heat loss by somewhere between 20 and 40 percent. (Commercial growers sometimes use two layers of polyethylene separated by forced air from a small fan.) There are also special double- and even triple-walled greenhouses on the market, which do tend to cut down on light. Some manufacturers of glass houses are offering a new, double-walled glazing material from Rohm and Haas called Tuffax-Twinwal. This is tough and is said to cut down heat loss by 40 percent. Any extra layer of glazing material will*

The interior of a lean-to greenhouse.

cut light by between 10 and 15 percent, but this isn't a serious problem. There's also a bubble film, similar to that used in shipping, that can be stuck to the glass in fall, then removed in spring.

Q: *Which is better for a small greenhouse, roof vents or an exhaust fan?*

A: *It depends on the greenhouse. I'd like to see both. But whichever route you go, give serious consideration to automatic ventilation. Commercial growers can be around all day to watch vents and make changes as needed. Most homeowners can't. Exact placing of vents is an engineering problem. Generally speaking, though, you want a vent down low to let cool air in, as well as one up high to remove the heated air. A nice compromise system is to have manually controlled roof vents and an automatic exhaust fan. This way, the fan can take care of most situations, and on really warm days there won't be any harm in opening roof vents early and leaving them open all day.*

Q: *When I saw a greenhouse kit advertised for $2,400, I was nearly ready to buy when a friend warned me to be careful. She said there were a lot of "hidden extras." Are there?*

A: *The price of the kit isn't the only thing you should consider. Kit prices usually include just the greenhouse frame and covering. Here's a list of other things you must count on in most installations: 1. a permanent foundation; 2. extension of home heating system or purchase of a separate heater; 3. an automatic ventilation system; 4. benches; 5. extension of home electric system so you have lights and at least one outlet for a soil cable and maybe a standby electric heater; 6. installation of running water (you'll want at least a hose, and a sink with cold and hot water running into a single faucet is especially handy); 7. shading; 8. in some climates, a humidifier or evaporative cooler is needed. Finally, you may need to hire someone to put the greenhouse together. In short, approach the purchase of a home greenhouse with your eyes open. Remember, you are making an investment that not only can add to your pleasure, but will increase the value of your property.*

Roof vents on a lean-to greenhouse. The pulleys in front are for controlling exterior shades that protect the plants from the full blast of the summer sun.

SELECTING A GREENHOUSE

GREENHOUSE ACCESSORIES

Automatic ventilation is great for those who can't keep their eyes on a greenhouse or cold frame all day long. But what do you do when there's no electric power to your greenhouse or cold frame?

The answer comes in a simple package now showing up in more and more cold frames and greenhouses. These devices are designed to open vents, or lift the covers of cold frames and hotbeds, using nothing but the power of the sun. The principle is simple: fill a cylinder with a heat-sensitive compound. When that compound expands, have it push a piston. Then harness the force of the piston and you have a lifting arm to open your vent. If the piston is designed to work against a spring, closing the vent is no problem, for as soon as the compound cools in the cylinder, the spring pulls the vent closed, pushing the piston back inside the cylinder.

This also makes a handy backup system for a greenhouse that may already have automatic electric ventilation. (After all, what happens if the power fails?) The simplicity of the system means there's relatively little to wear out and you don't have to worry about a separate thermostat. I've found these especially useful in cold frames and window greenhouses which, because of their small volume of air, tend to heat up, or cool off, fast. Such small units can go through several major temperature changes in a day.

The two ventilator openers shown here are easy to install, requiring just a screwdriver, a small wrench, and perhaps 30 minutes spare time. Directions are clear and simple to follow.

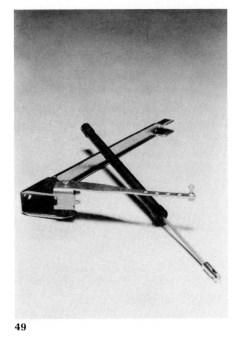

49

Automatic Ventilator Control,
"THERMOFOR,"
IMPORTED BY BRAMEN, $50.00–55.00
(49)

3-piece metal and plastic unit, base 16¼ inches long; uses heat-activated cylinder that lifts up to 30 pounds to maximum opening of 12 inches.

There is a method of coarse adjustment on this device so the vent can be made to start opening at different temperatures in a range of 55 to 80 degrees. The length of opening is adjustable to 12 inches. The vent opens slowly, starting at the minimum temperature it is set for, and reaches full extension when the temperature is 20 degrees higher. This prevents plants from getting a sudden blast of cold air. It is guaranteed for five years. Several units can be operated together to open a long, heavy ridge vent. A spring protects the vent from being blown open accidentally.

Automatic Ventilator Control,
"SOLARVENT,"
DALEN PRODUCTS, $25.00–28.00   **(48)**

Metal 3-piece ventilation system, includes heat-activated cylinder that will lift up to 9 pounds to maximum opening of 7 inches; counterbalance spring available to increase lifting power to 20 pounds.

This unit is designed to open when the temperature reaches 68 degrees in the area of the vent. The thermal assembly is guaranteed for three years. Two coil springs protect the window and unit from forcing, wind buffeting, or locking. Installation directions are simple and time to install is minimal. Heavier loads can be lifted by a series of these vents adjusted to work in unison or by the addition of a counterbalance spring. The amount of opening is easily adjusted, and by twisting one nut, the unit can be disconnected for manual operation of the vent.

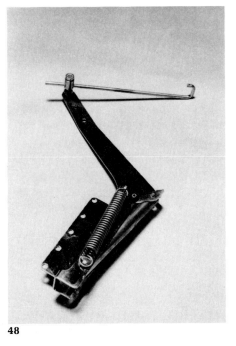

48

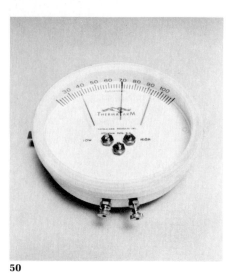

50

Temperature Alarm, "THERMALARM,"
DISTRIBUTED BY E. C. GEIGER,
$28.00–31.00   **(50)**

*6-inch-diameter thermometer in
waterproof metal case with adjustable
minimum and maximum temperatures in a range of 20–110 degrees
Fahrenheit.*

Here's an inexpensive form of indoor
crop insurance — a thermometer that
can be set to sound an alarm whenever the temperature in your greenhouse or plant room climbs too high
or low. The Thermalarm is just the
temperature sensing unit. You still
need a 6-volt dry cell battery and a
bell, such as an ordinary door bell,
plus wire to connect the system. The
idea is simple. The temperature indicator is a metal rod. You set two similar metal rods at the maximum and
minimum temperature by adjusting
two lock nuts on the outside of the
case. Then wire your bell into the circuit using a 6-volt battery. When the
temperature-indicating rod touches
one of the others, the circuit is completed and your bell rings until shut
off. Wiring diagram is included, and
since there are just two wires and a 6-
volt dry cell, there shouldn't be any
need to involve an electrician. The
alarm is waterproof, but should be
mounted out of the direct sun. With
this unit, you don't have to worry
about someone leaving a vent open by
mistake, a pane of glass getting bro-

ken in the middle of the night, the
heating system failing, or the automatic ventilation system dying. Without an alarm, any of these things
could destroy every plant in a greenhouse. With it, you can be warned in
time to take action.

Insulating Material,
"AIRCAP BARRIER COATED BUBBLES,"
SEALED AIR, $26.00–29.00 a roll *(no
photo)*

*Two layers of polyethylene bonded
together with one side flat and the
other like a muffin tin with tiny,
sealed air bubbles; comes in various-
sized rolls; price above is for 16-
inch × 300-foot (400 square feet) roll.*

AirCap may be more familiar to you
as a packing material used to reduce
breakage when shipping fragile items.
It now is being used to reduce heat
loss through the side walls and gable
ends of greenhouses. There are two
ways to apply it. It will adhere to wet
glass if the cracks between the panes
of glass are tight, or you can use a
double-sided tape applied around the
perimeter of dry glass. Much of the
heat loss through a glass house is
through the minute cracks between
panes of glass. This effectively seals
that escape route and the dead-air
space in the bubbles (about $^3/_{16}$ inch)
provides additional insulation.

Deluxe Exhaust Fan, "FUG FIGHTER,"
AGENT VENT-AXIA, $220.00–240.00
(51)

*7½-inch-diameter fan designed to op-
erate in the high humidity of a greenhouse; will exhaust 300 cubic feet of
air per minute; operates on three different speeds.*

Here's a smooth, quiet exhaust fan
with louvers that you open when
the fan is on. Most of the parts are
weather-resistant plastic, and the fan
can be mounted in an 8½-inch-diame-
ter hole cut in glass or plastic, or in a
greenhouse wall. This size fan is recommended for a greenhouse of about
60 square feet. The company also
makes 6-inch, 9-inch, and 12-inch

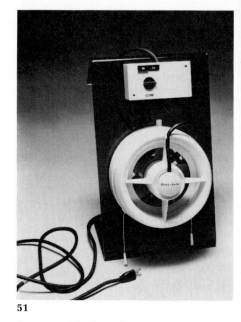

51

fans suitable for other sizes of greenhouses. These fans are manufactured
in England and have a wide variety of
applications besides greenhouses.

If you purchase such a fan, a thermostat will be needed to make the installation automatic. You will also
want some other type of vent set up
elsewhere in the greenhouse to let
fresh air in when the fan is exhaust-
ing hot, stale air. The usual method is
to try to mount the exhaust fan in a
high position (where there's the most
hot air) at one end of a greenhouse.
Ordinary metal louvers can be
mounted at the other end so that they
swing inward. In this way, the louvers
should open because of the change in
air pressure when the exhaust fan
goes on. In some installations, such
louvers are operated by a small electric motor attached to the same thermostat as the fan. In a small greenhouse, an exhaust fan can handle the
ventilation entirely, but many prefer
to have roof vents as a supplementary,
or backup, system if electric power
fails. Also consider using an exhaust
fan to pump excess solar heat from
the greenhouse to your home in the
wintertime.

APPENDIX: MANUFACTURER'S ADDRESSES

AIRGUIDE INSTRUMENT COMPANY
2210 Wabansia Avenue
Chicago, Ill. 60647

AKKO INC.
Dundee Park
Andover, Mass. 01810

ALLEGRETTI & CO.
9200 Mason Avenue
Chatsworth, Calif. 91311

AMERACE CORP.
Swan Hose Division
8929 Columbus Pike
P.O. Box 509
Worthington, Ohio 43085

AMERICAN OPTICAL CORP.
Safety Products Division
14 Mechanic Street
Southbridge, Mass. 01550

AMERICAN STANDARD CO.
1 West Street
Plantsville, Conn. 06479

AMES
A McDonough Company
Box 1774
Parkersburg, W. Va. 26101

AMI MEDICAL ELECTRONICS INC.
Division of Distinctive Devices Inc.
2165 Fifth Avenue
Ronkonkoma, N.Y. 11779

ANIMAL REPELLENTS, INC.
P.O. Box 999
Griffin, Ga. 30224

A.O.W. INDUSTRIES
Accord, N.Y. 12404

ANNAPOLIS VALLEY PEAT MOSS CO. LTD.
Berwick, Nova Scotia BOPIEO

ARCHITECTURAL POTTERY
P.O. Box AP
3601 Aviation Boulevard
Manhattan Beach, Calif. 90266

ARNO ADHESIVE TAPES, INC.
P.O. Box 301
Michigan City, Ind. 46360

BALLBARROW
1320 Ardmore Avenue
Itasca, Ill. 60143

BARTLETT MANUFACTURING CO.
3003 East Grand Boulevard
Detroit, Mich. 48202

BAUSCH & LOMB
P.O. Box 450
Rochester, N.Y. 14602

BEAGLE MANUFACTURING CO., INC.
4377 Baldwin Avenue
El Monte, Calif. 91731

L. L. BEAN INCORPORATED
Freeport, Me. 04033

BEAIRD-POULAN DIVISION
Emerson Electric Co.
5020 Greenwood Road
Shreveport, La. 71109

BEH HOUSEWARES CORP.
1150 Broadway
New York, N.Y. 10001

DOROTHY BIDDLE SERVICE
DBS Building
8 & 12 Broadway
Hawthorne, N.Y. 01532

BIRCH MEADOW FARMS
Box 188
Concord, Mass. 01742

BISHOP CO., INC.
Box 387
Bath, Me. 04530

BLACHER BROTHERS, INC.
299 Carpenter Street
P.O. Box 1417
Providence, R.I. 02901

BRAMEN CO., INC.
P.O. Box 70
Salem, Mass. 01970

BROCKTON CUTTING/DIE & MACHINE CO.
Memorial Drive
Avon, Mass. 02322

BROOKSTONE CO.
Vose Farm Road
Peterborough, N.H. 03458

BURGESS VIBROCRAFTERS, INC.
Grayslake, Ill. 60030

D. V. BURRELL SEED GROWERS CO.
P.O. Box 150
Rocky Ford, Colo. 81067

BUZZA CO.
P.O. Box 136
Cambridge, Mass. 02142

CALIFORNIA FLEXRAKE CORP.
4307 Rowland Avenue
El Monte, Calif. 91731

CARE FREE GARDEN PRODUCTS
P.O. Box 383
1400 Harvester Road
West Chicago, Ill. 60185

CARLTON CO.
3901 S.E. Naef Road
Milwaukie, Ore. 97222

CENTRAL QUALITY INDUSTRIES, INC.
Polo, Ill. 61064

CHEYENNE CORP.
30961 Agoura Road, Suite 311
Westlake Village, Calif. 91361

CHOPPER INDUSTRIES
P.O. Box 87
Easton, Pa. 18042

WALTER E. CLARK & SON
550 Grassy Hill Road
Orange, Conn. 06477

COLEMAN TREE PRUNERS
Tioga Center, N.Y. 13845

COLLINS AXE
P.O. Box 351
Lewiston, Pa. 17044

COLORITE PLASTICS CO.
101 Railroad Avenue
Ridgefield, N.J. 07657

L. E. COOKE CO.
26333 road 140
Visalia, Calif. 93277

CORONA CLIPPER CO.
14200 East Sixth Street
P.O. Box 730
Corona, Calif. 91720

CRANE PRODUCTS
8432 Birchbark Avenue
Pico Rivera, Calif. 90660

THE CYCLONE SEEDER CO., INC.
Urbana, Ind. 46990

DALEN PRODUCTS, INC.
201 Sherlake Drive
Knoxville, Tenn. 37922

DAMART THERMAWEAR, INC.
1811 Woodbury Avenue
Portsmouth, N.H. 03805

DARE PRODUCTS, INC.
860 Betterly Road
Battle Creek, Mich. 49016

THE DESIGN FACTORY INC.
180-10 93rd Avenue
Jamaica, N.Y. 11433

DEXOL INDUSTRIES
1450 West 228th Street
Torrance, California 90501

DISSTON, INC.
P.O. Box 3000 Rt. 29N
Danville, Va. 24541

DOVER STAMPING CO.
427 Plymouth Avenue
Fall River, Mass. 02722

THE DRAMM CO.
P.O. Box 528
Manitowoc, Wisc. 54220

DRIP GUARD CO.
P.O. Box 2352
Costa Mesa, Calif. 92626

E. I. DUPONT DE NEMAURS
Customer Service Center (Vexar)
Chestnut Run
Wilmington, Del. 19898

DYNAMIC FORM SYSTEMS, INC.
P.O. Box 103
Scotch Plains, N.J. 07076

EARTHWAY PRODUCTS, INC.
P.O. Box 547
Bristol, Ind. 46507

EASCO TOOLS, INC.
6721 Baymeadow Drive
Glen Burnie, Md. 21061

EDWARDS MANUFACTURING CO.
Tru Chek Rain Gauge Division
P.O. Box 166
Albert Lea, Minn. 56007

ELLISCO INC.
American and Luzerne Streets
Philadelphia, Pa. 19140

EQUIPMENT CONSULTANTS & SALES
2241 Dunwin Drive
Mississauga, Ontario L5L 1A3

ERIE IRON WORKS CO. LTD.
99-101 Edward Street
St. Thomas, Ontario, Canada

THE FANNO SAW WORKS
P.O. Box 628
224 West Eighth Avenue
Chico, Calif. 95927

F. & R. FARRELL CO.
6810 Biggert Road
P.O. Box 133
Harrisburg, Ohio 43126

FEATHER HILL INDUSTRIES, INC.
Box 41
Zenda, Wisc. 53195

THE FIBRE-METAL PRODUCTS CO.
Baltimore Pike at Brinton Lake Road
P.O. Box 248
Concordville, Pa. 19331

FILFAST CORP.
Pope Industrial Park
Pope Road
Holliston, Mass. 01746

THE FLETCHER CO.
Division of The Fletcher Enamel Co.
P.O. Box 67
Dunbar, W. Va. 25064

FLORALIFE, INC.
7 Salt Creek Lane
Hinsdale, Ill. 60521

FOGG-IT NOZZLE CO.
P.O. Box 16053
2308 Vicente Street
San Francisco, Calif. 94116

FRIEND MANUFACTURING CORP.
Gasport, N.Y. 14067

THE GARDEN WAY COUNTRY KITCHEN
CATALOG
Garden Way Research
Charlotte, Vt. 05445

E. C. GEIGER
Box 285
Harleysville, Pa. 19438

GENERAL ELECTRIC CO.
95 Hathaway Street
Providence, R.I. 02907

GERMAIN'S, INC.
P.O. Box 3233
Los Angeles, Calif. 90051

GILBERT & BENNETT
Georgetown, Conn. 06829

GILMOUR MANUFACTURING CO.
Division of R. M. Smith, Inc.
Somerset, Pa. 15501

THE BF GOODRICH CO.
Engineered Systems Division
500 South Main Street
Akron, Ohio 44318

GOOD-PROD SALES, INC.
825 Fairfield Avenue
Kenilworth, N.J. 07033

GOSERUD PRODUCTS MANUFACTURING
CO.
Division of Wynn Manufacturing Co.
568 Burgess Street
St. Paul, Minn. 55103

JOHN H. GRAHAM & CO., INC.
617 Oradell Avenue
Oradell, N.J. 07649

GRANBERG INDUSTRIES, INC.
200 S. Garrard Boulevard
Richmond, Calif. 94804

GREAT OUTDOORS
Consumer Division of Slater Products
301 Riverside Avenue
Westport, Conn. 06880

GREEN GARDE
Division of Encap Products Co.
P.O. Box 278
Mt. Prospect, Ill. 60056

GREEN HABIT ENTERPRISES, INC.
29 N.E. 148th Avenue
Portland, Ore. 97230

GREEN INK
P.O. Box 6142
Cincinnati, Ohio 45206

HALL INDUSTRIES, INC.
2323 Commonwealth Avenue
North Chicago, Ill. 60064

HANDY FOLDING PAIL CO., INC.
96-104 Spring Street
New York, N.Y. 10012

HARDWARE & INDUSTRIAL TOOL CO.,
INC.
2607 River Road
Cinnaminson, N.J. 08077

HARRISON-HOGE INDUSTRIES, INC.
104 Arlington Avenue
St. James, Long Island, N.Y. 11780

HAYES EQUIPMENT CORP.
P.O. Box 266
150 New Britain Avenue
Unionville, Conn. 06085

HAYES PRODUCTS
1035 Watsoncenter Road
Carson, Calif. 90745

HMC
22133 South Vermont
Torrance, Calif. 90502

HOLD-ALL MANUFACTURING CO., INC.
3 Cross Street
Suffern, N.Y. 10901

MANNING HOLOFF CO.
14600 Arminta Street
Van Nuys, Calif. 91402

HOMELITE DIVISION OF TEXTRON INC.
P.O. Box 7047
Charlotte, N.C. 28217

THE HOMESTEADER & ARNOLD CO.
Salem, N.Y. 12865

HORTISCAPE
Pilot Plastics, Inc.
7866 Second Street
Dexter, Mich. 48130

H. D. HUDSON MANUFACTURING CO.
500 North Michigan Avenue
Chicago, Ill. 60611

ILLINOIS B & G CORPORATION
1920 Waukegan Road
Glenview, Ill. 60025

INTERDESIGN CRAFT INC.
P.O. Box 22128
Beachwood, Ohio 44122

JACKSON MANUFACTURING CO.
P.O. Box 1649
Harrisburg, Pa. 17105

JEMCO TOOL CORP.
60 State Street
Seneca Falls, N.Y. 13148

JOHNSON'S INDUSTRIAL SUPPLY CO.
1941 Karlin Drive
St. Louis, Mo. 63131

JUDSEN RUBBER WORKS, INC.
4107 W. Kinzie Street
Chicago, Ill. 60624

KAZ, INC.
614 West 49th Street
New York, N.Y. 10019

LAB SYSTEMS
1330 Grove Street
Berkeley, Calif. 94709

LAMOTTE CHEMICAL PRODUCTS CO.
Chestertown, Md. 21620

A. M. LEONARD INC.
P.O. Box 816
Piqua, Ohio 45356

LITTLE WONDER
Division of Schiller-Pfeiffer, Inc.
1028 Street Road
Southampton, Pa. 18966

LONDON GARDEN ASSOCIATES, LTD.
Box 333
Ridgefield, Conn. 06877

LUDLOW CORP.
145 Rosemary Street
Needham Heights, Mass. 02194

MCDONOUGH POWER EQUIPMENT
535 Macon Highway
McDonough, Ga. 30253

THE GEO. W. MCGUIRE CO., INC.
150-31 12th Avenue
Whitestone, Long Island, N.Y. 11357

MCHUTCHINSON & CO., INC.
695 Grand Avenue
Ridgefield, N.J. 07657

MECHANICAL APPLICATIONS, INC.
P.O. Box 266
Wiscasset, Me. 04578

MELNOR INDUSTRIES
Moonachie, N.J. 07074

MERKLE INDUSTRIES
52 Reservoir Drive
Danvers, Mass. 01923

MICRO ESSENTIAL LABORATORY INC.
4224 Avenue H
Brooklyn, N.Y. 11210

MILWAUKEE ELECTRIC TOOL CORP.
13135 West Lisbon Road
Brookfield, Wisc. 53005

MINE SAFETY APPLIANCES CO.
600 Penn Center Boulevard
Pittsburgh, Pa. 15235

MOLDED FIBER GLASS TRAY CO.
East Erie Street
Linesville, Pa. 16424

NANCRAFT INC.
Pumpkin Hook Road
R.D. #1
Jordanville, N.Y. 13361

NATURE WORKS
P.O. Box 120
Boston, Mass. 02101

NELSON MCCOY
A Lancaster Colony Company
Roseville Floraline
451 Gordon Street
Roseville, Ohio 43777

L. R. NELSON CORP.
7719 N. Pioneer Lane
Peoria, Ill. 61614

NICOL & ASSOCIATES
65 Newtown Avenue
Stratford, Conn. 06497

NICHOLSON FILE CO.
The Cooper Group
P.O. Box 728
Apex, N.C. 27502

NORTHERN WIRE PRODUCTS, INC.
P.O. Box 70
St. Cloud, Minn. 56301

NORTON CO.
Worcester, Mass. 01606

OLEY TOOLING
Oley, Pa. 19547

OMARK INDUSTRIES
9701 S. E. McLoughlin Boulevard
Portland, Ore. 97222

OPUS INC.
P.O. Box 1387
Framingham, Mass. 01701

ORTHO DIVISION OF CHEVRON
   CHEMICAL COMPANY
200 Bush Street
San Francisco, Calif. 94104

C. S. OSBORNE & CO.
Harrison, N.J. 07029

LAWN-BOY
A Division of Outboard Marine Corp.
Gale Products
Galesburg, Ill. 61401

GEO. W. PARK SEED CO., INC.
P.O. Box 31
Greenwood, S.C. 29647

PARKER MCCRORY MANUFACTURING CO.
3175-3187 Terrace Street
Kansas City, Mo. 64111

PAW PAW EVERLAST LABEL CO.
P.O. Box 93
Paw Paw, Mich. 49079

PERFEX CORP.
Poland, N.Y. 13431

PIPER INDUSTRIES, INC.
Planet Jr. Division
Building G-11
P.O. Box 1188
Freeport Center
Clearfield, Utah 84016

PROEN PRODUCTS CO.
Ninth and Grayson Street
Berkeley, Calif. 94710

PRO-GROW SUPPLY CORP.
5557 North 124th Street
Butler, Wisc. 53007

RACKY'S ENTERPRISES
P.O. Box 866
Lake Arrowhead, Calif. 92352

RADIO STEEL & MANUFACTURING CO.
6515 West Grand Avenue
Chicago, Ill. 60635

RAIN BIRD NATIONAL SALES CORP.
7045 North Grand Avenue
Glendora, Calif. 91740

RAINDRIP
14675 Titus Street
Panorama City, Calif. 91402

RINGER CORP.
6860 Flying Cloud Drive
Eden Prairie, Minn. 55343

ROBERTS IRRIGATION PRODUCTS
700 Rancheros Drive
San Marcos, Calif. 92069

ROOT-LOWELL CORP.
Division of Root Lowell
   Manufacturing Co.
1000 Foreman Road
Lowell, Mich. 49331

ROSS DANIELS, INC.
P.O. Box 430, 1720 Fuller Road
West Des Moines, Iowa 50265

ROTOCROP (USA) INC.
604 Aero Park
Doylestown, Pa. 18901

ROWE ENTERPRISES, INC.
P.O. Box 1224
343 S. Kellogg Street
Galesburg, Ill. 61401

RUGG MANUFACTURING CO.
105 Newton Street
P.O. Box 507
Greenfield, Mass. 01301

SACKNER PRODUCTS
901 Ottawa Avenue
Grand Rapids, Mich. 49503

RAY SANDERS & CO.
396 S. Pasadena Avenue
Pasadena, Calif. 91105

SANDVIK, INC.
Distributed by Disston, Inc.
Saws & Tools Division
1702 Nevins Road
Fair Lawn, N.J. 07410

SCHRADE CUTLERY CORP.
1776 Broadway
New York, N.Y. 10019

O. M. SCOTT & SONS
Marysville, Ohio 43040

SCOVIL HOE CO.
A Division of The Samoa Corp.
Scovil Road
Higganum, Conn. 06441

SEALED AIR CORP.
Park 80 Plaza East
Saddle Brook, N.J. 07662

SHELBURNE FARMS
Shelburne, Vt. 05482

H. B. SHERMAN MANUFACTURING CO.
Division of the Citation Companies,
  Inc.
207 West Michigan Avenue
Battle Creek, Mich. 49014

L. L. SHROYER ENTERPRISES
306 Railroad Street
Union City, Mich. 49094

SILENT STEAM BLACKSMITHS
P.O. Box 640
Cobleskill, N.Y. 12043

ALLEN SIMPSON MARKETING & DESIGN
  LTD.
Albert Street
Eden Mills, Ontario NOB 1PO

SKODCO, INC.
P.O. Box 242
10 Lewis Street
Greenwich, Conn. 06830

D. B. SMITH & CO., INC.
Main Street
Utica, N.Y. 13503

HIRAM A. SMITH WHETSTONE, INC.
1500 Sleepy Valley Road
Hot Springs, Ark. 71901

SEYMOUR SMITH·& SON, INC.
Oakville, Conn. 06779

SNOW & NEALLEY CO.
155 Perry Road
Bangor, Me. 04401

SOLAR CAPS INC.
P.O. Box 150
Port Edwards, Wisc. 54469

SOLO MOTORS INC.
P.O. Box 5030
5100 Chestnut Avenue
Newport News, Va. 23605

SOUHAN DESIGN, INC.
1726 Plantation
P.O. Box 36384
Dallas, Tex. 75235

THE SPECIALTY MANUFACTURING CO.
2356 University Avenue
St. Paul, Minn. 55114

SPEEDLING INC.
P.O. Box 7098
Sun City, Florida 33586

SPOOL TOOL CO.
P.O. Box 2268
Waco, Tex. 76703

STANLEY HARDWARE
Stanley Tools
Division of The Stanley Works
New Britain, Conn. 06050

STAPLE HOME GARDEN PRODUCTS
A Division of Staple Sewing Aids
  Corp.
141 Lanza Avenue
Garfield, N.J. 07026

STIHL INC.
536 Viking Drive
Virginia Beach, Va. 23452

SUDBURY LABORATORY, INC.
Sudbury, Mass. 01776

TAYLOR INSTRUMENT
Consumer Products Division
Sybron Corp.
Arden, N.C. 28704

TEXAS NOVACHEM CORP.
11055 Dennis Road
Dallas, Tex. 75229

THOMPSON MANUFACTURING CO.
A Division of Jennison Enterprises,
  Inc.
2251 East Seventh Street
Los Angeles, Calif. 90023

TILTON EQUIPMENT CO.
300 Lafayette Road, Rt. 1
Rye, N.H. 03870

TOPPING LADDER CO., INC.
36 Van Auker Street
Rochester, N.Y. 14608

THE TORO CO.
8111 Lyndale Avenue South
Minneapolis, Minn. 55420

TROY-BILT
Garden Way Manufacturing Co., Inc.
102nd Street & 9th Avenue
Troy, N.Y. 12180

TRUE FRIENDS GARDEN TOOLS INC.
100 State Street
Teaneck, N.J. 07666

TRUE TEMPER CORP.
Hardware Division
A Wilkinson Match Group Co.
1623 Euclid Avenue
Cleveland, Ohio 44115

THE TURNER ASHBY CO.
252 College Street
Burlington, Vt. 05401

THE UNION FORK AND HOE CO.
500 Dublin Avenue
Columbus, Ohio 43216

VANDERMOLEN CORP.
119 Dorsa Avenue
Livingston, N.J. 07039

VAUGHAN & BUSHNELL
  MANUFACTURING CO.
11414 Maple Avenue
Hebron, Ill. 60034

VENT-AXIA
Crown Vent
Dundee Park
Andover, Mass. 01810

VITRI PRODUCTS CORP.
58-01 37th Avenue
Woodside, N.Y. 11377

WAFLER FARMS
R.D. 2
Wolcott, N.Y. 14590

WALLACE MANUFACTURING CORP.
Enfield, Conn. 06082

WARP BROTHERS
100 North Cicero Avenue
Chicago, Ill. 60651

THE WARREN GROUP
Division of Warren Tool Corp.
P.O. Box 68
Hiram, Ohio 44234

WATROUS & CO., INC.
172 Euston Road
Garden City, N.Y. 11530

WEED EATER, INC.
Subsidiary of Emerson Electric Co.
10515 Harwin Drive
Houston, Tex. 77036

WELLS & WADE HARDWARE
P.O. Box 1161
Wenatchee, Wash. 98801

WEST RINDGE BASKETS, INC.
P.O. Box 24
Rindge, N.H. 03461

WHITE FLOWER FARM
Litchfield, Conn. 06759

WILCOX ALL-PRO TOOLS & SUPPLY
Montezuma, Iowa 50171

WILKINSON SWORD, INC.
55 Old Field Point Road
Greenwich, Conn. 06830

WILLSON SAFETY PRODUCTS
Division of INCO
P.O. Box 1733
Reading, Pa. 19603

THE ROLLIN WILSON CO.
P.O. Box 7433
1213 Empire Avenue
Memphis, Tenn. 38107

WISCONSIN MARINE, INC.
P.O. Box 28
Lake Mills, Wisc. 53551

WOLVERINE GLOVE
A Division of Wolverine World Wide,
  Inc.
P.O. Box 166
Reed City, Mich. 49677

WOODINGS-VERONA
A Subsidiary of The Budd Co.
P.O. Box 126
Verona, Pa. 15147

WOODSTREAM CORP.
P.O. Box 327
Lititz, Pa. 17543

YARD-MAN CO.
5389 West 130th Street
Cleveland, Ohio 44111

YOUNG INDUSTRIES
1033 Wright Avenue
Mt. View, Calif. 94043

THE ZANESVILLE STONEWARE CO.
309 Pershing Road
Zanesville, Ohio 43701

INDEX